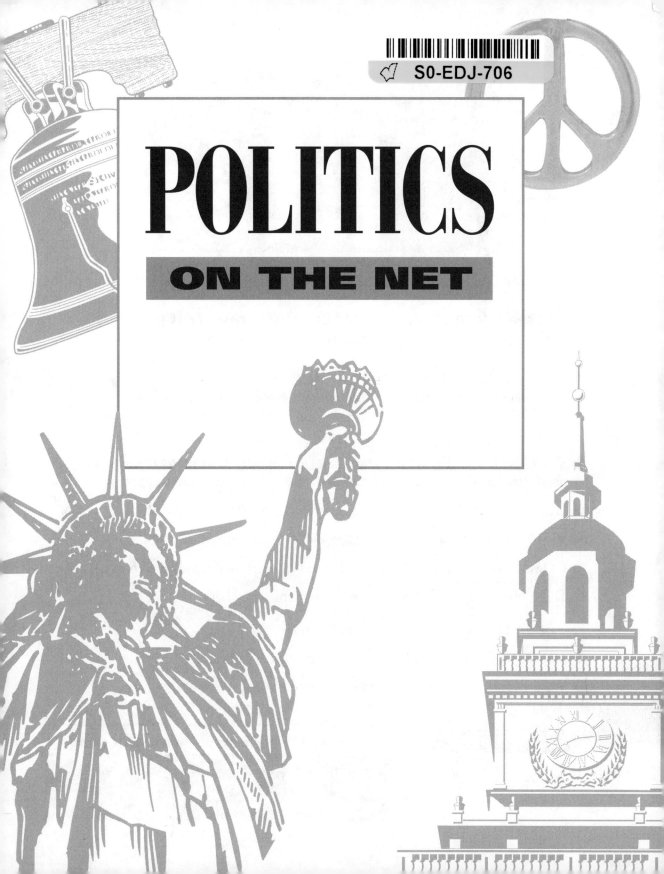

POLITICS

ON THE NET

PLUG YOURSELF INTO...

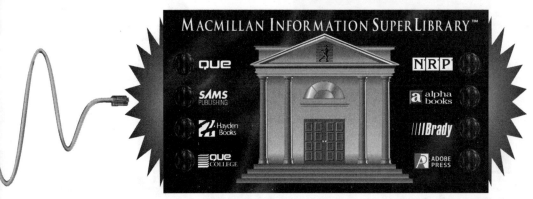

THE MACMILLAN INFORMATION SUPERLIBRARY™

Free information and vast computer resources from the world's leading computer book publisher—online!

FIND THE BOOKS THAT ARE RIGHT FOR YOU!

A complete online catalog, plus sample chapters and tables of contents give you an in-depth look at *all* of our books, including hard-to-find titles. It's the best way to find the books you need!

● **STAY INFORMED** with the latest computer industry news through our online newsletter, press releases, and customized Information SuperLibrary Reports.

● **GET FAST ANSWERS** to your questions about MCP books and software.

● **VISIT** our online bookstore for the latest information and editions!

● **COMMUNICATE** with our expert authors through e-mail and conferences.

● **DOWNLOAD SOFTWARE** from the immense MCP library:
  - Source code and files from MCP books
  - The best shareware, freeware, and demos

● **DISCOVER HOT SPOTS** on other parts of the Internet.

● **WIN BOOKS** in ongoing contests and giveaways!

TO PLUG INTO MCP: ➤   WORLD WIDE WEB: **http://www.mcp.com**

GOPHER: gopher.mcp.com

FTP: ftp.mcp.com

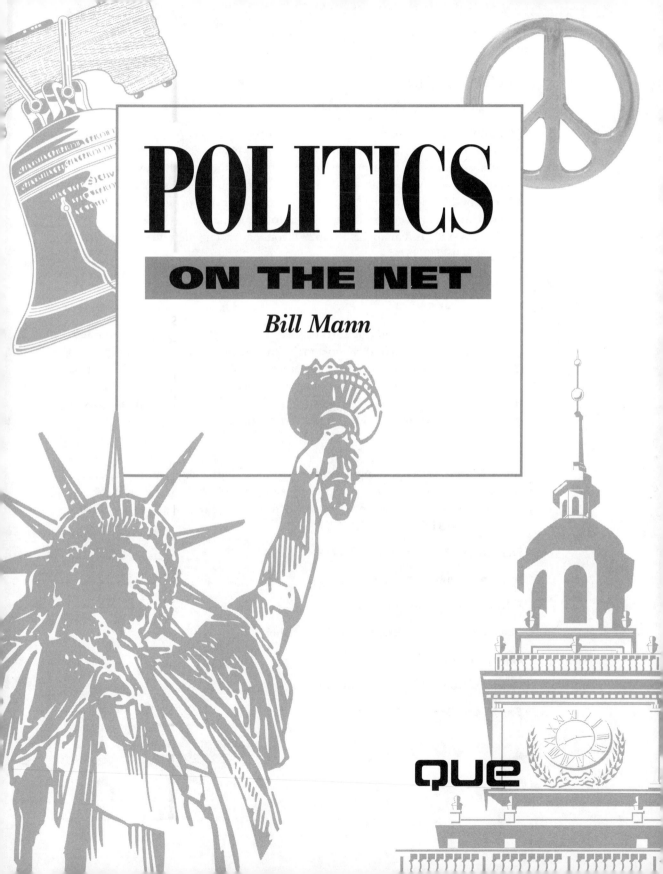

POLITICS

ON THE NET

Bill Mann

que

POLITICS ON THE NET

Copyright© 1995 by Que® Corporation

Library of Congress Catalog No.: 95-67675

ISBN: 0-7897-0286-x

98 97 96 95   4 3 2 1

Interpretation of the printing code: the rightmost double-digit number is the year of the book's printing; the rightmost single-digit number, the number of the book's printing. For example, a printing code of 95-1 shows that the first printing of the book occurred in 1995.

President and Publisher: Roland Elgey

Associate Publisher: Stacy Hiquet

Publishing Director: Brad R. Koch

Director of Editorial Services: Elizabeth Keaffaber

Managing Editor: Sandy Doell

Director of Marketing: Lynn E. Zingraf

Senior Series Director: Chris Nelson

CREDITS

Publishing Manager
Thomas H. Bennett

Acquisitions Editor
Beverly Eppink

Acquisitions Coordinators
Ruth Slates
Andrea Duvall

Production Editor
Nanci Sears Perry

Copy Editors
Danielle Bird
Kelli M. Brooks
Noelle Gasco
Julie A. McNamee
Jeff Riley

Technical Writers
Noel Estabrook
Bob Temple

Technical Editor
Alp Barker

Book Designers
Ruth Harvey
Sandra Schroeder

Graphic Image Specialists
Brad Dixon
Dennis Clay Hager
Jason Hand
Clint Lahnen
Michael Reynolds
Laura Robbins
Cari Skaggs
Craig Small

Production Team
Steve Adams
Claudia Bell
Carol Bowers
Amy Cornwell
Ann Dickerson
Maxine Dillingham
Chad Dressler
Amy Durocher
Joan Evan
Karen Gregor
Barry Jorden
Daryl Kessler
Bob LaRoche
Brenda Sims
Michael Thomas
Scott Tullis
Susan Van Ness

Indexer
Rebecca Mayfield

TRADEMARKS

All terms mentioned in this book that are known to be trademarks or service marks have been appropriately captialized. Que cannot attest to the accuracy of this information. Use of a term in this book should not be regarded as affecting the validity of any trademark or service mark.

ABOUT THE AUTHOR

Bill Mann is a writer, engineer, and software developer. His interest in the impact of new technology on society makes *Politics on the Net* a natural subject for him.

A former resident of Arizona, he's moved his family and his company, Desert Frog Software, to New Hampshire, where the political action is. This is his third book.

You can reach Bill on the Net at `wpmann@ix.netcom.com`.

ACKNOWLEDGMENTS

My thanks to everyone at Que for doing the behind-the-scenes work that turned my scribbles into a book. Special thanks go to Patti and Jennifer for putting up with me during this project, Jim for all those newspaper clippings and NPR reports, and Ralph for his insightful ideas and ever-partisan opinions.

DEDICATION

This book is for Patti, who puts up with my schemes and helps me live my dreams.

WE'D LIKE TO HEAR FROM YOU!

As part of our continuing effort to produce books of the highest possible quality, Que would like to hear your comments. To stay competitive, we *really* want you, as a computer book reader and user, to let us know what you like or dislike most about this book or other Que products.

You can mail comments, ideas, or suggestions for improving future editions to the address below, or send us a fax at (317) 581-4663. For the online inclined, Macmillan Computer Publishing now has a forum on CompuServe (type **GO QUEBOOKS** at any prompt) through which our staff and authors are available for questions and comments. In addition to exploring our forum, please feel free to contact us on CompuServe at 72410,2077 to discuss your opinions of this book.

Thanks in advance—your comments will help us to continue publishing the best books available on computer topics in today's market.

CONTENTS AT A GLANCE

TABLE OF CONTENTS

II Issues   103

6 Political People   105

7 Issues Related to the Bill of Rights   133

9 The Economy and Trade   185

III Political Places and Things   231

11 The Branches of Government   233

13 The End Product: Laws and Other Documents   273

IV The International Scene   293

14 Political Hot Spots   295

15 Other Interesting International Locations   311

V Getting Going and Keeping Up   327

16 Getting Going and Keeping Up on the Net   329

17 Getting Going and Keeping Up on the Online Services   345

Index   355

Introduction

In cyberspace—the Net and online services—politics is a major topic of discussion. The federal and state governments are putting information and other resources on the Net continually. Political parties and organizations are discovering that the Net is an inexpensive, efficient way to communicate with their members, and make their views known to a wide audience. Individuals are participating in newsgroups, and creating their own personal political Web sites. Virtually any significant political issue or subject is covered somewhere on the Net—the trick is finding it.

Politics on the Net is your guide to what's where in cyberspace. This book examines dozens of sites on the Net and on the three major online services: America Online (AOL), CompuServe, and Prodigy. For each site, you'll find directions on how to get to it, a description of what it contains, and a screen shot that shows what you can expect to see if you decide to visit the site.

> **NOTE**
>
> One of our major goals in creating this book was to keep it unbiased. The depth of coverage for any party or subject is determined primarily by *the amount of online material for that party or subject*. For example, the Libertarian party coverage is more in depth than the Democrats or the Republicans because there is more Libertarian material on the Net.

What This Book Is About

This book covers the political resources that are available on the Net and the online services. The range of resources out there is enormous—finding what you need is the problem. This book is designed to help you find what you are looking for. In it, I've highlighted sites that I have found to be interesting and useful political resources. Whatever your level of access to the Internet—from a newsgroup reader to the latest Web browser—I have tried to provide you with something you can use in every chapter.

If you use one of the online services—America Online (AOL), CompuServe, or Prodigy—this book has a lot to offer you too. Each chapter includes coverage of related resources that are available on the online services. In addition, all three services give you access to parts of the Net. They all have Web browsers, UseNet newsgroups, Gopher, and e-mail. It won't be long until you have full access to all the political resources on the Net, as well as on your online service.

The Types of Political Information on the Net

Political activity on the Net comes in many forms. The following list describes the five main forms of political activity.

- *Real News.* You can get political news stories from major services like the Associated Press and Reuters. These stories are available as UseNet newsgroups if your Internet Service Provider subscribes to the ClariNet e.News service. Some Gopher and World Wide Web sites also give you access to new stories from these and other sources.

- *Opinions and Debates.* UseNet newsgroups and mailing lists serve as forums for debate. With most newsgroups and mailing lists, anyone can post their opinions and comments, sharing their views with people all over the world.

- *Government Documents and Agencies.* Federal, state, and local government agencies all make information and resources available on the Net. You can find out what the Department of Justice does or what bills are being considered by the state legislature this week. Also, you can get a copy of the latest decisions of the Supreme Court, or a transcript of the speech the President gave an hour ago.

  Foreign governments are putting their agencies and information on the Net, too. It's almost as easy to find information and documents from the Japanese or South African governments as it is to find information from your home state.

- *Political Parties.* Many political parties have seen the advantages of being active on the Net. A Gopher or World Wide Web site is a great way to make your positions known to the public. Newsgroups, mailing lists, or plain old e-mail are fast, inexpensive ways to communicate with party members virtually anywhere on the planet.

- *Other Political Organizations.* Politically oriented groups, like the League of Women Voters, gain the same advantages from the Net that political parties get. They can make their voices heard and communicate with members and like-minded groups without spending a lot of money.

IN RECESS

What Is Covered

The decision as to which parties or subjects were covered was based primarily on which things I felt were important to examine and that you would find interesting. If you think I missed something important, let me know and we will consider it for the next edition of *Politics on the Net*. My e-mail address is **wpmann@ix.netcom.com**.

How This Book Is Organized

I've tried to organize this book in a way that makes it easy for you to find the information you need. Here is a sketch of what you will find in each section of the book.

- Chapter 1, "Getting Involved as an Electronic Political Activist." The Net is a potent tool for political activists. This chapter looks at online resources that will help you become politically active—on or off the Net.

Part I: Parties

Part one dedicates two chapters to the two major parties—the Democrats and Republicans. Another chapter covers the Libertarian Party. Although only a fraction of the size of the two major parties, the Libertarians are the third largest party in the country, and a surprisingly visible entity on the Net.

The last chapter in this part looks at several other parties and groups that are on the Net. It includes coverage of United We Stand America (UWSA), a group that will instantly become the third largest party in the U.S. if it decides to register as an official party.

Each chapter in this part of the book ends with a list of Net sites related to the material in the chapter.

- Chapter 2, "The Republican Party." From college groups to official party resources, the Republicans are a growing presence on the Net. Use this chapter as a guide to what they're doing in cyberspace.
- Chapter 3, "The Democratic Party." The President and Vice President see the Net as an important part of future politics. This chapter looks at what their party is doing on and with the Net.
- Chapter 4, "The Libertarian Party." The Libertarians are the third largest political party in America. The party and its members are on the Net in a big way. This chapter looks at Libertarian sites.
- Chapter 5, "Other Parties." Numerous smaller political parties have a presence on the Net, as do other political organizations. Socialists, United We Stand America, and the League of Women Voters are a few of the groups with interesting information for Net surfers.

Part II: Issues

Most of major political issues appear in some form on the Net; this section points you to Net and online sites that deal with them. But before getting into political issues, there's a chapter that profiles some of the people who are important to Net politics.

- Chapter 6, "Political People." Despite its technology, the Net is about people. This chapter looks at some people who are important to Net politics.

- Chapter 7, "Issues Related to the Bill of Rights." This chapter addresses political issues that can be found on the Net. It covers sites that deal with tough issues like gay rights, privacy, and censorship.

- Chapter 8, "Policies and Programs." Government policies and programs such as AIDS policy, immigration, and health care reform are issues on the Net. This chapter looks at sites that deal with various policies and programs.

- Chapter 9, "The Economy and Trade." The Net has information on just about everything—even the U.S. economy and trade. We all interact with the economy every day and the Net can help us understand it.

- Chapter 10, "Foreign Affairs." From diplomacy to military action, many foreign affairs sites on the Net contain interesting and informative resources.

Part III: Political Places and Things

The federal government has three branches: Executive, Judicial, and Legislative. Their Internet presence is covered in this section. Between the three branches of government, there are thousands of state and local governments, and hundreds of the states have some sort of presence on the Net. The next chapter looks at some of these state and local sites. The federal, state, and local governments generate millions of documents—and thousands of them are available online. The final chapter in this part shows you where to find more government documents than you could ever read.

- Chapter 11, "The Branches of Government." All three branches of the U.S. Government are online. This chapter covers what resources they offer and what scandals they've been involved in recently.

- Chapter 12, "State and Local Politics." More state and local political entities get on the Net every day. This chapter shows what some of the state and local governments are up to and how to find what your state and local politicians are doing.

- Chapter 13, "The End Product: Laws and Other Documents." The government produces vast numbers of documents. This chapter shows you some places on the Net—both official government sites and others—where you can find copies of government documents.

Part IV: The International Scene

The Net is a worldwide phenomenon, as are U.S. political interests. This part of the book is dedicated to interesting international political sites.

- Chapter 14, "Political Hot Spots." The cold war may be over, but the world isn't a peaceful place. Use the Net to get information and news about places where peace hasn't broken out yet.
- Chapter 15, "Other Interesting International Locations." This chapter is a grab bag of political sites from around the world that caught my attention. Find out about indigenous peoples, emu export regulations, and bizarre political theories.

Part V: Getting Going and Keeping Up

This final part of the book has two goals. One is to provide basic information on getting connected to the Internet or one of the online services. The second is to give you some resources you can use to keep up with the changing political resources in cyberspace. The first chapter is for Net users; the second is for users of the online services.

- Chapter 16, "Getting Going and Keeping Up on the Net." Learn about the ways you can get on the Internet. Once on, you can use the tips in this chapter to keep up with the changing political resources.
- Chapter 17, "Getting Going and Keeping Up on the Online Services." Learn about the big three online services—America Online, CompuServe and Prodigy—and how to get connected. Pick up some tips on keeping up with the service's changing political coverage, too.

What This Book Is Not About

This book is not a manual on how to use the Internet. The Internet itself is the subject of many books, including other books published by Que—*Using the Internet, Easy Internet,* and *Special Edition Using the Internet,* Second Edition.

And this book certainly isn't about pushing my political views on you.

Conventions Used in This Book

Because of the nature of this book, we didn't need to use as many conventions as other computer books. We've kept it as simple as possible.

This book is packed with electronic addresses. Each of these addresses is listed in boldface type (**`like this`**) to set it off from the rest of the text. We also provide icons next to these addresses that show you what type of address we've listed (see the following table).

Icon	Address Type
America Online	America Online
CompuServe	CompuServe
Mailing List	LISTSERVs (mailing lists)
PRODIGY	Prodigy
gopher	Gopher
USENET	UseNet
WWW	World Wide Web (WWW)

The Internet is a strange and wonderful place where sites come and go as they please (because they are often run by individuals). If you try to reach an address mentioned in this book that no longer exists, don't get too frustrated. We've supplied you with many, many addresses, and there's bound to be another that suits your needs.

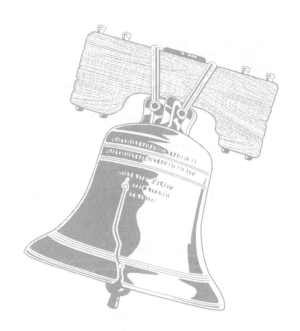

Chapter 1
Getting Involved as an Electronic Political Activist

This chapter is a guide to tools for the online activist.

In this chapter

- *News about online activism*
- *Sources of activist information on the Internet*

In other chapters

→ *The Right Side of the Web is a resource for conservative activists. It is covered in Chapter 2.*

→ *The Democratic Senatorial Campaign Committee Web site was designed by IDI, a company featured here. You can see the site in Chapter 3.*

→ *State and Local politics are a prime area for grassroots activism. Chapter 12 has useful background information.*

→ *The goal of most activism is to affect laws; Chapter 13 is another good source of information.*

Thomas Jefferson was a political activist. As one of the founding fathers of the United States, Jefferson knew that the key to successful political action was persuading the public to see things his way. Unlike the politicians of Jefferson's time, today's political activists have an amazing array of tools at their disposal, but the job of persuading the public remains the same.

Modern political activism tends to be a grassroots activity, with activists trying to organize locally.

One of the most important tools for modern political activists is propaganda. Good communications are critical if propaganda is to be effective. If few people are exposed to it, propaganda has little effect. Fortunately for activists, the types and availability of communication media have exploded in recent years. The fastest growing of all the media is the Internet.

> **NOTE**
>
> Although the word has negative connotations, propaganda is merely the distribution of ideas and information designed to affect people's attitudes. Public interest announcements, leaflets, staged news events, protest marches, and advertising are all forms of propaganda used by activists.

The Net has several advantages as a communication medium for activists:

"Enlighten the people generally, and tyranny and oppressions of body and mind will vanish like evil spirits at the dawn of day."

Thomas Jefferson
from the Ask Thomas Jefferson Web page

- *Demographics.* According to the February 27, 1995 issue of *Newsweek*, the demographics of the Net are largely better-educated people who have higher incomes than the general public.

- *Inexpensive.* The cost to maintain a World Wide Web page or a Gopher directory, sites that can be reached by tens of millions of Internet users, can be as low as tens of dollars a month. A television ad that can reach tens of millions of viewers probably costs tens, or even hundreds, of thousands of dollars a month. And the television ad is only visible at certain times, while the Internet site is available 24 hours a day.

- *Interactive.* The Net is also interactive. An activist's Web page or Gopher site can be designed to give a visitor additional information at the click of a mouse button. Online discussions involving any number of people, located anywhere in the world, can be conducted by a UseNet newsgroup, or by e-mail, much faster than by postal mail, and much less expensively than by telephone. In short, the Net is an ideal medium for political activism.

Newsgroups and Mailing Lists

Newsgroups and mailing lists are great ways for activist groups to communicate with the public and among themselves. They also require less powerful computers than the World Wide Web, making them ideal tools for grassroots activists.

There are quite a few activist newsgroups and mailing lists. I've included two newsgroups and one mailing list here, and many more in the list at the end of the chapter.

 An Unmoderated Activism Newsgroup

`alt.activism.d`

This is the newsgroup to join for general discussions of political activism, both on and off the Net. It's unmoderated, with a high volume of messages. Although most of the traffic comes from liberals, other users, including moderates and conservatives, also contribute. Figure 1.1 shows some titles of recent threads.

With the subjects covered in this newsgroup, and the fact that anyone at all can post to it, the discussions sometimes deteriorate into name calling and flaming. Even so, most of the threads are quite readable and contain some useful information.

 A Moderated Activism Newsgroup

`alt.activism`

This newsgroup is the moderated counterpart of `alt.activism.d`. This newsgroup contains announcements and controlled discussions of activist issues. Like `alt.activism.d`, most of the messages here deal with progressive activism.

Even though some discussions deteriorate to name calling, the unmoderated activism newsgroups contain useful information.

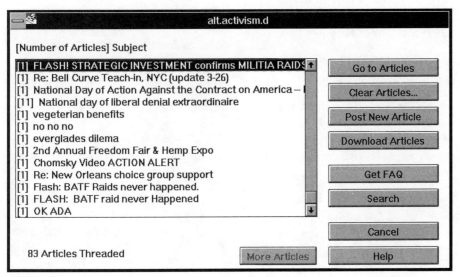

Figure 1.1 `alt.activism.d`
This newsgroup carries unmoderated activist discussions.

What Is a Moderated Newsgroup?

Most newsgroups allow anyone to add a message directly to the newsgroup, without any limitations. This means that I could add a message about a computer game or my dinner to a discussion about political activism, with no one to prevent it. Such irrelevant messages, as well as messages that attack others posting to the group, disrupt the discussions.

A *moderated newsgroup* avoids these problems by controlling which messages get posted. Messages posted to a moderated newsgroup automatically go to the moderator instead of directly into the stream of messages. The moderator is an individual or group that examines every message that comes in. They discard messages that don't belong in the group, and may edit or combine messages. Only messages approved by the moderator make it into the newsgroup.

 ### The Progressive Activism Mailing List

ACTIV-L LISTSERV Address:
listserv@mizzou1.missouri.edu

ACTIV-L is a moderated mailing list concerned with progressive political action. Messages that appear in this mailing list also appear in the **misc .activism.progressive** newsgroup.

Activist Resources on the Net

The Internet contains every kind of useful resource for political activists. The information at the Net sites addressed in this chapter is more general than that in later chapters. They've been selected because they provide resources that will be of use to most political activists.

The Online Activism Resource List

WWW Address: **http://www.eff.org/ pub/Activism/activ_resource.faq**

This has to be the most complete list of online activist resources available. I printed a copy of version 4.07. It's a 30-page listing of UseNet newsgroups, Internet mailing lists, and other resources for activists. Version 4.07 contained 78 mailing lists or publications transmitted by mailing lists, 87 UseNet newsgroups, and a variety of other electronic and printed items.

For some of the resources, the document includes a complete description of the resource and the topics it addresses. In other cases, there may be a limited description, or none at all. For users who prefer Gopher or the Web, many of the mailing lists have such addresses.

Three documents are particularly helpful in getting you started as a political activist. One covers online activism exclusively, one online and offline activities, and one offline exclusively. Between the three of them, they cover the full spectrum of political activism and can serve as a guide for anyone who wants to be politically active. The next three sections describe these documents, and the sites that contain them.

 The Activist's Oasis

`http://www.matisse.net/`
`politics/activist/`
`activist.html`

The Activist's Oasis describes itself as a source of "Practical Tools for Troublemakers," and a place to "relax, put your feet up and remember why you care" (see fig. 1.2).

The Oasis is primarily a large collection of links to Net sites of interest to activists. Although the site leans toward liberal views, most of its resources will help any online activist.

One of these resources is the AP Wire search tool. Part of the site's News and Media Resources section, the tool lets visitors do keyword searches on Associated Press stories. By combining this search tool with links to news sources like the CNN News Server and the White House, the Oasis becomes a powerful way to keep up to date on current events.

In keeping with its billing as a place to relax, the Oasis offers a relaxation

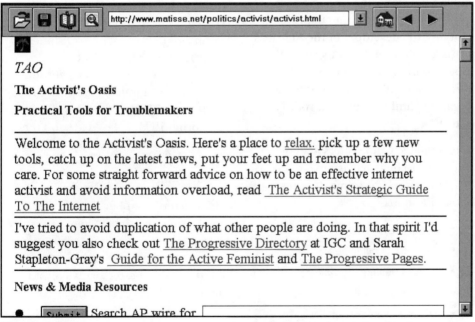

Figure 1.2 `http://www.matisse.net/politics/activist/activist.html`
The Activist's Oasis is a good way to keep up to date with current events.

page. This page contains links to various distractions, everything from the Egyptian Book of the Dead to the joke religion Discordianism. There is even a collection of online games.

For the novice online activist, the most useful resource at the Activist's Oasis is the Activist's Strategic Guide to the Internet. The guide was created by Kathy Watkins, the developer of the Activist's Oasis.

 An Activist's Strategic Guide to the Internet

`http://www.matisse.net/politics/activist/actguide.html`

One problem with using the Internet is the size and diversity of it. While you can find just about anything on the Net, you can also get lost, or spend so much time exploring that you never get anything useful done. Kathy Watkins, the developer of the Activist's Oasis, created An Activist's Strategic Guide to the Internet in response to this problem; it's a guide to staying organized and in control of your Net activities.

The Strategic Guide offers a set of questions to help activists make the best use of their Net time. It poses seven questions:

- Who's on your side?
- Who else is out there?
- Who's listening?
- What is my goal?
- Where is the cool stuff?
- Where am I?
- When do I start?

By answering these questions, activists can prepare to get the most out of their time on the Net.

Besides offering its seven questions, the document contains tips for answering them. The tips remind you that while the Net is composed of computers and wires, the people on the Net are what is really important. Although it is written for a specific audience, An Activist's Strategic Guide to the Internet is useful reading for anyone who wants to make effective use of the Net.

 Jim Warren's Gopher

`gopher://gopher.path.net 8102`

Jim Warren is a veteran online activist. He led Californians in a successful campaign to make state government information freely available online. The winner of the Electronic Frontier Foundation's Pioneer Award and the Professional Journalists—Northern California 1994 James Madison Freedom-of-Information Award, Mr. Warren is also a proponent of online access to government, and electronic privacy.

Mr. Warren's Gopher site is a collection of electronic newsletters covering political action, government access, cryptography, and privacy. The Political Action directory is shown in figure 1.3.

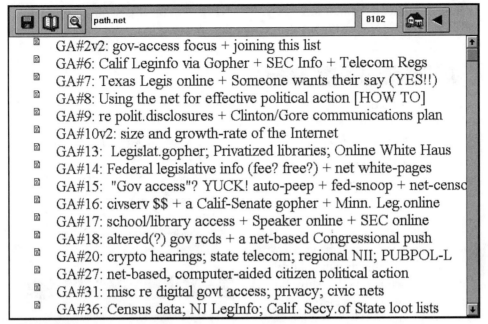

```
[disk][book][search]  path.net                                    8102  [home] ◀
```

GA#2v2: gov-access focus + joining this list
GA#6: Calif Leginfo via Gopher + SEC Info + Telecom Regs
GA#7: Texas Legis online + Someone wants their say (YES!!)
GA#8: Using the net for effective political action [HOW TO]
GA#9: re polit.disclosures + Clinton/Gore communications plan
GA#10v2: size and growth-rate of the Internet
GA#13: Legislat.gopher; Privatized libraries; Online White Haus
GA#14: Federal legislative info (fee? free?) + net white-pages
GA#15: "Gov access"? YUCK! auto-peep + fed-snoop + net-censo
GA#16: civserv $$ + a Calif-Senate gopher + Minn. Leg.online
GA#17: school/library access + Speaker online + SEC online
GA#18: altered(?) gov rcds + a net-based Congressional push
GA#20: crypto hearings; state telecom; regional NII; PUBPOL-L
GA#27: net-based, computer-aided citizen political action
GA#31: misc re digital govt access; privacy; civic nets
GA#36: Census data; NJ LegInfo; Calif. Secy.of State loot lists

Figure 1.3 gopher://gopher.path.net
The Political Action directory on Jim Warren's Gopher currently contains 16 newsletters.

Currently, the directory contains 16 newsletters. All are interesting, but two in particular focus on activism and the Net:

- *GA#8*. Using the Net for effective political action [HOW TO] is a December 1993 column from *BoardWatch* magazine. It describes the way the Internet was used to help ensure the passage of California Assembly Bill 1624, the bill that put California government information online.

- *GA#27*. Takes the material in GA#8, generalizes it, and expands upon it to create a guide to grassroots political action using the Net as well as leaflets and letter-writing campaigns. Following is a description of the newsletter:

How Citizens Can Pursue Net Grassroots Political Activism

gopher://gopher.path.net:8102

Select the following directories:

```
Government Access
Political Action
GA#27: net-based, computer-
    aided citizen political
    action
```

This document is a guide to individual political action combining online and offline activities. The basic outline was developed in 1993, during the campaign to get free online access to California's legislative and statutory information. Filled with new ideas and refinements, the document was published on the Net in 1994.

The text begins with background information on subjects like political math—the calculations that show how most U.S. House of Representatives elections are decided by less than 20,000 votes. Combined with insights into the things that motivate most politicians, the material sets the stage for the introduction of Warren's system.

The system calls for a reasonably powerful PC with Net access and a high-quality printer. The Net is used for information gathering, and communicating with other activists; while the printer allows the activist to create leaflets that can be physically distributed to voters. Anyone interested in Net activism should read How Citizens Can Pursue Net Grassroots Political Activism.

 The Space Activism Site's Guidelines for Effective Activism Page

`http://muon.qrc.com/space/guidelines/activ_onlinefaq.html`

To assist in pro-space political action, the Space Activism site maintains a page called Guidelines for Effective Activism (see fig. 1.4). While some of the articles there are specifically related to space activism, two of them are of interest for any activist:

- *How Citizens Can Pursue Net Grassroots Political Action.* A guide to political activism, online and off.
- *Lobbying/Advocacy Techniques.* A guide for political action in the physical world.

 Lobbying/Advocacy Techniques

`http://muon.qrc.com/space/guidelines/lobby_techniquesfaq.html`

Although you can reach a lot of people online, most voters and politicians spend their time in the physical world. Lobbying/Advocacy Techniques is a guide for real-world lobbying at the state and regional level.

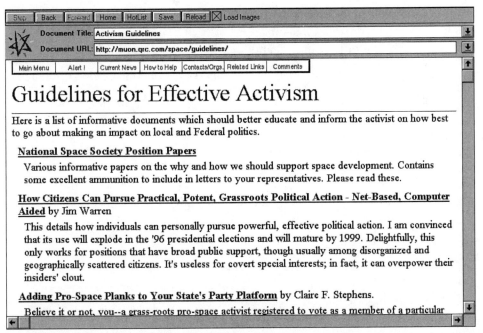

Figure 1.4 `http://muon.qrc.com/space/guidelines/`
The Guidelines for Effective Activism page on Prodigy.

The guide takes readers step-by-step through the entire lobbying process. It starts at the most basic level: determining who you represent, what you want, and who else is involved. From there, it moves to crucial details like the proper format for letters to legislators, and how to deal with their staffs. Extensive guidelines take the activist up to, and beyond, giving testimony before the legislature.

The detailed instructions in Lobbying/ Advocacy Techniques supplement the strategy in How Citizens Can Pursue Net Grassroots Political Action. By combining these documents with An Activist's Strategic Guide to the Internet, an electronic activist can assemble a complete guide to his trade.

 The Activist Toolkit at the WELL

`gopher://gopher.well.sf.ca.us`

Select the following directories:

> **Politics**
> **Activist Toolkit**

The Whole Earth 'Lectronic Link (WELL) is a computer conferencing system in the San Francisco Bay Area. It was founded by the creators of the Whole Earth Catalog, and is one of the more famous online communities in the world. The Activist Toolkit is part of the WELL's Gopher site.

The Activist Toolkit directory contains the Citizens Guide to the Net. Although it's not clear from the title, this large document is actually about online activism. It contains a massive amount of information on political and government online resources. There is contact information for activist groups like the Electronic Frontier Foundation (EFF), and the Computer Professionals for Social Responsibility (CPSR). There are the names of lists of newsgroups and mailing lists and Gopher sites and even the List of Lists. And there is basic information on what all this stuff is and how to use it.

The other thing you'll find in the Activist Toolkit is a directory with the concise title of How To Win: A Practical Guide to Defeating the Radical Right (see fig. 1.5).

 How To Win: A Practical Guide to Defeating the Radical Right

`gopher://gopher.well.sf.ca.us`

Select the following directories:

> **Politics**
> **Activist Toolkit**
> **How To Win: A Practical**
> **Guide to Defeating the**
> **Radical Right**

This directory contains 31 text files and a tool for searching those files. Two files in this document are of particular interest to any activist:

- Tips for Winning Elections
- Media Tools and Strategies

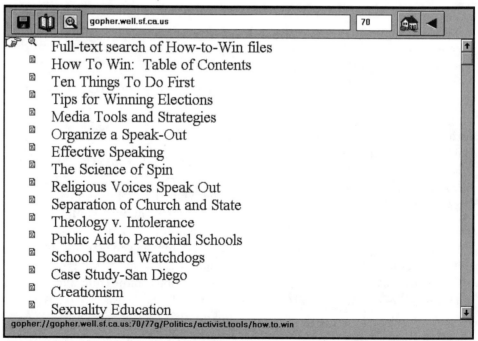

Figure 1.5 `gopher://gopher.well.sf.ca.us`
How To Win: A Practical Guide to Defeating the Radical Right is part of the Activist Toolkit at the WELL. This site has information that is helpful for any activist.

Tips for Winning Elections is a case study of techniques that liberal activists in San Diego used to win several victories in the 1992 elections. While the specific details are liberal versus radical right, techniques like identify your allies, create a list of principles and beliefs you can present to the public, and take advantage of polling data, can be used by any activist.

Media Tools and Strategies contains advice on dealing with the media. It advocates that you plan ahead by knowing what you want to say, who you want to say it to, and how to phrase it. Beyond that, it guides you in preparing documents for the media and other such practical matters.

 IDI, Professional Electronic Advocates

`http://idi.net/services.html`

All of the groups covered so far in this chapter are similar in that they are motivated by some cause. Whether that cause is something specific, like space exploration, or something more general, like online democracy, their

members are activists because they believe in their cause. Issue Dynamics, Inc. (IDI) is different. You might call them activists for hire.

IDI is a consumer and public affairs consulting company that helps groups take advantage of the Net. They can get a group online and help it use the power of the Net for lobbying and grassroots organizing. The IDI home page is one example of their work (see fig. 1.6).

IDI can provide some valuable benefits to its clients. It can monitor the Net for discussions and references to a particular subject. A pro-gun group, for example, could get a daily summary of Net activity related to gun control. IDI also serves as an electronic advocate, helping clients reach important individuals and groups, creating and distributing electronic petitions, and performing interactive online lobbying.

Recommended Sites to See

The following lists contain addresses of the Net sites discussed in this chapter, as well as numerous others that may also be of interest. The lists are broken

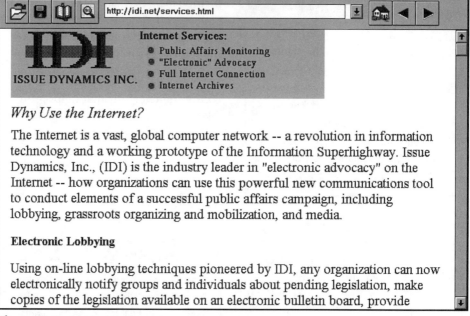

Figure 1.6 `http://idi.net/services.html`
The IDI home page includes a link to a number of IDI client pages.

up into the same sections as the body of the chapter.

Newsgroups and Mailing Lists

Unmoderated activist discussions.

UseNet Address: `alt.activism.d`

Moderated activist discussions and announcements.

UseNet Address: `alt.activism`

Moderated progressive activist information and discussions.

LISTSERV Address: `ACTIV-L`
`listserv@mizzou1.missouri.edu`

The UseNet version of the ACTIV-L mailing list.

UseNetAddress:
`misc.activism.progressive`

Discussions of political reform.

UseNet Address:
`alt.politics.reform`

The Electronic Frontier Foundation. Covers many topics, including activism.

UseNet Address:
`comp.org.eff.talk`

Activist Resources on the Net

The Online Activism Resource List WWW address.

WWW Address: `http://`
`www.eff.org/pub/Activism/`
`activ_resource.faq`

The Online Activism Resource List Gopher address.

> Gopher Address: `gopher://gopher.eff.org`

> > Select the following directories:
> > ```
> > Electronic Frontier Founda-
> >    tion files & information
> > Issues
> > Activism
> > activ_resource.faq
> > ```

The Activist's Oasis home page.

> WWW Address: `http://www.matisse.net/politics/activist/activist.html`

The Activist's Strategic Guide to the Internet.

> WWW Address: `http://www.matisse.net/politics/activist/actguide.html`

Jim Warren's Gopher site.

> Gopher Address: `gopher://gopher.path.net:8102`

How citizens can pursue grassroots political action Gopher site.

> Gopher Address: `gopher://gopher.path.net:8102`

> > Select the following directories:
> > ```
> > Government Access
> > Political Action
> > GA#27: net-based, computer-
> >    aided citizen political
> >    action
> > ```

How Citizens can Pursue Grassroots Political Action Web site.

> WWW Address: `http://muon.qrc.com/space/guide-lines/activ_onlinefaq.html`

The Space Activism site's Guidelines for Effective Activism.

> WWW Address: `http://muon.qrc.com/space/guidelines`

A guide to Lobbying/Advocacy Techniques.

> WWW Address: `http://muon.qrc.com/space/guidelines/lobby_techniquesfaq.html`

The Activist Toolkit at the WELL.

> Gopher Address: `gopher://gopher.well.sf.ca.us`

> > Select the following directories:
> > ```
> > Politics
> > Activist Toolkit
> > ```

How To Win: A Practical Guide to Defeating the Radical Right.

> Gopher Address: `gopher://gopher.well.sf.ca.us`

> > Select the following directories:
> > ```
> > Politics
> > Activist Toolkit
> > How To Win: A Practical
> >    Guide to Defeating the
> >    Radical Right
> > ```

IDI, Professional Electronic Advocates.

> WWW Address: `http://idi.net/services.html`

The Political Participation Project's Political Activism links.

WWW Address: `http://www.ai.mit.edu/projects/ppp/polact.html`

The Right Side of the Web, a resource for conservative activists.

WWW Address: `http://www.clark.net/pub/jeffd/index.html`

The Conservative Generation X Electronic Democracy page.

WWW Address: `http://www.teleport.com/~pcllgn/id.html`

The Lead or Leave page.

WWW Address: `http://www.cs.caltech.edu/~adam/lead.html`

Feminist activist resources on the Net.

WWW Address: `http://www.igc.apc.org/women/feminist.html`

The Online Political Information Network.

WWW Address: `http://www.ai.mit.edu/projects/ppp/opin.html`

A collection of environmental activist links.

WWW Address: `http://www.einet.net/galaxy/Community/The-Environment/Environmental-Activism.html`

PART I

Parties

Chapter 2

The Republican Party

The sites covered in this chapter are a comprehensive look at what's available on the Net for Republicans today.

In this chapter

- *How to get the news on Republican issues and activities*
- *The Republican and conservative materials on the Net*
- *Other groups and materials related to Republicanism*

In other chapters

→ *The Libertarian party, which shares many beliefs with parts of the Republican party, is covered in Chapter 4.*

→ *You can find a profile on Newt Gingrich in Chapter 6.*

→ *The Thomas Legislative Information Service is described in Chapter 11.*

The Republican party is one of two parties that has dominated American politics in this century. Founded in 1854, the original mission of the party was to end slavery. In most cases, the Republican party is more conservative than its major opposition, the Democrats.

Since Republican views are popular on the Net, you would think that the Republican party would have a large presence online. In reality, it doesn't. If you do a Gopher search, or ask a Web robot to find the word Republican, you'll get a pretty good response. But after you sort out duplications, entries that are no more than a single document, and documents and sites that happen to contain the word, there isn't much left.

This situation may change soon. House Speaker Newt Gingrich is a big advocate of the Net and online democracy, as are other prominent Republicans, like Presidential candidate Lamar Alexander. With such high-level interest, it seems only a matter of time before more Republican-specific material appears on the Net. When it does, it will likely be announced in a UseNet newsgroup first.

Newsgroups and Mailing Lists

UseNet newsgroups and mailing lists are ideal ways to keep up with the Republican party. They carry the latest information and require less computer power than the Web.

Given that the Republican party is one of the two largest political parties in the United States, it's surprising that there aren't more newsgroups and mailing lists for it. The following sections describe newsgroups and mailing lists that contain useful material for Republicans.

This is best single spot to get news on the Republican party. **Alt.politics.usa.republican** is a general discussion group that covers anything to do with the Republican party or beliefs. Figure 2.1 shows the titles of some typical message threads. As you can see, the threads are relatively short, and mainly cover current events in Washington.

Unfortunately, the diversity of articles here works against you. If you just want official party announcements and information, you'll have to sort through the articles yourself.

Discussions about the U.S. Republican Party

`alt.politics.usa.republican`

The Republican Liberty Caucus Mailing List

LISTSERV address: `rlc-news-request@tomahawk.welch.jhu.edu`

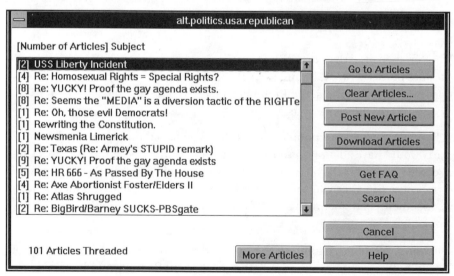

Figure 2.1 `alt.politics.usa.republican`
Typical threads in the Republican newsgroup.

The Republican party includes a small but growing Libertarian wing. To get the current news on what this group is up to, try this newsgroup. It contains news-only articles on the Republican Liberty Caucus, the organization of Libertarian Republicans. The RLC is covered in more detail later in this chapter.

 A Conservative Mailing List

`alt.society.conservatism`

This newsgroup features articles on general conservative topics. The article threads here tend toward long, wordy debates on subjects like a gold-backed currency and media bias. There is some overlap with `alt.politics.usa.republican`.

Republican and Conservative Material on the Net

The Republican party doesn't have a large presence on the Net, but there are still items of interest to Republicans. The sites covered in this chapter are a comprehensive look at what's available on the Net for Republicans today.

Some of the best Republican resources online are not officially related to the Republican party. For a great example of the way one individual can have an impact on the Net, read the following section, "The Right Side of the Web."

NOTE

You'll find that Republicanism and Conservatism are frequently tied together on the Net. I've done the same in this chapter, so don't be surprised at the number of times you see the word conservative.

 The Right Side of the Web

`http://www.clark.net/pub/jeffd/index.html`

It always helps to have a point of departure for exploring the Net. For Republicans and other conservatives, that point is the Right Side of the Web. Liberal and Libertarian sensibilities are common on the Net. (There's more on the Libertarians in Chapter 4.) The Right Side of the Web was created as a counterpoint to those sensibilities (see fig. 2.2).

Designed "to make up for all of the socialism and moral anarchy...on the Net," this page gathers pointers to conservative and Republican resources. As you might expect, the politics are on the conservative side.

The page starts off with some personal views and opinions by the author of the page, Jeff Donels. Beyond that, the resources are more generally useful. There is a copy of the Republicans'

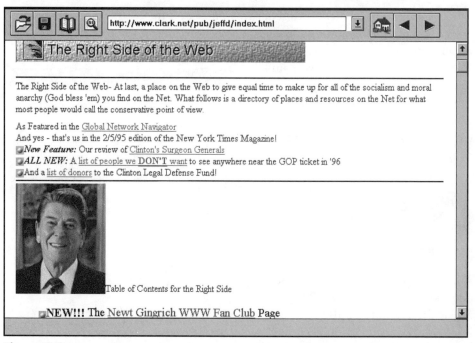

Figure 2.2 `http://www.clark.net/pub/jeffd/index.html`
The Right Side of the Web home page.

Contract with America, set up as a checklist to keep track of the passage of each portion; a Newt Gingrich WWW Fan Club, which is covered in more detail later; and a page of pointers to other conservative resources on the Net that lets you explore further.

This site is constantly being updated with new links. Among the regular links are:

- The Question of the Week
- The Rush Limbaugh Information Page
- A list of people whom the Right Side doesn't want to see on the GOP ticket in 1996
- A list of people whom the Right Side would like to see run in 1996

This is a great place to get the latest on what's hot in Washington, as it includes status reports on a variety of bills of interest to the Republican party.

> **NOTE**
>
> The Right Side of the Web has achieved an amazing amount of publicity. Aside from features in Internet locations, such as the Whole Internet Catalog and the Global Network Navigator, they broke into print media with coverage in *Newsweek*, the *National Journal* and the *New York Times* (and now *Politics on the Net*).

Ronald Reagan: Republican Icon

One of the most prominent Republicans on the Net today hasn't held a political office for years. Revered by friends, reviled by foes, Ronald Reagan, our 40th President, is a much discussed topic on the Net.

His name is used by both the left and the right, either as part of a description like "the post-Reagan years," or as a criticism, "almost as bad as Reagan." The best online source of information on President Reagan is the Ronald Reagan home page on the WWW (see fig. 2.3) at **http://www.erinet.com/ bkottman/reagan.html**.

The Ronald Reagan home page is dedicated to "the greatest peace-time expansion in U.S. history." The page takes a positive look at the economic expansion that coincided with Reagan's Presidency.

The bulk of the page deals with economic expansion, providing statistics to counter the belief that the Reagan years were harmful to America. There is detailed information on standards of living, social spending, job growth and more, all hyperlinked in the text.

Some of the material deals more directly with President Reagan. You can retrieve the text of some of his speeches, as well as a file of quotes. A large scan of him during his Presidency and notes on how to contact him round out the site.

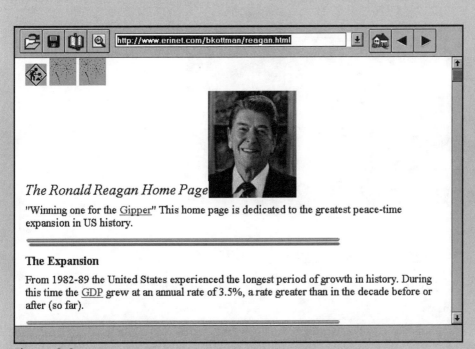

Figure 2.3 http://www.erinet.com/bkottman/reagan.html
The Ronald Reagan home page looks at economic expansion during the Reagan Presidency.

The Republican Primary Page

`http://www.umr.edu/~sears/primary/main.html`

The Republican party has a number of members who are anxious to challenge President Clinton in 1996. But first, they must win the party's nomination. This page is dedicated to providing information about Republicans who are vying for that nomination—as well as those who may yet run (see fig. 2.4). This site is rich in information, as the next few paragraphs will show.

The Republican Primary page consists of links to information about each candidate, potential candidate, and non-candidate. The specific information varies from individual to individual, but you can expect to find some of the following: a Time-Warner Web page for the candidate, biographical note, little known facts, legislation introduced, rankings by special interest groups, quotes, and speeches.

Some candidates also have buttons that search databases of Congressional data for information like the legislation the candidate introduced in the 103rd Congress. Before you can access some of the information, you must become a member of Time-Warner's Pathfinder system. The membership is free.

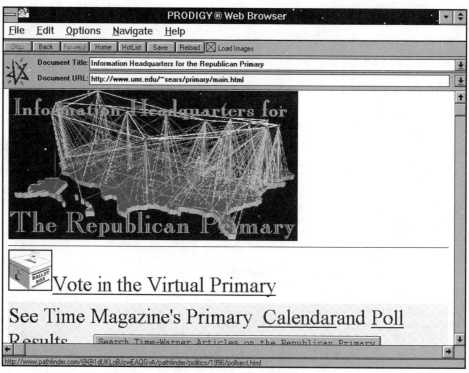

Figure 2.4 `http://www.umr.edu/~sears/primary/main.html`
The Republican Primary Information page.

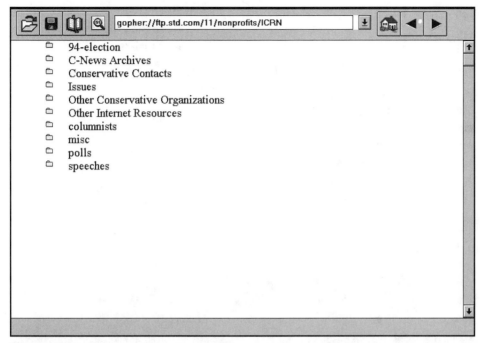

gopher://ftp.std.com/11/nonprofits/ICRN

- 94-election
- C-News Archives
- Conservative Contacts
- Issues
- Other Conservative Organizations
- Other Internet Resources
- columnists
- misc
- polls
- speeches

Figure 2.5 gopher://ftp.std.com
The Internet Conservative Resource Network.

The Republican Primary Information page sports some other fun and useful features. Some of the candidates' pages have links to their home pages elsewhere on the Net. There's a Virtual Primary, where you can vote for your favorite Republican candidate, and tools that let you read and post messages to an election newsgroup and a Republican mailing list. There are also links to other sites, such as the Right Side of the Web.

 The Internet Conservative Resource Network (ICRN)

gopher://gopher.std.com

Select the following directories:

Non-Profit Organizations Internet Conservative Resources Network

The Internet Conservative Resource Network (ICRN) Gopher site pulls together several types of Republican and Conservative information in one central location. The information available ranges from C-News (Conservative News) archives, to phone and e-mail contact numbers, to a list of other conservative organizations. Figure 2.5 shows the main ICRN directories.

Two directories on the ICRN are of particular relevance to this chapter: the House and Senate Republican Conferences Directory, and the Republican

National Committee (RNC) directory. Both of these directories are located under the Other Conservative Organizations directory.

Both of these directories are similar. They contain the plain text of press releases, briefs, and commentary for each of their organizations. One feature of the RNC directory is a brief copy, and the full text of the "Contract with America." There also is a subdirectory that contains the full text of the various bills described in the Contract.

Berkeley College Republican

`http://www.berkeleyic.com/`
`conservative/`

One place where the Republican party seems to be flourishing is on college campuses. Whether this is a reflection of a conservative turn by the nation's youth, or just an example of their greater comfort with technology, the strongest Republican presence on the Net is that of Republic student groups.

IN RECESS

Getting Involved in Republican Politics

The Internet Conservative Resource Network is a great place for people who want to get involved in Republican politics. There is a complete collection of phone, fax, and e-mail contact information for Republicans and others involved in politics (see fig. 2.6).

If you want to join the Republican party, you can start by phoning or faxing the offices of the State Republican party chairperson. If you want to register your opinion on a subject, use the contact person listed in the ICRN Contact directory shown in figure 2.6.

An easy way to send e-mail to your Congressperson or another important politician is through the Interactive Democracy page at the CGX site. For more information on CGX, see "CGX—The Conservative Generation X Home Page," later in this chapter.

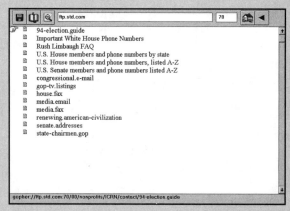

Figure 2.6 `gopher://ftp.std.com`
Conservative Contacts on the ICRN.

The Grand Old Page

"I am not a Conservative, I am a Revolutionary."

--Bret Schundler, First Republican Jersey City Mayor in 80 years

The Grand Old Page Bulletin Board

Figure 2.7 `http://www.berkeleyic.com/conservative/`
The Berkeley College Republican page is a good example of what college groups are capable of.

The Berkeley College Republican page is an outstanding example of what these groups are capable of (see fig. 2.7). The site has many useful and unusual resources. There is a copy of the "Contract with America," as well as a bulletin board for information specific to the Berkeley College Republicans. Of more interest are unique options such as the Conservative Multimedia Archive. The Multimedia Archive is a collection of images and sound clips. Ronald Reagan is prominent here, as are classic images such as the Statue of Liberty and the GOP elephant.

NOTE

Time-Warner's Pathfinder system is a fine source for quality information about the candidates. Unfortunately, Pathfinder requires users to be registered if they want to use many features of the system. I found this to be a slow, cumbersome process, perhaps because the system uses some advanced HTML features that my Web browsers had trouble with.

Once I acquired a Web browser that understood the version of HTML used by Pathfinder and registered, I could access the system as long as I entered my "official" screen name and password every time.

The Berkeley College Republican page has dozens of other links to Republican and conservative information and pages. One link lets you create and send a fax to Rush Limbaugh. Another lets you send e-mail to members of the House of Representatives. The Berkeley College Republican page is definitely worth a visit.

Other Conservative Groups

You'll notice that most of the material here is the product of individuals and small groups, rather than a group like the Republican National Committee. The Net is an ideal publishing medium for those who don't have the budget or audience size to take advantage of traditional media. Thus, you find groups like the Republican Liberty Caucus or the Berkeley College Republicans as the biggest Republican presence on the Net.

One of the best features of CGX *is its Interactive Democracy (ID) page.*

 ### CGX—The Conservative Generation X Home Page

```
http://www.teleport.com/
~pcllgn/cgx.html
```

CGX is a zine created by and for conservative members of Generation X. The CGX Web page is the online embodiment of the zine. If you're wondering what language I'm speaking, you should read the Buzzword Translation sidebar that follows. If you know what I'm talking about, skip the sidebar and find out what the CGX Web page has to offer.

The creators of the CGX Web page, and the zine of the same name, feel that they "offer the Conservative faction of Generation X means to express themselves in ways previously not possible" (see fig. 2.8). One goal of the creators is to counter the media perception that Generation X consists of a bunch of immature, whining Clintonites. While I'm not sure how much impact *CGX* has on the mass media, the page does have some useful resources for Republicans and conservatives.

IN RECESS

Buzzword Translation

Sometimes the people and sites you encounter on the Net are speaking (or typing) in some language other than English. At other times, it just seems that way. The following is Internet lingo that you may come across:

Zine is derived from magazine, and is used to describe small self-published periodicals like CGX.

Generation X is the media label for the generation that follows the Baby Boomers.

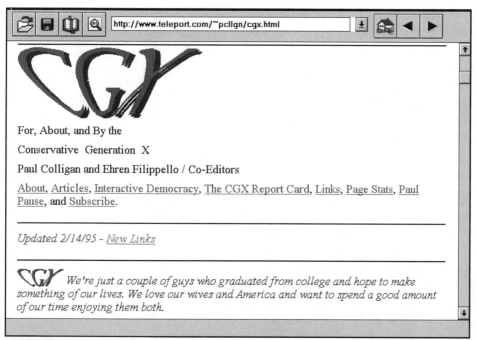

Figure 2.8 `http://www.teleport.com/~pcllgn/cgx.html`
The CGX Web page has useful resources for Republicans and conservatives.

One of the best features of *CGX* is its Interactive Democracy (ID) page. Designed for use with Web browsers that support e-mail, the ID page makes it easy to send e-mail to prominent politicians, talk radio personalities, and various media outlets. This innovative page is one of the easiest ways to make your voice heard on the political scene.

Another useful feature of this site is the "best of CGX" link. The link takes you to some of the best articles published in *CGX*, and provides one way to get a better understanding of what Generation X is thinking. Another is the Links page, which leads to a number of other conservative and Republican locations on the Net.

 The Republican Liberty Caucus

`http://w3.ag.uiuc.edu/liberty/rlc/index.html`

Libertarians and Libertarian ideas have been in and out of vogue within the Republican party over the last few decades. Barry Goldwater's 1964 Presidential campaign attracted the support of many Libertarians. Some Reagan administration officials pushed Libertarian economic ideas, and today academics such as Dr. Thomas Sowell and sociologist Charles Murray push Libertarian solutions to national problems.

The Republican Liberty Caucus (RLC) is an organization of Libertarian Republicans. It was founded in North Carolina in 1988, went national in 1990, and now in 1995 has affiliates in over two dozen states. The RLC, and its political action committee, the Republican Liberty Federal Campaign Fund, aim to increase the number of Libertarian Republicans in office.

The Republican Liberty Caucus page on the Web is an unofficial site for the RLC (see fig. 2.9). It provides background information on the group, and contains a copy of the RLC's Statement of Principles. After you read the chapter on the Libertarian party (LP), come back to the RLC page and reread the statement of principles. You won't find much difference between the official Libertarian party and RLC positions.

The RLC Web page also contains a partial list of the Republican Liberty Caucus's Board of Advisors. The board is comprised of prominent citizens, and former and current Senators and Congressmen. The final link on this page goes to Bob Reinhardt's Republican Liberty Caucus page.

Reinhardt's page is primarily a collection point for news and information about the RLC. The information on this page ranges from e-mail messages about RLC activities to excerpts from printed articles.

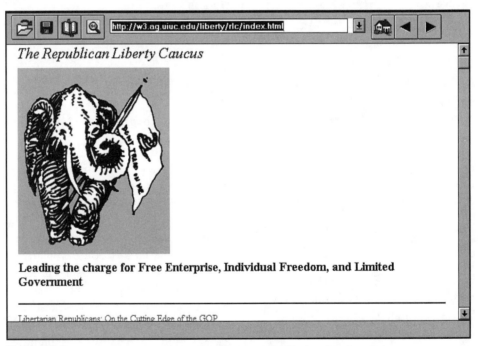

Figure 2.9 `http://w3.ag.uicu.edu/liberty/rlc/index.html`
The Republican Liberty Caucus Web page.

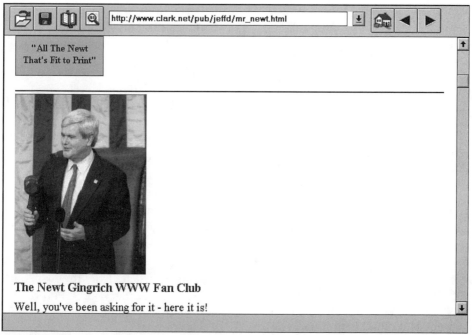

Figure 2.10 http://www.clark.net/pub/jeffd/mr_newt.html
The Newt Gingrich WWW Fan Club is one place on the Net to learn more about the Speaker of the House.

The other feature here is complete instructions on joining RLC's electronic mailing lists. The **RLC-NEWS** mailing list carries official RLC news from the Caucus headquarters. **RLC-DISCUSS** is the discussion list for RLC-related topics.

 Newt Gingrich WWW Fan Club

http://www.clark.net/pub/jeffd/ mr_newt.html

As Speaker of the House of Representatives, Newt Gingrich is creating quite a ruckus. As a historian, Gingrich sees a world in the midst of a great transformation from an industrial society to an information-based society. This vision drives Mr Gingrich's policies. Because he is such a force in the Republican party, understanding him is a key to understanding where the party is trying to go.

> **NOTE**
>
> There is a profile of Newt Gingrich in Chapter 6, "Political People," for those who want to learn more about him.

The Newt Gingrich WWW Fan Club is one place to learn more about the Speaker (see fig. 2.10). This page points to a number of sites that have helpful information. Links to several of Gingrich's speeches and public remarks let you see his ideas in his own words. Links to a Contract with America Page and to the Thomas Legislative information service detail his vision for the future.

> **NOTE**
>
> The Thomas Legislative information service is covered in much greater detail in Chapter 11, "The Branches of Government."

Two interesting links, the Progress and Freedom Foundation link and the George Gilder link, help you understand the basic ideas that drive the Speaker's actions. The Progress and Freedom Foundation (PFF) sponsors Mr. Gingrich's television show on National Empowerment Television. The PFF's Web page contains extensive writings derived from the works of Dr. Alvin Toffler, George Gilder, and other future-oriented thinkers. The George Gilder link takes you to a collection of articles by George Gilder. The collection was published in a special edition of *Forbes* magazine, and was hosted to the Net with permission from the copyright holders.

The Republicans on the Online Services

The Republican party seems to have decided to focus its online efforts on CompuServe. That's where you'll find the Republican National Committee's Republican Forum. It's a great place for Republicans to get information or share their thoughts on the issues of the day.

Neither America Online nor Prodigy has much in the way of formal Republican party coverage. AOL has a directory for the party in its Capital Connection, but there are only two files in it. A better source here is the Heritage Foundation/Policy Review forum. This area is dedicated to conservative political views and has information of use to Republicans. Besides the text of news articles from the Associated Press and other sources, Prodigy has little specific political coverage.

 The Republican Forum on CompuServe

Go: CIS:REPUBLICAN

The Republican Forum on CompuServe is the place to go for Republican party information on the online services (see fig. 2.11). There is a mass of information on the Republican National Committee (RNC), the organization that governs the Republican party. There's membership information, RNC Chairman's Reports, and more. The RNC Monday Briefings provide information on current events and issues, while their Talking Points provide grist for debates and discussions.

The Republican Forum also has libraries of reports from the Republicans in the House and Senate. Up-to-date e-mail lists for Senators and

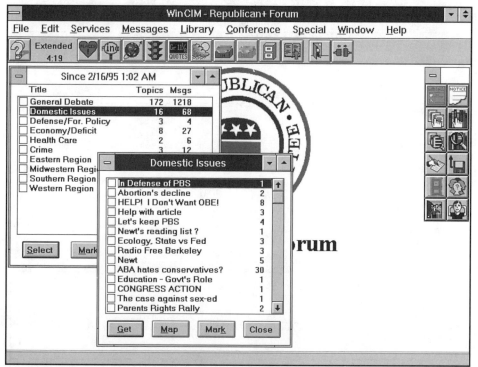

Figure 2.11 Go: CIS:REPUBLICAN
The Republican Party forum on CompuServe.

Congressmen are available, so you can talk directly to your elected representatives. State party information is also included.

The Republican Forum also provides 10 different message sections for discussions. Major issues such as defense, the economy, and health care have their own sections. Regional issues are covered in one of the four regional message sections. The general debate section carries the bulk of the action.

The Heritage Foundation/Policy Review Forum on AOL

Keyword: HERITAGE FOUNDATION

The Heritage Foundation/Policy Review forum is the place for conservative political thought on AOL. The forum is divided into four sections. One section contains information about *Policy Review* magazine. The third section is a list of 250 conservative quotations that the magazine believes were excluded from recent editions of *Bartlett's Familiar Quotations* due to the political bias of the current editor, Justin Kaplan.

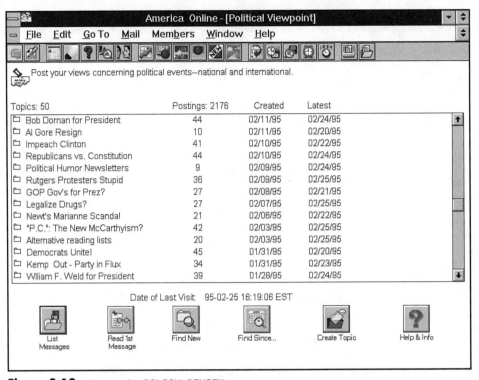

Figure 2.12 Keyword: POLICY REVIEW
The Policy Review Political Viewpoint message board at AOL.

The other two sections are more interesting. The *Policy Review* magazine directory contains the text of the magazine's articles. Republicans will enjoy articles such as, "Ready, Fire, Aim: Clinton's Left-Footed Foreign Policy."

The last section is the Political Viewpoint message board. Some typical articles from this board appear in figure 2.12. As you can see, with articles like "Republicans vs. Constitution," or "GOP Gov's for Prez?," this message board will also be of interest to Republicans.

Recommended Sites to See

The following list contains addresses of Net sites discussed in this chapter, as well as numerous others that might be of interest. The list is broken up into the same sections as the body of the chapter.

Newsgroups and Mailing Lists

Republican Party newsgroup.

UseNet address: `alt.politics.usa.republican`

News from Libertarian Republicans.

LISTSERV address: `rlc-news-request@tomahawk.welch.jhu.edu`

General talk about conservatism.

UseNet address: `alt.society.conservatism`

The Rush Limbaugh newsgroup.

UseNet address: `alt.rush-limbaugh`

Discussions of Newt Gingrich and his policies.

UseNet address: `alt.politics.usa.newt-gingrich`

Political news stories.

UseNet address: `clari.news.politics`

Anti-Gingrich political views.

UseNet address: `alt.politics.newt.grinch.grinch.grinch`

Republican and Conservative Material on the Net

The Right Side of the Web.

WWW address: `http://www.clark.net/pub/jeffd/index.html`

An archive of Republican and conservative information.

Gopher address: `gopher://ftp.std.com/`

Select the following directories:
`Non-Profit Organizations`
`Internet Conservative`
`Resource Network`

ICRN contact information.

Gopher address: `gopher://ftp.std.com`

Select the following directories:
`Non-Profit Organizations`
`Internet Conservative`
`   Resource Network`
`Conservative Contacts`

The Berkeley College Republican page.

WWW address: `http://www.berkeleyic.com/conservative/`

The Republican Primary page.

WWW address: `http://www,umr.edu/~sears/primary/main.html`

The Conservative Generation X page.

WWW address: `http://www.teleport.com/~pcllgn/cgx.html`

CGX's Interactive Democracy page.

WWW address: `http://www.teleport.com/~pcllgn/id.html`

The Republican Liberty Caucus
(unofficial).

WWW address: `http://`
`w3.ag.uiuc.edu/liberty/rlc/`
`index.html`

The Rush Limbaugh home page.

WWW address: `http://`
`eskimo.com/~jeremyps/`
`limbaugh-info.html`

Reinhardt's RLC page.

WWW address: `http://`
`tomahawk.welch.jhu.edu:1080/`
`rlc.html`

The Newt Gingrich WWW Fan Club.

WWW address: `http://`
`www.clark.net/pub/jeffd/`
`mr_newt.html`

The Progress and Freedom Foundation.

WWW address: `http://`
`www.pff.org/`

George Gilder on the Information
Superhighway.

WWW address: `http://`
`www.seas.upenn.edu/~gaj1/`
`ggindex.html`

Pro Life News.

WWW address: `http://`
`www.pitt.edu/~stfst/pln/`
`AboutPLN.html`

Ronald Reagan Fan Club.

UseNet address:
`alt.fan.ronald-reagan`

Dan Quayle Fan Club.

UseNet address:
`alt.fan.dan-quayle`

An unsympathetic view of the
Whitewater affair.

WWW address: `http://`
`www.cs.dartmouth.edu/~crow/`
`whitewater/`
`whitewater.html`

Free-market think tanks.

WWW address: `http://`
`chat.carleton.ca/~nlocklin/`
`tory/`
`conserv.dir`

Ronald Reagan home page.

WWW address: `http://`
`www.erinet.com/bkottman/`
`reagan.html`

Chapter 3
The Democratic Party

This chapter is your guide to exploring Democratic party resources on the Net.

In this chapter

- *Getting the news on the Democratic party*
- *The Democratic party and related resources on the Net*
- *The Democratic party on the Online Services*

In other chapters

→ *Democratic Socialists of America, a group that sometimes works with the Democratic party, is covered in Chapter 5.*

→ *Office of First Lady Hillary Clinton is examined in Chapter 8.*

→ *There is a profile of the White House, the current home of the top Democrat, Bill Clinton, in Chapter 11.*

The Democratic party was formed in the 1790s in support of Thomas Jefferson. Originally known as the Republican party (but unrelated to the Republican party we know today), the name evolved to the Democratic-Republican party and then to the Democratic party. The party originally supported individual liberty and a limited federal government. Today, the Democratic party is often viewed as the party of unions, minorities, and big government.

Democratic party resources on the Net are relatively scarce. Most of what you find on the Internet about the Democratic party is related to Senators, several of whom were defeated in 1994. However, expect more information to find its way onto the Net before the next election.

There are several forces that will drive this improvement. One is the team in the White House. Both the President and Vice President are strong believers in technology. This is, after all, the Administration that proposed the National

Information Infrastructure. Additional support for using the Net comes from the staff of Senator Edward Kennedy. The Senator opened a home page and a campaign page on the Web before the 1994 election. Since the election, many other Democrats have contacted the Senator's staff for help in setting up their own Web sites.

Getting the Newsgroups and Mailing Lists

Democrats on the Net keep up with, and comment on, party activities through UseNet newsgroups. Although there are about a half-dozen newsgroups with the word Democrat in the name, a few of them are inactive, or have a low volume of messages.

The fact that there is a Democrat in the White House gives the party a number of additional newsgroups to work with. I've included two of them here.

 A Democratic Discussion Newsgroup

`alt.politics.democrats.d`

This is the place to go for discussions of Democratic party politics. It appears to be the most active of the Democratic newsgroups. A wide variety of subjects are discussed here, as you can see in figure 3.1.

The intellectual level of the discussions varies. Some of the threads are little

more than name-calling between Democrats and people with other political beliefs. I've seen everyone from anarchists to conservatives contribute to this newsgroup at one time or another.

 White House News Stories

`clari.news.usa.gov.white_house`

This newsgroup covers the White House and related news stories. It is provided by the ClariNet **e.News** service and contains only news stories from major sources like Reuters and the Associated Press. Figure 3.2 shows the titles of some recent articles.

> **NOTE**
>
> For more information on ClariNet, see the "What is ClariNet?" sidebar in Chapter 11, "The Branches of Government."

Since all the articles here are news stories, the tone of this newsgroup is very different from that of `alt.politics.democrats.d`. There are no comments from the general public, and no threads discussing the topics. While a ClariNet newsgroup lacks the interactivity of a normal newsgroup, it compensates with the authoritative, professional information it does contain.

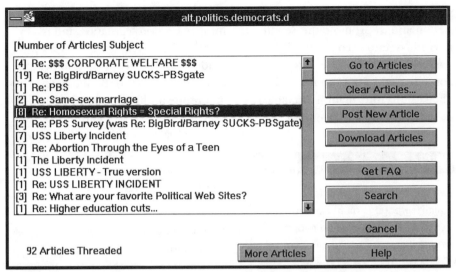

Figure 3.1 `alt.politics.democrats.d`
This Democratic discussion newsgroup covers a wide variety of subjects.

 ### Discussions about President Clinton

`alt.president.clinton`

This group is for discussions about the President and his policies. It is similar to `alt.politics.democrats.d`, with the addition of some threads related specifically to Mr. Clinton and other Presidents.

Democratic Party Resources on the Net

Right now, only two sites on the Net are run by the Democratic party. Both of them are run by Senate committees.

The other sites examined in the following sections are all related to the

Democratic party in some way. Since the President is a Democrat, the online Office of the President is included. There are Democratic student organizations, so I've included the Web site for the Indiana University College Democrats. The Political Participation Project is linked to by some of the Democratic pages, and is included here on that basis. A profile of Senator Edward Kennedy, the first Senator on the Web, completes the picture.

 ### The Democratic Policy Committee

`ftp://ftp.senate.gov/committee/`
`Dem-Policy/general/dpc.html`

As an arm of the Democratic party leadership, the task of the Senate's Democratic Policy Committee (DPC) is to provide information on current legislation and to promote the Senate Democratic Agenda. To accomplish this task, the DPC publishes information on bills and important issues. It now makes this information available to the general public through the Net.

> **NOTE**
>
> The address for the Democratic Policy Committee page is an FTP address. Even so, the DPC page is a hypertext document and works like a normal Web page. Your Web browser should be able to handle this and treat the page like a regular Web page.

The DPC Web page has five types of information on legislation and issues (see fig. 3.3). Weekly Reports keeps readers up to date on current Senate activities. Legislative Bulletins provides an outline and background for legislation. Special Reports features research and analysis on hot issues. Talking Points consists of Democratic party commentary on issues and current legislation. Background Briefs helps the reader place events in context.

The page has some other resources of general interest to Democrats. There is a hyperlinked list of Senate Democrats who have Web pages or directories on the Senate gopher. Another link connects to a collection of basic information for each Democratic party senator.

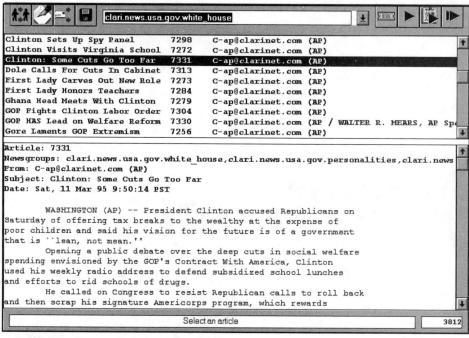

Figure 3.2 `clari.news.usa.gov.white_house`
White House news stories can be found on this ClariNet newsgroup.

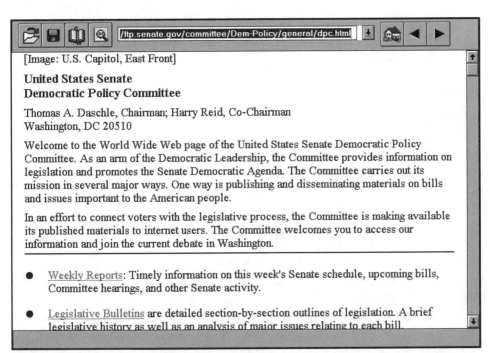

[Image: U.S. Capitol, East Front]

United States Senate
Democratic Policy Committee

Thomas A. Daschle, Chairman; Harry Reid, Co-Chairman
Washington, DC 20510

Welcome to the World Wide Web page of the United States Senate Democratic Policy Committee. As an arm of the Democratic Leadership, the Committee provides information on legislation and promotes the Senate Democratic Agenda. The Committee carries out its mission in several major ways. One way is publishing and disseminating materials on bills and issues important to the American people.

In an effort to connect voters with the legislative process, the Committee is making available its published materials to internet users. The Committee welcomes you to access our information and join the current debate in Washington.

● Weekly Reports: Timely information on this week's Senate schedule, upcoming bills, Committee hearings, and other Senate activity.

● Legislative Bulletins are detailed section-by-section outlines of legislation. A brief legislative history as well as an analysis of major issues relating to each bill.

Figure 3.3 ftp://ftp.senate.gov/committee/Dem-Policy/general/dpc.html
The Democratic Policy Committee page has five types of information on legislation and issues.

The Democratic Senatorial Campaign Committee

`http://www.dscc.org/d/dscc.html`

The Democratic Senatorial Campaign Committee (DSCC) exists to raise money for the support of Democratic party Senate candidates. According to President Clinton, the DSCC is, "...by far the most important single source of support for Democratic party candidates for the United States Senate." The committee uses the money it raises in several ways: to provide direct financial support of candidates, assist with media coverage, provide state-of-the-art strategies for communicating with voters, and more.

The DSCC Web page is one of the state-of-the-art communication strategies they employ (see fig. 3.4). While it has some overlap with the DPC page, the DSCC page has a number of unique resources. One of the resources is a collection of opinion polls. Taken from a variety of sources, these polls help the Democrats keep up with the public's varying views on candidates and issues.

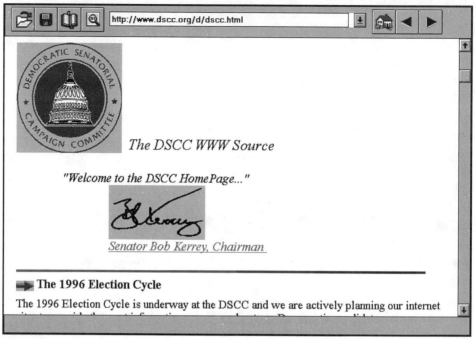

Figure 3.4 `http://www.dscc.org/d/dscc.html`
The Democratic Senatorial Campaign Committee has resources that deal directly with campaigns.

> **NOTE**
>
> The DSCC page is growing and changing. Several new features and resources are planned by the end of 1995, with even more additions likely as the 1996 elections approach.

In keeping with the DSCC's campaign support role, some of its resources deal directly with campaigns. The Morning Line reports on campaign issues.

There's also the Quotebook, which is a collection of quotes taken from Democratic and Republican campaigns.

There's even a collection of campaign press releases, endorsements, position papers, and similar items.

The DSCC also has a Gopher site with a large collection of public documents—this page links you to it. Other links take you to the home pages of many Democratic party senatorial campaigns, other political sites, and some general government resources. One thing that both the DSCC and the DPC pages have in common is a link to the home page of Senator Edward Kennedy. For more on Senator Kennedy, see the following Celebrity Profile.

Edward Kennedy: First Senator on the Web

WWW Address: `http://` `www.ai.mit.edu/projects/iiip/` `Kennedy/homepage.html`

Senator Edward Kennedy is one of the Democratic party's survivors of the 1994 elections. Senator Kennedy was the first Senator to have a World Wide Web page and, according to members of his staff, it helped him win re-election. With all the high technology in Massachusetts, a presence on the Web couldn't have hurt the Senator's standing with the voters. Figure 3.5 shows Senator Kennedy's home page.

Senator Kennedy's home page contains a range of material. A page lists online sources of Kennedy press releases—Gopher, FTP, and WWW sites, as well as UseNet newsgroups and New England-based Bulletin Board Systems. Constituents can send the Senator e-mail, and receive a response by United States mail if they include their mailing address. A section of the page covers Massachusetts Net and Web resources and includes a clickable map of the state. You can click the map to display a larger map of Massachusetts WWW resources.

Beyond state politics, the page links to some national resources. Some of the resources are found on other Democratic party Web pages, but others, like those related to the Information Infrastructure, are not.

The Senator also had a re-election page at WWW Address: `http://www.dscc.org/d/ma.html`

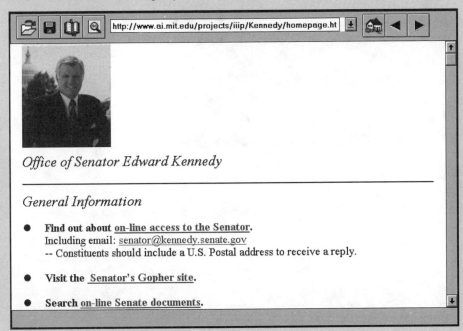

Figure 3.5 `http://www.ai.mit.edu/projects/iiip/Kennedy/homepage.html`
Senator Edward Kennedy was the first Senator on the Web.

The Political Participation Project

`http://www.ai.mit.edu/projects/ppp/home.html`

The PPP is a nonprofit, nonpartisan project to improve the public's participation in the political process through the use of interactive media like the Internet. The project is affiliated with MIT's Intelligent Information Infrastructure Project (IIIP). The IIIP Web page has numerous links to an assortment of useful and interesting political sites (see fig. 3.6).

One of the best links takes you to OPIN, the Online Political Information Network. OPIN is a directory of links to even more political resources, covering conventional political topics and topics such as Political Activism and Community networking. Other links take you to a directory of grassroots political organizations, conferences, publications, and a bibliography.

The Grassroots Directory is a concise list of information on dozens of grassroots organizations from both ends of the political spectrum. Liberal, conservative, and special-interest groups are all included on the list, with contact information, size, budget, and a one-sentence summary of purpose for each group.

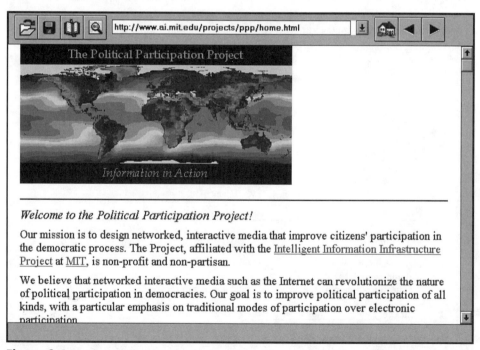

Figure 3.6 `http://www.ai.mit.edu/projects/ppp/home.html`
The Political Participation Project is an attempt to develop a general information distribution and retrieval system.

The Intelligent Information Infrastructure Project

WWW Address: `http://www.ai.mit.edu/projects/iiip/home-page.html`

The IIIP is an attempt to develop a general information distribution and retrieval system on the Net. One eventual goal of the project is to develop tools that can understand natural language requests for information.

The project started during the 1992 Presidential election as an automated way to distribute campaign information and gather input from the public. The system also helped volunteers to organize. The project remains involved in political communications, working with the White House and members of Congress, including Senator Kennedy.

The Office of the President

`http://www.whitehouse.gov/White_House/EOP/OP/html/OP_Home.html`

No look at Democratic party resources on the Net is complete without a stop at the office of the top Democrat, President Bill Clinton. Figure 3.7 shows the President's virtual office, part of the White House Web site. The page links to a list of the offices and agencies that report to the President and provides reports on highlights of the President's term in office.

Almost a dozen organizations are represented on the White House Offices and Agencies page. They range from high-powered groups such as the National Security Council to the office of the Staff Secretary. Each organization in the list has a hotlink to more information. Some of the links give you little more than a paragraph of text; others, such as the Office of Science and Technology Policy, are complete hypertext documents.

> **NOTE**
>
> The Office of the First Lady is one of the organizations represented on this page. It, too, is a complete hypertext document with significant information about Mrs. Clinton's activities. More information on the Office of the First Lady is in the Hillary Clinton profile in Chapter 7, "Issues Related to the Bill of Rights."

> **NOTE**
>
> You can get more information on the White House Web site in Chapter 10, "Foreign Affairs," where it is profiled.

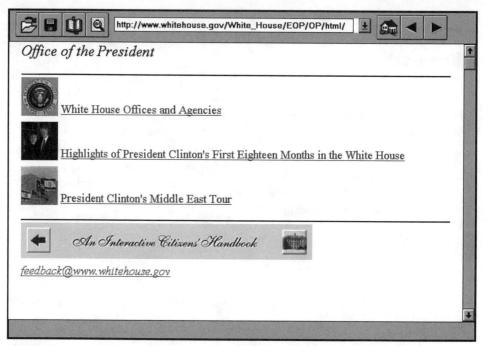

Figure 3.7 `http://www.whitehouse.gov/White_House/EOP/OP/html/OP_Home.html`
The Office of the President Web page has plenty of information about President Clinton.

The Highlights of President Clinton's First Eighteen Months in the White House link takes you to an illustrated document that details many of the President's accomplishments. When you click one of the images in this document, you get to see a larger version of the image. Hot links to the National Performance Review page and other sites give you access to more details on important subjects.

Another link from the President's Office takes you to a report on the President's 1994 Middle East tour. This document is similar in style to the Highlights one, but it contains fewer links to additional information. It does, however, contain lots of interesting photographs.

 Indiana University College Democrats

`http://www.indiana.edu/~iudems/home.html`

The Republican party is not the only party with college organizations on the Web. The Democrats have their own—although not as many as the Republicans. The Indiana University College Democrats page is one of the Democratic students' best sites (see fig. 3.8).

It has links to everything from campus activities to national political resources.

The Indiana University College Democrats are involved in a number of campus activities, from speeches to their Monthly Issue series. The group holds monthly meetings on issues of major importance. The goal is to get the members involved in debate and action on the subjects. Past debates have included issues such as the Balanced Budget Amendment and Voter Registration.

On a broader level, the page maintains links to state and national resources. The national Democratic party links connect to sites like the DSCC and DPC pages, and the nonpartisan links connect to many of the best national political resources. A link to the Gallup organization enables you to participate in an online Gallup poll.

The Democratic Party on the Online Services

The Democratic party has a presence on the three major online services. Both AOL and CompuServe have Democratic party forums. Each has a White House forum of some kind, with AOL and CompuServe providing the most complete coverage. The Democratic party is one political topic where the online services provide better information than the Net.

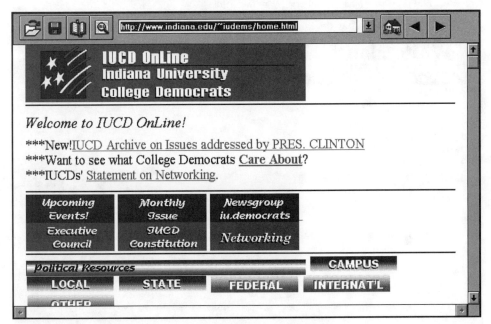

Figure 3.8 `http://www.indiana.edu/~iudems/home.html`
The Indiana University College Democrats Web page maintains links to local, state, and national resources.

The next sections cover the best Democratic forums on each service. AOL and CompuServe offer additional Democratic party information. To find this material, you can try **Keyword: CAPITAL** and look for the Democratic forum on AOL. Try **Go: CIS:WHITEH**, or **Go: CIS:POLITICS** on CompuServe.

 AOL's White House Forum

Keyword: **WHITE HOUSE**

The White House forum on America Online is a source for press releases and other documents from the White House's Office of Media Affairs (see fig. 3.9). The documents, which include Presidential speeches, remarks, and other statements, are organized for easy reference. The documents are divided into a number of sections, with each section addressing a different topic. A search program lets users find documents without browsing.

The additional features of the forum distinguish it from similar document archives on the Net. Seven message boards are dedicated to topics like The Economy, and Domestic and Foreign Affairs. With the message boards, AOL subscribers can comment on the information and issues covered in the forum.

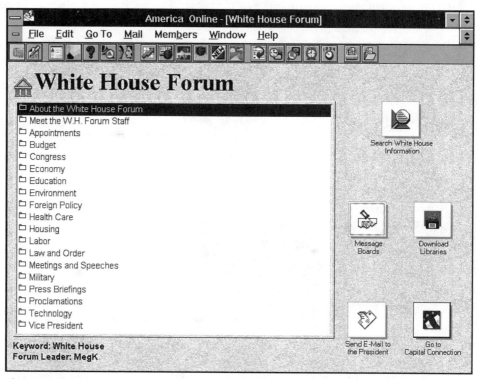

Figure 3.9 Keyword: WHITE HOUSE
AOL's White House Forum includes press releases and other informative documents.

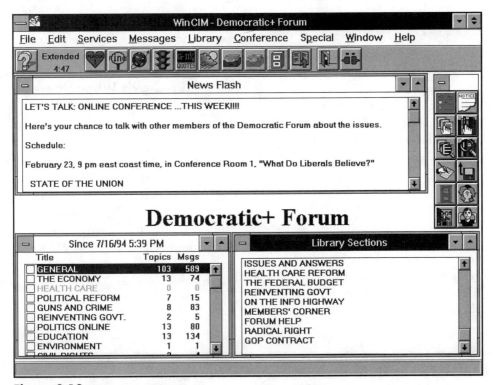

Figure 3.10 Go: `CIS:DEMOCR`
The Democratic forum on CompuServe is full of valuable information.

Three download libraries store documents not included in the main database. Two of these are for older or larger files that come from the White House. The third one is a place where visitors can upload their files on issues or administration.

There's even a button that lets anyone send e-mail to the President. A file called Welcome to the White House Forum, found in the folder About the White House Forum, provides instructions on how to do it.

 **CompuServe's Democratic Forum**

Go: `CIS:DEMOCR`

The Democratic Forum on CompuServe is full of useful party information (see fig. 3.10). The message sections are divided by subject matter, as well as by geographic location. Specific topics include health care, education, and welfare, as well as the conservative right. From what I've seen, the debate here is of decent quality, with reasonable discussions and little flaming.

The library sections in the forum carry a lot of information from the Democratic National Committee and other sources. The coverage ranges from items specifically of interest to Democrats—like the Party, Party, Party library—to general interest material. There's even a copy of the Republican's Contract with America, and the specific Acts that would implement it.

 Prodigy's White House Memo Forum

Jump: WHITE HOUSE

The White House Memo forum on Prodigy carries the same White House documents as the White House Forum on AOL (see fig. 3.11). Like AOL, Prodigy gets documents from the White House Office of Media Affairs and groups them by subject. Prodigy uses six groups rather than the dozen plus on AOL. You can browse the message groups or search them.

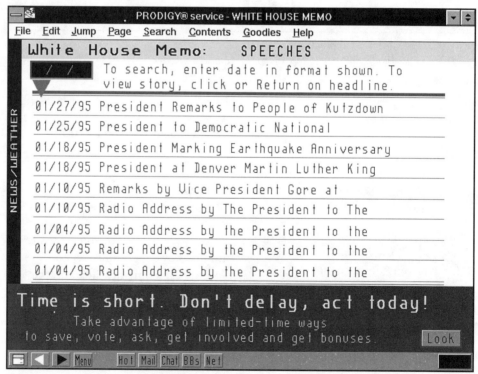

Figure 3.11 Jump: WHITE HOUSE
Prodigy's White House Memo forum gets documents from the White House Office of Media Affairs.

Recommended Sites to See

The following lists contain the addresses of the Net sites discussed in this chapter and others that might be of interest. The lists are divided into the same sections as the body of the chapter.

Newsgroups and Mailing Lists

Discussions of the Democratic party and related issues.

> UseNet Address:
> `alt.politics.democrats.dd`

News stories related to the White House and President Clinton.

> UseNet Address:
> `clari.news.usa.gov.white_house`

The President and his policies.

> UseNet Address:
> `alt.president.clinton`

General politics and press releases from Senator Kennedy.

> UseNet Address:
> `talk.politics.misc`

Low-volume newsgroups.

> UseNet Address:
> `alt.politics.democrats`

> UseNet Address:
> `alt.politics.democrats.clinton`

Low-volume newsgroup about Democrats in the House of Representative.

> UseNet Address:
> `alt.politics.democrats.house`

Low-volume newsgroup about Democrats in the Senate.

> UseNet Address:
> `alt.politics.democrats.senate`

The New England political scene and Senator Kennedy's press releases.

> UseNet Address: `ne.politics`

Democratic Party Resources on the Net

The Democratic Policy Committee.

> FTP Address: `ftp://`
> `ftp.senate.gov/committee/Dem-`
> `Policy/general/dpc.html`

The Democratic Senatorial Campaign Committee.

> WWW Address: `http://`
> `www.dscc.org/d/dscc.html`

Senator Edward Kennedy's home page.

> WWW Address: `http://`
> `www.ai.mit.edu/projects/iiip/`
> `Kennedy/homepage.html`

Senator Kennedy's 1992 Campaign page.

> WWW Address: `http://`
> `www.dscc.org/d/ma.html`

The Political Participation Project.

WWW Address: `http://www.ai.mit.edu/projects/ppp/home.html`

The Intelligent Information Infrastructure Project page.

WWW Address: `http://www.ai.mit.edu/projects/iiip/home_page.html`

The Office of the President.

WWW Address: `http://www.whitehouse.gov/White_House/EOP/OP/html/OP_Home.html`

The Indiana University College Democrats.

WWW Address: `http://www.indiana.edu/~iudems/home.html`

Senator Kennedy's Gopher site.

Gopher Address: `gopher://ftp.senate.gov`

Select the following directories:
`Available Documents Distributed by Member`
`Massachusetts`
`Senator Edward Kennedy`

Gopher access to DSCC.

Gopher Address: `gopher://info.tamu.edu`

Select the following directories:
`Browse by Subject`
`Political Science & Politics`
`Democratic Senatorial Campaign Committee`

White House document summaries.

WWW Address: `http://eos.esusda.gov/wh/whsum.html`

The Information Infrastructure Task Force.

WWW Address: `http://iitf/doc/gov/`

The California Democratic Committee newsletter.

Gopher Address: `gopher://sypal.org`

Chris Casey, developer of Web sites for politicians.

WWW Address: `http://www.ai.mit.edu/people/casey/casey.html`

Senator Daschle, first Senator with a web page on a congressional server.

FTP Address: `ftp://ftp.senate.gov/member/sd/daschle/general/daschle.html`

The White House.

WWW Address: `http://www.whitehouse.gov/`

The First Lady's office.

WWW Address: `http:/www.whitehouse.gov/White_House/EOP/First_Lady/html/HILLARY_Home.html`

Vice-President Gore's National Performance Review.

WWW Address: `http://www.npr.gov`

The University Democrats of the University of Texas at Austin.

WWW Address: `http://www.utexas.edu/students/unidems/.html/main.html`

The Clinton Administration's National Information Infrastructure proposal.

WWW Address: `http://sunsite.unc.edu/nii/NII-Table-of-Contents.html`

Chapter 4
The Libertarian Party

This chapter lets you see what the Libertarians are up to on the Net.

In this chapter

- *Getting the news on the Libertarian party*
- *A look at official Libertarian party materials and pages*
- *Unofficial Libertarian pages and resources*
- *One-of-a-kind pages related to Libertarianism*

In other chapters

← *For more information on the Republican Liberty caucus and Progressive Young Republicans, see Chapter 2.*

→ *For a look at individual Rights and Responsibilities, see Chapter 7.*

→ *For coverage of current government policies and programs, see Chapter 8.*

→ *For current economic and trade policies, see Chapter 9.*

→ *For US relations with the rest of the world, see Chapter 10.*

The Libertarian party (LP) is the third largest political party in the United States. The party strives to provide a real alternative to the Democrats and Republicans by focusing tightly on individual liberty. To Libertarians, personal freedom and civil liberties are paramount. The government exists merely to protect the citizens from force or fraud.

Libertarianism is a popular topic on the Net. This being the case, there is a mass of Libertarian material available in just about any form you might want.

The LP runs its own Web page, as do individuals and groups interested in Libertarianism. Some of these pages are little more than collection points for online documents; other pages are more interesting, with extensive hypertext links and scanned images. If your Web browser can handle forms, you can even take an online quiz designed to tell you where you fit into the political universe.

Fortunately, you don't need to be able to use the Web to get Libertarian material online. With FTP or Gopher, you can reach most of the important Libertarian documents. Net users can find several newsgroups that cover Libertarianism or related topics, or choose from a set of mailing lists.

Newsgroups and Mailing Lists

People interested in Libertarianism have a number of newsgroups and mailing lists that they can turn to for current information. Several of them are described here.

 **Libertarian Newsgroup**

`alt.politics.libertarian`

This newsgroup is the place to talk about Libertarian philosophy, issues, and movements. Figure 4.1 shows some typical discussion threads.

 **Libertarian Announcements**

LISTSERV Address: `libernet-request@dartmouth.edu`

This mailing list is for Libertarian announcements and statements. It is not

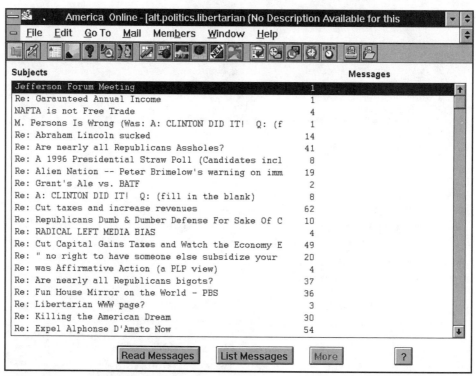

Figure 4.1 `alt.politics.libertarian`
This site is a place to discuss Libertarian philosophy, issues, and movements. Both Libertarians and people opposed to Libertarianism meet here, making for lots of arguments.

a place for discussions. Discussions of Libertarian issues are held in the `libernet-d` mailing list.

Official Libertarian Party Materials

With its ability to move information across the entire planet at virtually no cost, the Net is an ideal tool for the Libertarian party. The LP makes good use of this tool. The party has two pages on the Net: one representing its headquarters, and one serving as the LP home page. These pages have extensive links to official and unofficial resources: party documents, current activities, and contact lists.

The LP has done a good job of moving official documents online. Many of its most important documents, things like the current party platform and its positions on major issues, have been converted to hypertext. In this form, the documents are easier to use, and are more useful than the printed versions. Other documents are available as plain text, so they can be captured and read by people without Web access.

The Current Activities page is a good place to find out about the activities of the Libertarian party. You'll find things like press releases and the party's alternatives to Clinton Administration proposals. One very important activity of the party is petition drives to get its candidates on state ballots. This page links you to current ballot efforts.

The LP maintains a number of contact lists on the Net, and they are vitally important to its membership. There is a list of Libertarian Party Committee members and their e-mail addresses. There are lists of the state and local LP affiliates. There also is an up-to-date list of every elected Libertarian in the country. As you read through the chapter, you'll learn where to find these lists.

 The Libertarian Party Headquarters Page

`http://access.digex.net/~lphq/`

The place to start exploring official Libertarian party resources is the Libertarian Party Headquarters page on the Web (see fig. 4.2). This page has links to many of the Libertarian resources, and points you to information on how to join the party.

The Libertarian Party Headquarters page has direct links to copies of recent LP platforms, the party's stand on major issues, and hypertext copies of press releases. A link is also provided to a page of directories that contain e-mail contact information for national, state and local parties, and officials. The directory also includes a list of all the LP members currently in office in the United States.

> **NOTE**
>
> There is an FTP site that serves as an archive for Libertarian party press releases and other official documents. You can reach it by FTP at `ftp://ftp.digex.net` `/pub/access/` `lphq/`.

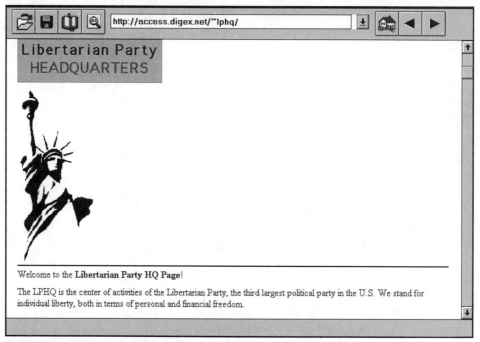

Welcome to the **Libertarian Party HQ Page**!

The LPHQ is the center of activities of the Libertarian Party, the third largest political party in the U.S. We stand for individual liberty, both in terms of personal and financial freedom.

Figure 4.2 `http://access.digex.net/~lphq/`
The Libertarian Party Headquarters page has links to many Libertarian resources.

Some of the other interesting links on this page lead to a list of LP products you can buy, the electronic Libertarian resource list, and a link to the Libertarian party home page.

 ### The Libertarian Party Home Page

`http://www.lp.org/lp/`

A link from the LP Headquarters page takes you to the Libertarian party home page. On this page, you get pointers to just about anything you want to know about the Libertarian party—its history to what it's up to today (fig. 4.3).

The material linked to this page is easily accessible, well-written, and up-to-date. The next few sections look at some of the pages you can link to.

 ### The Party Overview Page

`http://www.lp.org/lp-overview.html`

To get a good background on Libertarianism and its goals, try the Libertarian Party Overview page. You can reach this page directly at the preceding address, or by clicking the Overview hotlink on the LP home page. However you get there, you'll see something like figure 4.4.

One link on the Party Overview page offers a number of convenient ways to join the Libertarian Party. There's an online membership form you can fill out, as well as information on joining by e-mail, phone, or U.S. mail. If you're not sure about joining, another link from the Party Overview page takes you to a collection of introductory material.

The last link goes to the Libertarian FAQ page. This page contains answers to ten of the most commonly asked questions about Libertarians and Libertarianism.

 The Current Activities Page

`http://www.lp.org/lp/ lp-curr.html`

The Current Activities page lets you know what activities and projects the

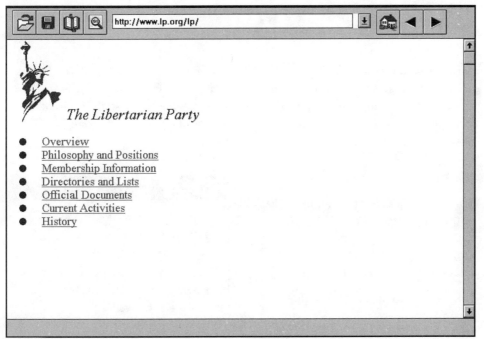

Figure 4.3 `http://www.lp.org/lp/` *The Libertarian Party Web home page.*

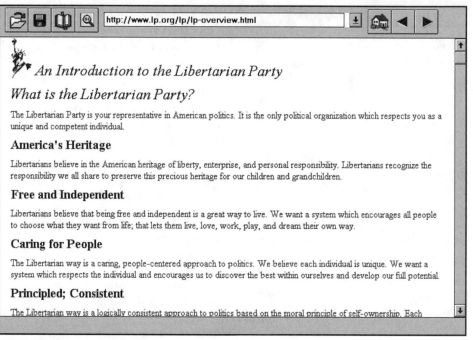

Figure 4.4 `http://www.lp.org/lp/lp-overview.html`
The Party Overview page.

party is pursuing today. This page is used to pull together a variety of activities that are ongoing. Figure 4.5 shows some of the activities that are underway.

LP News

The party makes its views on the issues of the day known using press releases and its monthly newspaper, *LP News*. On this page, you can reach these press releases and selected *LP News* articles.

Unlike the two major parties, the Libertarian Party is not automatically included on the ballot in all 50 states.

To get a spot on the ballot, the Party must conduct petition drives. The latest state-by-state ballot status is tabulated and available from this page (see fig. 4.6).

> **NOTE**
>
> An alternate source for LP press releases and other material is `ftp://ftp.digex.net/pub/access/lphq/`.
>
> The site contains text versions of most LP publications and documents, making the files accessible to those who can't use the Web.

Operation Safe Streets

Since crime is the number one concern of citizens today, the Libertarians developed Operation Safe Streets, a program to drastically reduce crime in America. A hotlink from the Current Activities page takes you to basic information about this program.

The Libertarians created Operation Safe Streets to drastically reduce crime in America. A hotlink on the Current Activities page takes you to basic information about the program.

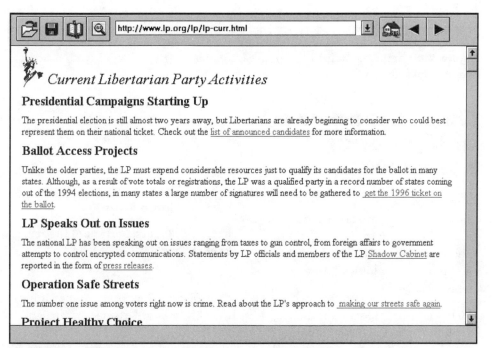

Figure 4.5 `http://www.lp.org/lp/lp-curr.html`
The Current Activities page.

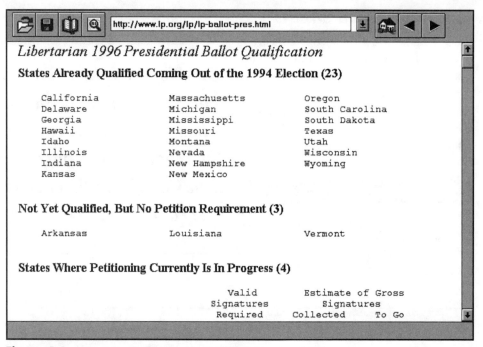

Figure 4.6 `http://www.lp.org/lp/lp-ballot-pres.html`
The LP Ballot Status on the WWW.

Other Collections of Libertarian Resources

Individuals, groups, clubs, and heaven knows who else, have taken advantage of the freedom of the Net to publish Libertarian materials. The work that went into these unofficial pages is impressive.

What is equally impressive is the vast amount of material linked into the pages. Besides the student and affiliated party pages included in this section, there are three different pages covering general Libertarianism. While they all cover some of the same

information, each one has some unique links.

 The Libertarian Web Home Page

`http://w3.ag.uiuc.edu/liberty/libweb.html`

The Libertarian Web is a product of the College Libertarians of the University of Illinois at Urbana-Champaign. Designed for newcomers to Libertarianism, as well as for veteran Libertarians, this page has links to some of the same resources as the official LP pages (see fig. 4.7).

Some of the links lead to liberty-minded groups like the Republican Liberty Caucus and DigitaLiberty. Other links lead to things like a source of Libertarian videotapes, or information on subscribing to *Reason* magazine, a pro-liberty publication.

This page also has links to documents on the philosophy of Libertarianism and the related philosophy of Objectivism.

 Other Good Libertarian Links

`http://www.mit.edu:8001/`
`activities/libertarians/`
`goodlinks.html`

The name of this page doesn't give an inkling of its value. As befits a page created by the minds at Massachusetts Institute of Technology (MIT), this page is a wide-ranging and comprehensive collection of Libertarian and liberty-related materials. Figure 4.8 shows the eight major topics covered by this page. Each of the topics leads to one or more links to other documents or other Web sites.

NOTE

At `http://www.vix.com/pub/objectivism/in-brief.html` Ayn Rand defines objectivism philosophy in the following way:

- Reason is man's only means of knowledge.
- Rational self-interest is the objective ethical code.
- Laissez-faire capitalism is the objective social system.

Getting Involved Nationally

You've decided to get involved in the Libertarian party, but how do you start?

For now, we'll look at getting in contact with the national Libertarian party (getting involved locally is covered later). The first step is to join the party. To do that, browse to the membership page at:

WWW Address: `http://www.lp.org/lp/lp membership.html`.

Once you've signed up, go to the directories and lists page at:

WWW Address: `http://www.lp.org/lp/lp-dirs.html`

This page gives you contact information for the Libertarian National Committee members, at-large members, and regional representatives.

IN RECESS

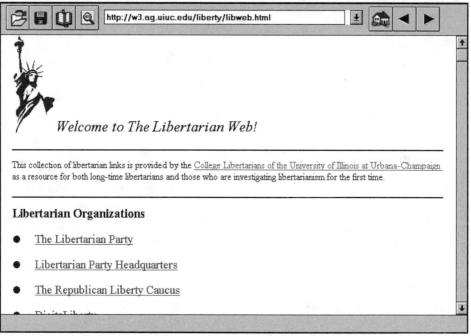

Figure 4.7 `http://w3.ag.uiuc.edu/liberty/libweb.html`
The Libertarian Web home page.

Libertarians value their privacy. The Cryptography and Technology Issues section of the Good Libertarian Links page covers online privacy resources. It links you to organizations that support online privacy, as well as a source for PGP, Pretty Good Privacy, a public domain encryption program.

Each of the other seven sections of the Good Libertarian Links page is similarly connected to useful resources. Some of them are addressed in this chapter, but many aren't. If you want to browse this site, you should leave yourself plenty of time for exploration.

> **NOTE**
>
> You can get more information on PGP and encryption in Chapter 6.

The Libertarian Student Clubs WWW Network Page

`http://w3.ag.uiuc.edu/liberty/libweb.html`

Libertarian student clubs have popped up at colleges and universities here and abroad. Some clubs are specifically Libertarian, while others, like the Pro-gressive Young Republicans, share views in common with the Libertarians. The best place to find out more about Libertarian student clubs is the Liber-tarian Student Clubs WWW Network home page (see fig. 4.9).

On the Libertarian Student Clubs WWW Network home page, you'll find links to more than a half-dozen

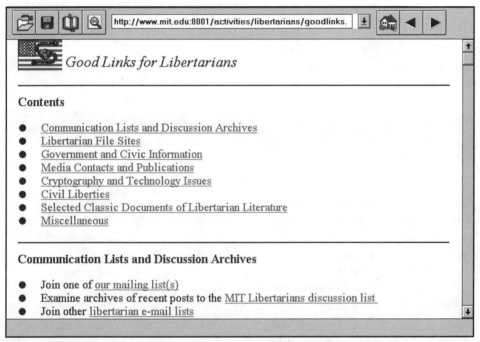

Figure 4.8 `http://www.mit.edu:8001/activities/libertarians/goodlinks.html`
Other good Libertarian links on the WWW.

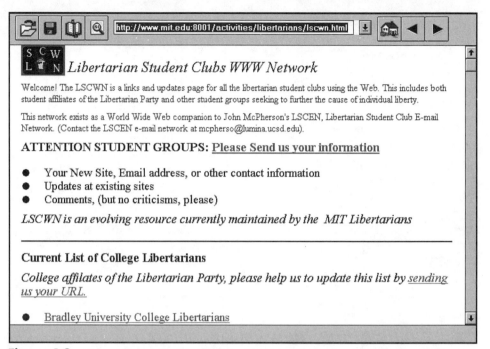

Figure 4.9 `http://www.mit.edu:8001/activities/libertarians/lscwn.html`
The Libertarian Student Clubs WWW Network home page.

Libertarian, or Libertarian-minded student groups. Some of these groups provide links to still other groups or materials; the connections that make the name World Wide Web so appropriate. This page also provides a link to the interactive version of the World's Smallest Political Quiz, and a collection of articles on political activism and organizing political groups.

 Affiliated Parties

`http://www.lp.org/lp/`
`lp-aff.html`

The Libertarian Party has affiliates in every state. These affiliates, while following basic Libertarian philosophy, are independent of the national organization and set their own policies and stake out their own positions on issues. Several of the affiliated groups have online information that can be reached from the LP's Affiliate Parties Web page (fig. 4.10).

If your local LP affiliate is online, the LP's Affiliate parties page is a great way to find out what's happening.

Related Sites and Sources

Because people interested in Libertarianism tend to be individualistic, it isn't surprising that there are some unusual Libertarian resources on the Net.

The next few pages will show you some interesting sites. These sites range from a page for those aspiring to become the LP Presidential candidate, to a set of arguments against Libertarianism. But first, it's time for a quiz.

The World's Smallest Political Quiz

`http://lydia.bradley.edu/`
`campusorg/libertarian/`
`wspform.html`

Perhaps you're wondering if you are or should be a Libertarian. Find out by taking the World's Smallest Political Quiz, created by the Advocates for Self-Government. The quiz consists of 10 multiple-choice questions, five dealing with personal issues and five with economic issues (see fig. 4.11). To take the quiz, a Web browser that can handle forms is needed.

In this version of the quiz, you need only check the answers that most closely match your beliefs, then click the Submit button to get it scored automatically. The results of the quiz are plotted on the Self-Government Compass, a diagram that places you within the political spectrum. The possible categories are liberal, centrist, conservative, authoritarian, and libertarian. The diagram allows for gradations

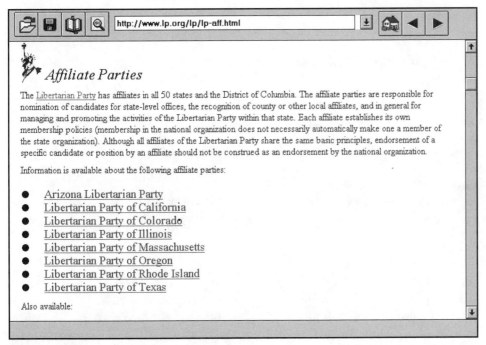

Figure 4.10 `http://www.lp.org/lp/lp-aff.html`
The LP's Affiliate Parties page.

within each category, so you might be classified as a conservative that tends toward Libertarianism, or an authoritarian liberal.

Give this quiz a try. It's fun, and who knows, you may be surprised by what you find.

 Laissez-Faire Books

`http://www.xmission.com/~legalize/lf/Laissez-Faire.html`

If you want Libertarian material that doesn't require a computer to read, cruise the Libertarian sites to search for references to books published by Laissez-Faire Books.

Laissez-Faire Books has been a prime source for Libertarian books and tapes for over two decades. It carries works that are not readily available in other places. Best of all, Laissez-Faire Books has an online catalog and accepts orders by e-mail. Figure 4.12 shows a portion of their WWW subject catalog.

> **NOTE**
>
> It's important to realize that the Internet has virtually no security. If you pass your credit card number over the Net, anyone with the right equipment can record it. Companies are working furiously to develop secure methods for using credit cards online, but until they do, think twice before sending your credit card number across the Net.

 The Presidential Nominations Page

`http://www.lp.org/lp/lp-cand-pres.html`

The Libertarian party has run a candidate for President since 1972. In 1992, the party's nominee, Andre Marrou, received just under 300,000 votes. The party hopes to capitalize on anti-government feelings to significantly improve its showing in 1996.

One of the candidates, Harry Browne, has his own Presidential Campaign Web page. Here you can find out who he is, what he stands for, and why he is running.

 Critiques of Libertarianism

`http://draco.centerline.`
`com:8080/~mrh/liber`

While the Libertarian party may be the third largest political party in the United States, it is still much smaller and less well known than the Democratic or Republican parties.

Because so much of the information about Libertarianism is written by

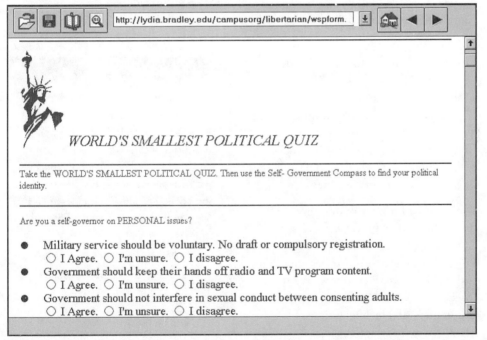

Figure 4.11 `http://lydia.bradley.edu/campusorg/libertarian/wspform.html` *The World's Smallest Political Quiz.*

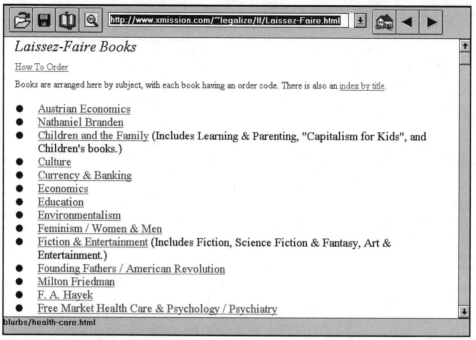

Figure 4.12 `http://www.xmission.com/~legalize/lf/Laissez-Faire.html`
The Laissez-Faire Books online catalog and order service.

Libertarians, Mike Huben created the Critiques of Libertarianism Web page, where non-Libertarians can debate, criticize, and learn more about Libertarian issues (see fig. 4.14). The non-Libertarian FAQ file is another place to get information about Libertarian political and social philosophies.

You'll find a number of documents at the Critiques of Libertarianism site. They range from rebuttals of common Libertarian arguments, to the complete text of historical documents, like the Declaration of Independence, that are frequently cited by libertarians.

Libertarian Harry Browne

If you've explored some of the Libertarian pages discussed earlier in this chapter, you have probably noticed the name Harry Browne. There are links to his Presidential campaign page from many Libertarian sites. While I can't say how popular Mr. Browne is among Libertarian voters, he has certainly established the strongest Net presence of any Libertarian candidate (see fig. 4.13).

The Harry Browne for President page is the central location for information on Mr. Browne and his campaign. The site lists members of his Presidential campaign committee and prominent members of the financial community who endorse him—in particular, Robert R. Prechter, Jr. and Mark Skousen.

This page also includes Mr. Browne's writings related to Libertarianism, government, and the Presidency. In addition, you will find Browne's biography and a transcript of his September, 1994 interview with LP News.

You can reach the Harry Browne for President site at:

WWW Address: `http://www.rahul.net/browne/`

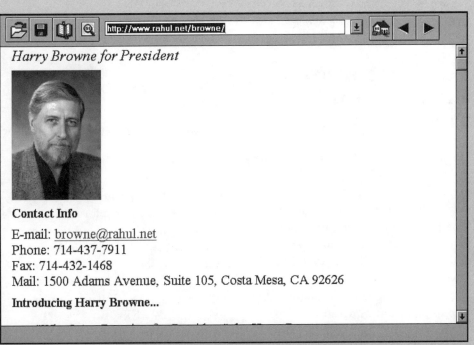

Figure 4.13 `http://www.rahul.net/browne/`
The Harry Browne for President page.

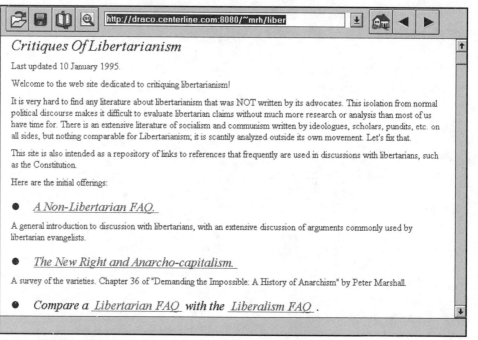

Figure 4.14 `http://draco.centerline.com:8080/~mrh/liber`
The Critiques of Libertarianism site.

The Libertarian Party on the Online Services

The Libertarian party presence on the online services varies greatly from one service to the other. America Online has a Libertarian forum of its own. CompuServe covers the subject in the Political Debate forum that is shared with other parties. Prodigy has little coverage of Libertarianism. The following sections cover the Libertarian AOL and CompuServe addresses.

 America Online

Keyword: LIBERTARIAN

When it comes to Libertarian coverage on the online services, America Online is the most comprehensive. AOL has a complete Libertarian forum that includes all the basics, like the Libertarian Party Platform. While it doesn't have the hypertext links of a Web page, this forum is the top choice for non-Internet Libertarian Party resources.

The Libertarian Party forum on America Online is part of the Capitol Connection, a central location for political materials. It's hosted by Jim Merritt, a member of both the California and National Libertarian Parties.

As you can see in figure 4.15, the party platform is just one of the resources AOL provides. Other available documents include LP press releases, and state and local announcements. These documents are in plain text so users can read them easily. The Libertarian Library contains an even larger collection of files, executable programs and more. These files are not in a form where you can read them on-screen while online. They need to be downloaded to your PC and decompressed, executed, or whatever is appropriate for the particular file.

The Libertarian Message Board is a place where AOL members can sound off on libertarian topics. It serves a

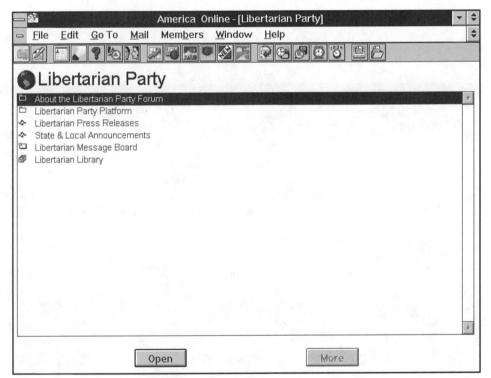

Figure 4.15 Keyword: LIBERTARIAN
AOL's Libertarian forum is part of Capitol Connection.

similar purpose as the libertarian newsgroups on UseNet, but has much lower traffic. On the day I signed on, there hadn't been any new messages in over two weeks.

 **CompuServe**

Go: `CIS:POLITICS`

While the Libertarian Party doesn't have its own forum on CompuServe, many LP officials maintain CompuServe accounts and provide their account numbers for use with LP-related e-mail.

The biggest point of LP activity on CompuServe is in the Political Debate forum. The party has its own message section and library (see fig. 4.16). The current Libertarian party platform and program are available in the library, while debates, discussions, and arguments appear in the message section.

The figure shows some of the contents of both the message section and the library. The box on the left contains the names of some of the discussion

Names of discussion threads   Available files

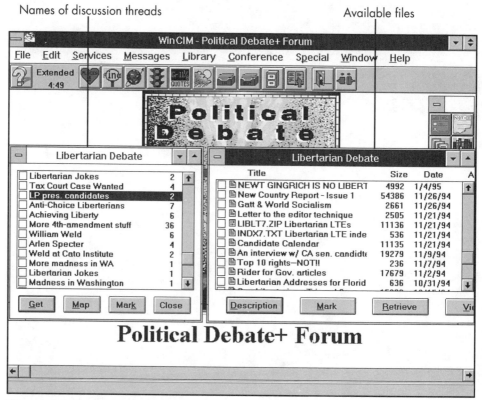

Figure 4.16 Go: `CIS:POLITICS`
CompuServe's Political Debate forum.

threads, while the box on the right shows some of the available files.

Recommended Sites to See

The remainder of this chapter consists of the addresses of Libertarian and liberty-minded sites on the Net. The addresses are divided into sections for each of the major sections of this chapter.

Each address is identified by its type and a very short description of what you can find there. Many of these addresses are discussed in more detail in the body of the chapter, so if you see one that looks interesting, skim through the appropriate section before logging onto the Net.

Newsgroups and Mailing Lists

Libertarian philosophy and issues.

UseNet Addresses: `talk.politics.libertarianism` and `alt.politics.libertarianism`

General civil liberty discussions.

UseNet Addresses: `alt.society.civil-liberties` and `alt.society.civil-liberty`

Access to LIBERNET and LIBERNET-D mailing lists.

LISTSERVE Address: `libernet-request@dartmouth.edu`

Extensive list of libertarian mailing lists.

WWW Address: `http://www.rahul.net/dehnbase/liberml/`

Last 5 days messages from LIBERNET & LIBERNET-D.

FTP Address: `ftp://coos.dartmouth.edu/Libernet`

Request access to LPUS mailing list.

LISTSERVE Address: `LPUS-request@dehnbase.fidonet.org`

Official Libertarian Party Materials

LP headquarters page.

WWW Address: `http://access.digex.net/~lphq/`

LP documents.

FTP Address: `ftp://ftp.digex.net/pub/access/lphq`

The LP home page.

WWW Address: `http://www.lp.org/lp/`

The LP home page by FTP.

FTP Address: `ftp://ftp.rahul.net/pub/lp/www/lp.html`

LP Overview.

WWW Address: `http://www.lp.org/lp/lpoverview.html`

Current LP activities page.

WWW Address: `http://www.lp.org/lp/lp-curr.html`

Operation Safe Streets.

WWW Address: `http://www.lp.org/lp/lp-oss.html`

LP membership information.

WWW Address: `http://www.lp.org/lp/lp-membership.html`

LP directories.

WWW Address: `http://www.lp.org/lp/lp-dirs.html`

National committee contact information.

WWW Address: `http://www.lp.org/lp/lp-lnc-dir.html`

FTP Address: `ftp://rahul.net/pub/lp/www/lp-lnc-dir.html`

General LP documents by FTP.

FTP Addresses: `ftp://think.com/pub/libernet` and `ftp://ftp.lp.org/pub/lp`

Other Resources

LP page on Yahoo.

WWW Address: `http://akebono.stanford.edu/yahoo/Politics/Parties_and_Groups/Libertarian_Party`

The Libertarian Web home page.

WWW Address: `http://w3.ag.uiuc.edu/liberty/libweb.html`

Links for Libertarians.

WWW Address: `http://www.mit.edu:8001/activities/libertarians/goodlinks.html`

LP affiliate parties.

WWW Address: `http://www.lp.org/lp/lp-aff.html`

FTP Address: `ftp://ftp.rahul.net/pub/lp/www/lp-aff.html`

LP state officials.

WWW Address: `http://www.access.digex.net/~lphq/state.lp.contacts`

A plain text LP resource list.

FTP Address: `ftp://shell.portal.com/pub/chan/libertarian/libertar.ian`

LP FAQ principles.

Gopher Address: `gopher.hike.te.chiba-u.ac.jp`

Once connected, navigate through the following directories: `news.answers archive... libertarian`

LP materials by Gopher.

Gopher Address:
`gopher.ocf.berkeley.edu`

Once connected, navigate
through the following directories:
`University of California`
`  at Berkeley`
`Berkeley College`
`  Republicans`
`  (BCR)`
`  Libertarian`

Related Sites

The world's smallest political quiz.

WWW Address: `http://`
`lydia.bradley.edu/campusorg/`
`libertarian/wspform.html`

The Laissez-Faire bookstore.

WWW Address: `http://`
`www.xmission.com/~legalize/`
`lf/Laissez-Faire.html`

Potential LP Presidential candidates.

WWW Address: `http://www.`
`lp.org/lp/lp-cand-pres.html`

Harry Browne for President.

WWW Address: `http://`
`www.rahul.net/browne/`

Critiques of Libertarianism.

WWW Address: `http://`
`draco.centerline.com:8080/`
`~mrh/liber`

The non-Libertarian FAQ.

WWW Address: `http://`
`draco.centerline.com:8080/`
`~mrh/liber/faq.html`

Chapter 5
Other Parties

The big political parties aren't the only groups using the Net—here are other parties and organizations present on the Net.

The two-party system has prevailed in the United States for most of this century. Under this system, the two major parties compete against each other for control of the government and totally dominate the political scene. On occasion, a third-party or independent candidate makes a decent showing, but, in general, the playing field belongs to the two major parties.

Beyond the major parties and their occasional challengers are a number of minor parties and nonparty organizations. Parties such as the Socialist Party USA and the

Greens do run candidates for office, but they mainly strive to make their views known in hopes of future gains. Nonparty political groups such as the League of Women Voters, Lead... or Leave, or the Concord Coalition don't run candidates, but they also seek to make their voices heard and influence the policies of the major parties.

This chapter looks at some of the other parties and nonparty organizations that participate in American politics today. Not all groups that fit this description are covered—this chapter is designed to give you an overview of what kind of groups are out there and profile some of the major ones. The groups included here range from the radical left (the Socialists and Greens) to the religious right (the Christian Coalition).

Newsgroups and Mailing Lists

Many of the minor parties and nonparty organizations take advantage of the Net to keep their members informed. In this section, you find newsgroups and mailing lists associated with most of the groups discussed in this chapter. These Internet areas enable you to access the most up-to-date information on alternative political parties and groups. You can find what a group is really like by reading the messages they exchange. As a result, these newsgroups and mailing lists are an excellent way to get the real story on a party or organization.

 **Green Party**

`alt.politics.greens`

This is the newsgroup for the discussion of international Green party activities. Many of the threads do deal with Green politics. But other threads drift off the topic.

When I was writing this chapter, there were threads about Rush Limbaugh, disbanding the IRS, Conservanazis (!), and more. There was also a message from Dale McMillen, the Green party Internet Coordinator, warning readers about the drift of this thread, and listing some sources of official Green information. Figure 5.1 shows the titles of some of these threads.

 The Socialist Party USA Mailing List

`majordomo@world.std.com`

SocNet is the discussion mailing list for the Socialist Party USA. You can subscribe by sending e-mail to the address shown here. The newsgroup carries discussions between members of the Socialist Party USA and socialists around the world. It is also the place to find out about Socialist Party activities.

Some Leftist Parties on the Net

Many small leftist parties make use of the Net. With their limited numbers of

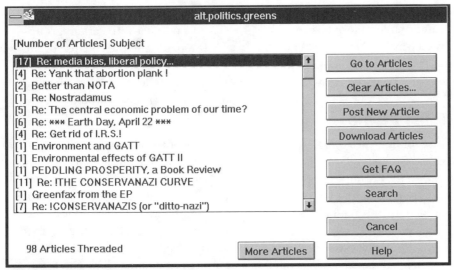

Figure 5.1 `alt.politics.greens`
Green party political discussions on the Net.

members widely dispersed across the country, and their ties to leftist parties in other countries, the Net is an ideal way for these groups to coordinate their activities and keep their members informed. This section looks at the leftist groups that are most active on the Internet.

Whatever the reason, a number of leftist parties are on the Net. These range from relative heavyweights such

Buzzword translation

When you look at secondary political parties like those shown here, the discussion quickly gets cluttered up with all sorts of *isms:* communism, socialism, capitalism, and so on. Here is a quick refresher on the isms to prepare you for the rest of this section.

- *Capitalism*—Private or corporate ownership of the means of production; profits; free markets.

- *Communism*—Collective ownership of the means of production for the common good of all members.

- *Marxism*—Marx's view of history as class struggles on the road from Capitalism to Socialism to Communism.

- *Populism*—The common man against the privileged elite.

- *Socialism*—Collective ownership of the means of production with political power for the whole community.

as the SPUSA and the Greens, to a number of smaller, more obscure groups such as Worker's World and the New party. This section looks at the Socialists and the Greens.

Socialist Parties

Of all the third parties that have appeared, the Socialists should have been given the award for perseverance. The first Socialist party in the United States was founded in 1901, and exists to this day (in the guise of the Socialist Party USA), even though it has never seriously challenged the Democrats or Republicans for power.

Socialism's vision of a world, where all production and distribution are owned by society and all of society has a voice in what is produced and distributed, remains popular with certain groups. This is so, despite the collapse of the Union of Soviet Socialist Republics (USSR) and the terrible problems of Socialist experiments around the world.

Two major socialist organizations in the United States are the SPUSA and the Democratic Socialists of America (DSA). According to documents from SPUSA, the DSA is involved with the liberal wing of the Democratic Party and the leadership of the AFL-CIO. Some DSA members have run for office as Democrats. SPUSA, on the other hand, concentrates on grassroots and local politics and often runs a Presidential ticket to educate the public about Socialism.

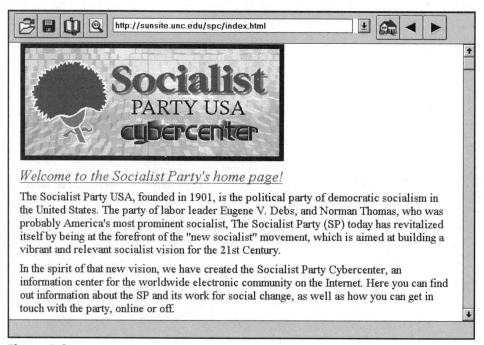

Figure 5.2 `http://sunsite.unc.edu/spc/index.html`
The Socialist Party USA Cybercenter is the online home of the Socialist Party USA.

Getting Involved with the Socialist Party

The two major Socialist organizations in America, The Socialist Party USA, and the Democratic Socialists of America, provide complete membership and contact information on their respective Web pages. You can go directly to Socialist Party USA material by setting your Web browser to:

> WWW Address: `http://sunsite.unc.edu/spc/Member.html`

The DSA also allows membership online. The DSA page has a link to a set of tips for organizing Socialists and other left-wing groups. To obtain membership information:

> WWW Address: `http://ccme-mac4.bsd.uchicago.edu/DSAJoin.html`

 ### The Socialist Party USA Cybercenter

`http://sunsite.unc.edu/spc/index.html`

This is the online home of the SPUSA. The Cybercenter is part of the party's attempt to reinvigorate itself for the twenty-first century.

The Cybercenter has background documents such as *The Socialist Party: Who We Are,* as well as a detailed history of Socialism in America (see fig. 5.2). The policies and principles of the party are laid out in a document entitled *Socialism as Radical Democracy: The SP Statement of Principles.*

This site includes assorted other material for visitors interested in learning more. Contact information is there for the Young People's Socialist League and the Socialist Institute. Subscription information for *The Socialist,* a magazine, and *SOCNET,* a socialist mailing list, helps you keep up-to-date on Socialist activities.

 ### The Democratic Socialists of America

`http://ccmemac4.bsd.uchicago.edu/DSA.html`

The DSA is the largest socialist organization in the United States. As an affiliate of the Socialist International, the DSA is linked to the worldwide Socialist movement. Its members' primary goal in this country is to promote what they call Democratic Socialism. The DSA Web page contains information on their campaign (see fig. 5.3).

This DSA should answer all your questions about democratic socialism and the DSA. There's a Brief Guide to DSA that contains details on the organization and goals of the party. The DSA Commissions and Locals page gives you contact information.

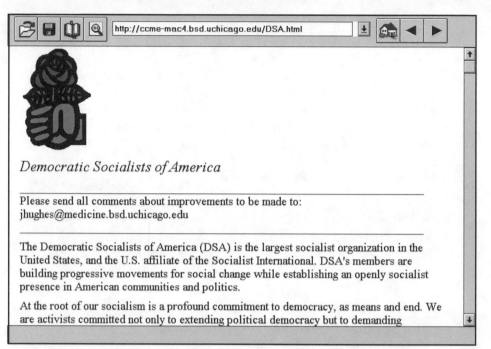

Figure 5.3 `http://ccme-mac4.bsd.uchicago.edu/DSA.html`
The Democratic Socialists of America page attempts to answer questions about Democratic Socialism and the DSA.

The DSA supports a number of hypertext documents on Socialism and society. You'll find titles like *Socialism Informs the Best of Our Politics, A Socialist Theory of Racism,* and *Toward a New Foreign Policy,* written by Democratic Representative Tom Dellums, Vice-Chair of the DSA.

> **NOTE**
>
> This page is chock full of information for anyone who wants to become a socialist or leftist activist. DSA organizational manuals are available, as are guides to inspirational leftist films and periodicals—there's even a collection of DSA songs.

 The Green Parties

`gopher://`
`ecosys.drdr.Virginia.EDU`

Once connected, navigate through the following directories:

```
The Library
General
GreenGopher, a Greens
  Resource
```

Green parties have appeared in the United States and around the world. Declaring themselves to be democratic, nonviolent, populist movements, they seek a fundamental restructuring of human civilization. This restructuring would reharmonize society with nature, eliminating the hierarchical, domineering western world view with some form of Socialism.

The Greens is a grassroots movement in the United States, organized in local committees. With little in the way of a central organization, there is no single Net site that serves as *the* spot for the Greens. Most of the Green material on the Net is related to the activities of local committees. Fortunately, there is a place where information from a number of these local groups is collected: The GreenGopher (see fig. 5.4).

The GreenGopher contains four directories, three of which contain Green-specific material. The U.S. Greens Greenprogram directory is one of these. Within this directory and its subdirectories you will find hundreds of files, covering environmental issues and everything from animal liberation to spirituality. One subdirectory specifically deals with Green party politics.

The Grassroots Groups of Greens directory is the place to go if you want to get involved in Green politics. The Greens have groups in 30 states, and this directory contains the nonelectronic contact information for all of them.

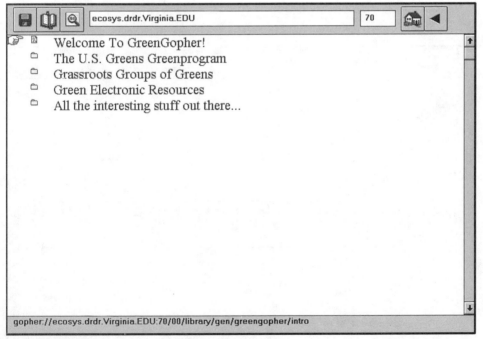

Figure 5.4 `gopher://ecosys.drdr.Virginia.EDU`
The GreenGopher is a Greens resource. The U.S. Greens Greenprogram is one of the directories available.

Nonparty Political Organizations

The Internet provides a low cost way for political organizations to reach many Americans. Moderate and conservative groups on the Net focus on educating the public, and serve as advocates for their views, but usually aren't official parties and don't run their own candidates. Even without official party status, these groups can have a big effect on American politics. Witness the impact of United We Stand America in recent years.

Political organizations on the Net represent varying political views. Several non-party political organizations, such as the Christian Coalition, are generally aligned with the Republican Party. Others, such as the League of Women Voters, are nonpartisan, supporting anyone who agrees with their views. And others, such as Lead… or Leave, are aligned along generational and economic lines rather than by party.

 The Christian Coalition

`http://www.infi.net/cc/`

The Christian Coalition considers itself one of the nation's leading pro-family organizations. Founded by Pat Robertson, the coalition is politically conservative and is generally aligned with the Republicans.

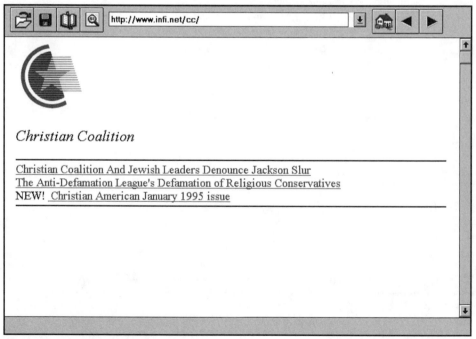

Figure 5.5 `http://www.infi.net/cc/`
The Christian Coalition page on the WWW.

The Christian Coalition Web site lists current events of interest to Coalition members and contains the text of the *Christian American,* the monthly magazine of the Christian Coalition (see fig. 5.5). The material at this site changes regularly.

A recent look at this Web site revealed the text of two press releases and the contents of the January 1995 edition of the *Christian American.* The press releases dealt with an alleged slur against the coalition by Jesse Jackson and one by the Anti-Defamation League of B'nai B'rith.

Another link on the page jumps to the text of the magazine. With articles like *GOP Set to Make Good on Pledge* and *Holy Spirit Moves Worldwide,* you can tell that this is a Christian organization.

 The Concord Coalition

`http://sunsite.unc.edu/concord/`

The Concord Coalition was formed in 1992 by Senators Paul Tsongas and Warren Rudman, along with former Commerce Secretary Pete Peterson. Stimulated by concerns about the nation's future economic health, the goal of the Concord Coalition is to end federal deficit spending. The coalition plans to do this by educating the public and building support and encouragement for politicians who are working to reduce the deficit. The Concord Coalition Web page is part of that effort (see fig. 5.6).

This page has links to complete information on the coalition and its mission. A number of documents provide the background and the basis for the coalition's positions. One such document is, "What does the debt cost us?" It lists some of the things the nation could do with the $213 billion in interest payments that the United States paid on the federal debt in 1993. Starting with job training for one million unemployed people, it runs through over a dozen more activities and projects. These include the complete funding for a number of federal agencies (like the FBI). The list is really disturbing, and brings home just how much the debt costs us.

The page also contains the coalition's Zero Deficit Plan, a proposal that would eliminate the federal deficit by the year 2000. The plan lists government programs that could be cut and calls for sacrifices from all but the poorest Americans.

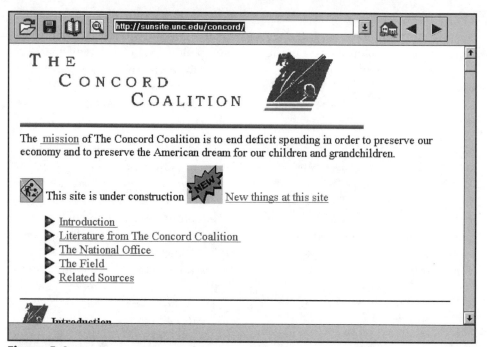

Figure 5.6 `http://sunsite.unc.edu/concord/`
The Concord Coalition Web page has links to information on the coalition and its mission.

 The League of Women Voters of Iowa Home Page

`http://lwvia.cornell-iowa.edu/`

The League of Women Voters (LWV) is a nonpartisan political organization that "encourages the informed and active participation of citizens in government, and influences public policy through education and advocacy." The specific goal of the LWV is to empower citizens to shape better communities worldwide.

Figure 5.7 shows the League of Women Voters of Iowa home page, an experimental Web site sponsored by the LWV of Iowa (LWVIA). The page distributes voting and governmental information for the state. Although most of the material at this site is specific to Iowa, some is of more general interest. One such item is the Citizen's Guide to the National Voter Registration Act of 1993, more commonly known as the Motor Voter Act. A fact sheet on the act lays out its basic requirements in an easy-to-understand form.

Adam Rifkin's Lead... or Leave Page

`http://www.cs.caltech.edu/`
`~adam/lead.html`

This page is maintained by Adam Rifkin to spread the word about Lead... or Leave (LOL), a Generation X political movement. LOL was formed by Rob Nelson and Jon Cowan to see that the needs of the younger generations are addressed by today's politicians. The organization claims almost a million members, with chapters in every state. Their basic premise is that no generation should be asked to pay for the excesses of another generation. LOL feels that current policies favor older and wealthier citizens over the younger and poorer citizens.

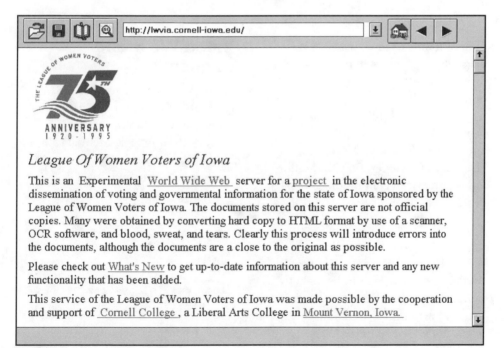

Figure 5.7 `http://lwvia.cornell-iowa.edu`
The League of Women Voters of Iowa home page.

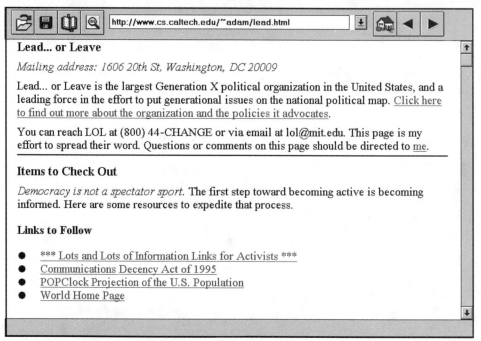

Lead... or Leave

Mailing address: 1606 20th St, Washington, DC 20009

Lead... or Leave is the largest Generation X political organization in the United States, and a leading force in the effort to put generational issues on the national political map. Click here to find out more about the organization and the policies it advocates.

You can reach LOL at (800) 44-CHANGE or via email at lol@mit.edu. This page is my effort to spread their word. Questions or comments on this page should be directed to me.

Items to Check Out

Democracy is not a spectator sport. The first step toward becoming active is becoming informed. Here are some resources to expedite that process.

Links to Follow

- *** Lots and Lots of Information Links for Activists ***
- Communications Decency Act of 1995
- POPClock Projection of the U.S. Population
- World Home Page

Figure 5.8 `http://www.cs.caltech.edu/~adam/lead.html`
Adam Rifkin's Lead... or Leave page contains a collection of general interest political documents.

Adam Rifkin's Lead... or Leave Web page, although not sanctioned by LOL, provides a link to some of the organization's ideals and materials (see fig. 5.8). Much of this material is drawn from the book *Revolution X,* by Nelson and Cowan. *Revolution X* proposes 13 challenges for Generation X, the thirteenth American generation. The page describes each of these challenges.

The Lead... or Leave page also contains a collection of general interest political documents and links. From here, you can reach an index of activist political organizations, contact information for Congress, and a form that lets you send e-mail to the White House Guest Book.

United We Stand America

United We Stand America (UWSA) is a grassroots organization dedicated to political and economic reform. Inspired by the 1992 Presidential campaign of Ross Perot, UWSA is growing rapidly and having an impact on American politics.

 UWSA

`http://www.telusys.com/
uwsa.html`

As their literature states, UWSA is not a political party. It is an educational, nonpartisan, nonprofit organization designed to inform the public about important issues facing the country. By banding together, members of the organization can have more impact on the way the nation is governed. Although no official numbers are available, UWSA membership is in the millions.

UWSA material is available in various locations on the Net. Their best site is the Web page for the online edition of the *United We Stand America National Newsletter,* shown in figure 5.9.

The UWSA site primarily contains hypertext forms of recent UWSA newsletters. These online newsletters let you see exactly where UWSA stands, with recent newsletters covering issues such as unfunded mandates, health care, and welfare. Ross Perot is a frequent contributor.

The site also runs articles on items of special interest at any given time. When I researched for this chapter, the topics were the Contract with America and the impact of NAFTA. The Contract with America page gives an in-depth analysis from the perspective of UWSA. The NAFTA Impact Update is a month-by-month list of negative affects of the North American Free Trade Agreement (NAFTA).

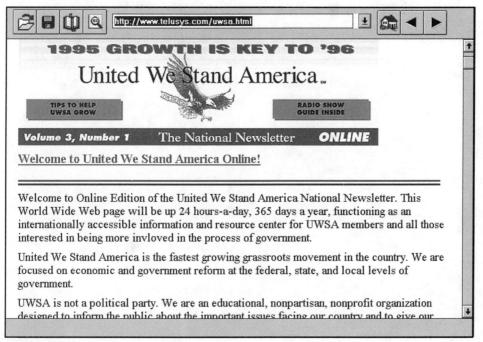

Figure 5.9 `http://www.telusys.com/uwsa.html`
The UWSA Newsletter on the Web contains hypertext forms of recent UWSA newsletters.

Billionaire Presidential Candidate Ross Perot

Billionaire businessman Ross Perot shook up the United States political scene with his 1992 Presidential campaign. Despite some unusual occurrences, and his temporary withdrawal from the race, Mr. Perot received over 19 million votes. Many people believe that Perot's strong showing gave Bill Clinton the presidency.

Perot's name appears throughout the Net, usually in relation to the 1992 election or United We Stand America. A number of archives contain the text of his book, *United We Stand,* including the one shown in figure 5.10.

Mr. Perot's physical appearance, sometimes controversial positions, and unor-

thodox political style make him a target for jokes and caricatures. His name appears in such online locations as The Nerd Test:

> WWW Address: `http://spider.lloyd.com/~dragon/nerdtest.html`

Despite such jokes and his reduced political stature since the election and passage of NAFTA, Mr. Perot and UWSA remain powerful political forces that may have an effect on the 1996 election. If UWSA does spawn a formal party and run a Presidential campaign, you can bet that you'll be seeing more of Ross Perot's name on the Net.

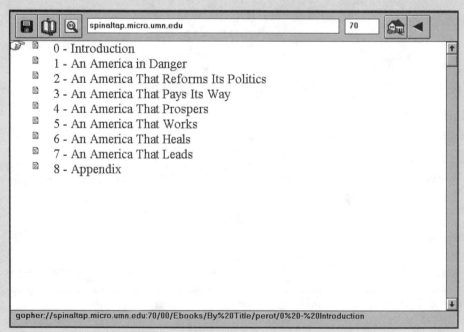

spinaltap.micro.umn.edu   70

0 - Introduction
1 - An America in Danger
2 - An America That Reforms Its Politics
3 - An America That Pays Its Way
4 - An America That Prospers
5 - An America That Works
6 - An America That Heals
7 - An America That Leads
8 - Appendix

gopher://spinaltap.micro.umn.edu:70/00/Ebooks/By%20Title/perot/0%20-%20Introduction

Figure 5.10   `gopher://spinaltap.micro.umn.edu`
The text of Ross Perot's book United We Stand America *is available at this Gopher site.*

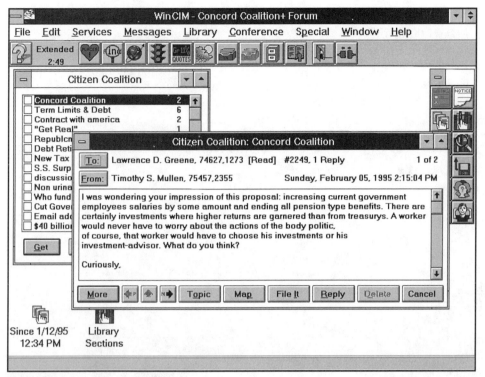

Figure 5.11 Go: CIS:CONCORD
The Concord Coalition Forum on CompuServe.

Other Parties and Organizations on the Online Services

Coverage of other parties and organizations is sparse on the online services. Only CompuServe has in depth coverage of groups discussed in this chapter. The League of Women Voters has its own area in the Political Debate Forum (**Go: CIS:POLITICS**). The Concord Coalition has its own Forum which is described in the next section.

 CompuServe

Go: **CIS:CONCORD**

The Concord Coalition is one of the few political organizations with its own CompuServe forum. As explained earlier in this chapter, the Concord Coalition is a grassroots organization dedicated to eliminating the federal deficit. The coalition's CompuServe forum was created to help in that effort.

The forum is a complete resource for interested visitors (see fig. 5.11).

The Message sections and Libraries are divided into six different sections, each addressing a different aspect of the Concord Coalition and it mission. The Message sections distinguish the CompuServe forums from the Web page on the Net. The messages here are mostly dignified and intelligent, with little of the flaming you see in other places.

Debtbusters 2000: Can You Balance the Budget?

Debtbusters 2000 is a shareware game from the Concord Coalition. The object of this DOS-based game is to analyze and prioritize government programs, with the end result being a balanced budget. Figure 5.12 shows a typical screen from the game.

The game was originally developed for use by the Concord Coalition as an interactive exercise for small groups. The computerized version lacks interaction with others, but benefits from several computer-aided analysis techniques not available in the original game.

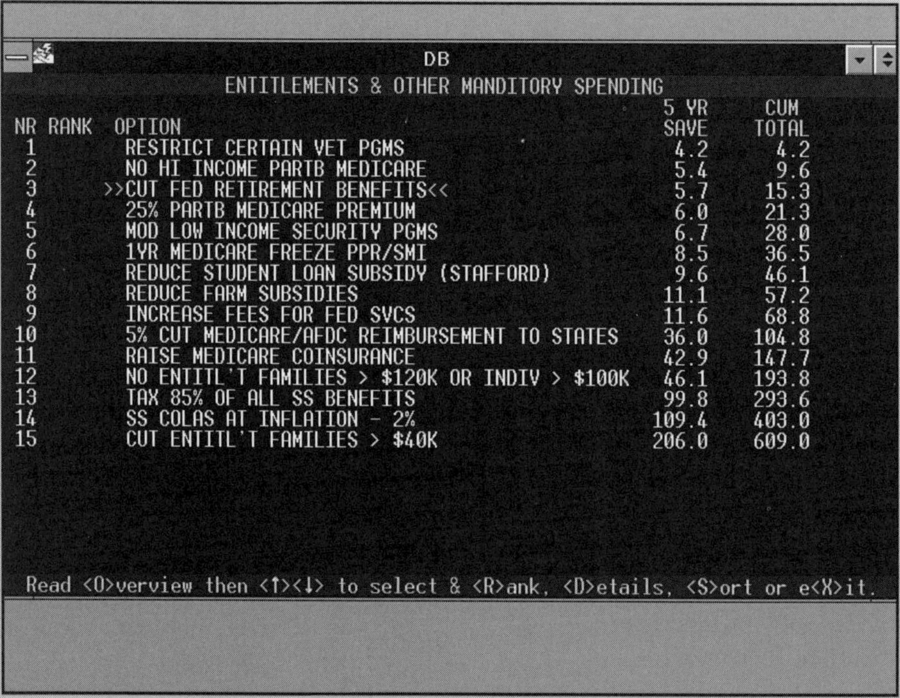

```
─ ▨                              DB                               ▼ ▲▼
              ENTITLEMENTS & OTHER MANDITORY SPENDING
                                                   5 YR      CUM
NR RANK  OPTION                                    SAVE      TOTAL
 1       RESTRICT CERTAIN VET PGMS                  4.2       4.2
 2       NO HI INCOME PARTB MEDICARE                5.4       9.6
 3       >>CUT FED RETIREMENT BENEFITS<<            5.7      15.3
 4       25% PARTB MEDICARE PREMIUM                 6.0      21.3
 5       MOD LOW INCOME SECURITY PGMS               6.7      28.0
 6       1YR MEDICARE FREEZE PPR/SMI                8.5      36.5
 7       REDUCE STUDENT LOAN SUBSIDY (STAFFORD)     9.6      46.1
 8       REDUCE FARM SUBSIDIES                     11.1      57.2
 9       INCREASE FEES FOR FED SVCS                11.6      68.8
10       5% CUT MEDICARE/AFDC REIMBURSEMENT TO STATES 36.0  104.8
11       RAISE MEDICARE COINSURANCE                42.9     147.7
12       NO ENTITL'T FAMILIES > $120K OR INDIV > $100K 46.1 193.8
13       TAX 85% OF ALL SS BENEFITS                99.8     293.6
14       SS COLAS AT INFLATION - 2%               109.4     403.0
15       CUT ENTITL'T FAMILIES > $40K             206.0     609.0




  Read <O>verview then <↑><↓> to select & <R>ank, <D>etails, <S>ort or e<X>it.
```

Figure 5.12
The Entitlements screen from the game Debtbusters 2000.

The forum's libraries contain historical documents, such as the coalition's first newsletter, as well as masses of budget and deficit information. There is even a shareware game that lets you try to balance the budget. The program Debtbusters 2000 is available in the Third Rail Library.

Recommended Sites to See

Each address of other political parties and organizations on the Net is identified by its type and a short description of what you can find there. Many of these addresses are discussed in more detail in the body of the chapter, so if you see one that looks interesting, skim through the appropriate section before logging onto the Net.

Newsgroups and Mailing Lists

The Socialist discussion mailing list.

LISTSERV Address:
`majordomo@world.std.com`
`subscribe SocNet`

Discussions of Green party politics.

UseNet Address:
`alt.politics.greens`

Generation X lifestyle and some politics.

UseNet Address:
`alt.society.generation-x`

Politics more or less related to Ross Perot.

UseNet Address:
`alt.politics.perot`

Discussions related to socialism and other leftist politics.

UseNet Address:
`alt.politics.radical-left`

Trotskyite socialist politics.

UseNet Address:
`alt.politics.socialism.trotsky`

Political/environmental discussions.

UseNet Address:
`talk.environment`

Anarchist discussions.

UseNet Address:
`alt.society.anarchy`

Leftist Parties

The SPUSA Cybercenter.

WWW Address:
`http://sunsite.unc.edu/spc/`
`index.html`

Membership information for the SPUSA.

WWW Address:
`http://sunsite.unc.edu/spc/`
`Member.html`

Full info on SocNet, the Socialist Party mailing list.

5

OTHER PARTIES

WWW Address:
`http://sunsite.unc.edu/spc/SocNet.html`

The DSA home page.

WWW Address:
`http://ccme-mac4.bsd.uchicago.edu/DSA.html`

DSA membership information.

WWW Address:
`http://ccme-mac4.bsd.uchicago.edu/DSAJoin.html`

Green party information.

Gopher Address: `gopher://ecosys.drdr.Virginia.edu`

Choose the following directories:

```
The Library
General
GreenGopher, a Greens
 Resource
```

Green Party resources.

FTP Address:
`ftp://ftp.rahul.net /pub/cameron/green-parties`

Membership form for the League of Conservation Voters.

WWW Address:
`http://www.econet.apc.org/lcv/lcv_info.html`

The Student Environmental Action Coalition.

WWW Address:
`http://www.psych.nwu.edu/biancaTroll/lolla/politics/seac/seac.html`

Nonparty Organizations

The Christian Coalition.

WWW Address:
`http://www.infi.net/cc/`

The Concord Coalition.

WWW Address:
`http://sunsite.unc.edu/concord/`

The Committee for a Responsible Federal Budget.

WWW Address:
`http://sunsite.unc.edu/concord/cc_crfb.html`

The Bipartisan Commission on Entitlements and Tax Reform.

WWW Address:
`http://www.charm.net/~dcarolco/`

The League of Women Voters of Iowa.

WWW Address: `http://lwvia.cornell-iowa.edu/`

Guide to the Motor Voter Act.

WWW Address: `http://lwvia.cornell-iowa.edu/National/EduFund/VoterAct/TOC.html`

The League of Women Voters mission statement.

WWW Address: `http://lwvia.cornell-iowa.edu/National/Mission/Mission.html`

Generation X Political movement.

WWW Address: `http://www.cs.caltech.edu/~adam/lead.html`

13 challenges for the 13th generation of Americans.

WWW Address: `http://www.cs.caltech.edu/~adam/LEAD/challenges.html`

United We Stand America's online newsletter.

WWW Address: `http://www.telusys.com/uwsa.html`

Subscribe Perot for UWSA information.

LISTSERV Address: `LISTSERV@MARIST.BITNET`

UWSA analysis of the Contract with America.

WWW Address: `http://www.telusys.com/contract/contract.html`

UWSA's NAFTA Impact Update page.

WWW Address: `http://www.telusys.com/nafta.impact/`

The text of Ross Perot's book United We Stand.

Gopher Address: `gopher://spinaltap.micro.umn.edu`

Select the following directories:
`Ebooks`
`By Title`
`United We Stand`

Political humor.

WWW Address: `http://spider.lloyd.com/~dragon/nerdtest.html`

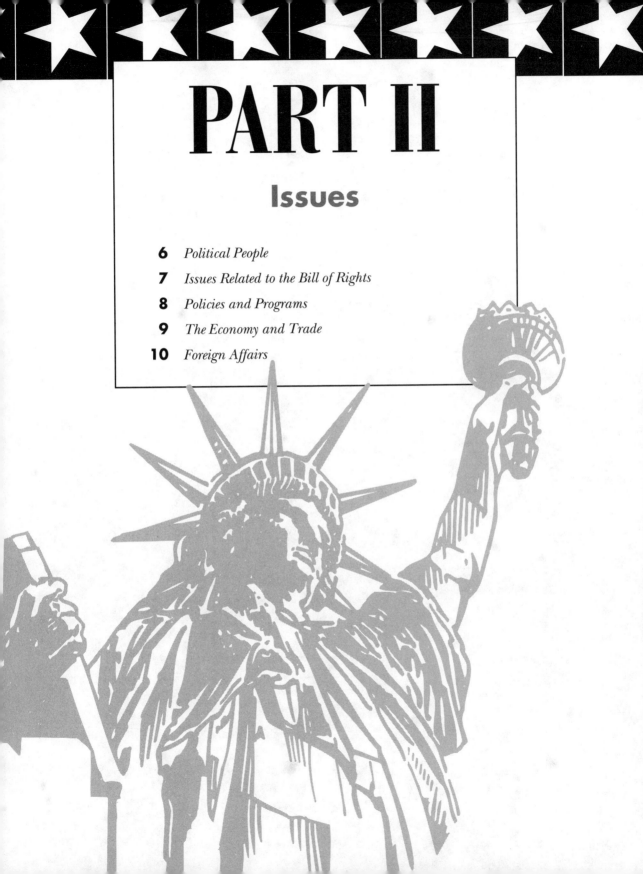

PART II

Issues

Chapter 6
Political People

Politics is as much a battle of personalities as policies. Here's where to find important political people on the Net and some sites that pertain to them.

The Internet is a world-spanning network of networks. It consists of tens of thousands of computers, millions of miles of copper wire and optical fiber, and uncountable bits of information. But in the end, it all comes down to individual people. That's particularly true of politics on the Net.

This chapter looks at five individuals who are politically important on the Net. Three of them are big-name politicians: President Clinton, Vice President Gore, and Speaker of the House Gingrich. The other two people are not politicians, but they impact online politics. Each does so indirectly: Rush Limbaugh through the actions of his supporters, and John Perry Barlow through his offline activities and the actions of his organization, the Electronic Frontier Foundation.

Newsgroups and Mailing Lists

A UseNet newsgroup might be the best way to keep track of the actions of an individual. People are much more dynamic than companies or government bureaucracies, and newsgroups can keep up with them.

This chapter covers individuals inside and outside of government. However, it's impossible to find a newsgroup or mailing list that covers them all. For news stories about government personnel, some of whom are important to the Net, you can turn to the ClariNet newsgroup **clari.news.usa. gov.personalities**.

ClariNet's Government Personalities Newsgroup

clari.news.usa.gov.personalities

This newsgroup contains stories about members of the U.S. government. The stories come from sources like the Associated Press, so they have more facts and useful information than typical UseNet postings. Figure 6.1 shows the titles of some recent articles, as well as a portion of text from the highlighted one.

Because the stories in this newsgroup don't deal specifically with the Net or people involved with the Net, you have to scan the titles to find relevant material. Even so, **clari.news.usa.gov. personalities** is the best newsgroup

Figure 6.1 `clari.news.usa.gov.personalities`
News stories about U.S. Government personalities can be found at this site.

for information on the people in this chapter.

As always with a ClariNet newsgroup, there are tradeoffs. You get more factual coverage of the people and events described, but the information only comes from a limited number of sources. You don't have to worry about unrelated messages or flame wars, but you can't comment on what you read—at least not in this newsgroup.

Clinton's Policy Discussions

`alt.politics.clinton`

This newsgroup is for discussions of President Clinton's policies. The threads that actually appear here don't stick too closely to the subject, and are often general conservative-versus-liberal arguments (see fig. 6.2). Even the small sample of threads shown in the figure ranges from RADICAL LEFT MEDIA BIAS to CONSERVANAZI bashing.

A lot of shouting goes on in this newsgroup. There is the Internet kind, where people use all capital letters to emphasize their words. And there's the more general kind, where people call each other names, use four-letter words, and argue past each other.

Subjects	Number
Re: Let Them Eat Block Grants/The GOP's n	10
Re: Laffer Curve	32
Re: stimulating the economy (Re: Clinton, Choice, a	3
Re: Unliberated Hillary	3
Re: BigBird/Barney SUCKS-PBSgate	46
Re: $$$ DEFICIT REDUCTION, or TAX CUTS FOR THE RICH	11
Re: The Hoax of School Lunches	94
Re: RADICAL LEFT MEDIA BIAS	61
Re: Is this purported ABORTION AMENDMENT	2
Re: Window on the World - Fight To Keep PBS	35
Re: Killing the American Dream	94
r	1
Re: Nazis are Altruists, can't you see?	90
Re: Fairness Doctrine (aka Get rid of Rush)	1
Re: !CONSERVANAZI FLAG AMENDMENT	18
Re: How to choose which 20 percent of school kids w	1

Figure 6.2 `alt.politics.clinton`
Discussions of President Clinton's politics are conducted within this UseNet newsgroup.

6

POLITICAL PEOPLE

A Newt Gingrich Newsgroup

`alt.politics.usa.newt-gingrich`

A comparison of this newsgroup with the `alt.politics.clinton` newsgroup points out one of the bad things about UseNet. People post the same messages to very different newsgroups. Because the President is a Democrat and Speaker Gingrich is a conservative Republican, the messages in their newsgroups should be very different. They aren't. Compare the thread titles in figure 6.3 with those in figure 6.2.

Fortunately, not all the messages in this newsgroup are the same as those in President Clinton's. Some of the threads deal specifically with issues Speaker Gingrich is involved with, like school lunch program funding.

Discussions of Rush Limbaugh

`alt.rush-limbaugh`

The threads in this newsgroup deal with Rush Limbaugh and his views. If anything, there is even more shouting, flaming, and swearing in this group than in the Clinton and Gingrich ones. Although most of the messages are from Limbaugh fans, some are from his opponents.

Important Politicians

Many politicians have a presence on the Net. Some of them have their own Web pages. Others appear in pages on a government server. And some make a big, but short-lived, splash.

Senator James Exon, a Democrat from Nebraska, is one making a splash right now. He is the author of the Communications Decency Act, which has half the Net in a frenzy. But once the Act is implemented or killed, his name will disappear into the background. Other politicians make a more enduring impact on the Net.

Subjects	Number
Re: Laffer Curve.	26
Re: The Hoax of School Lunches	82
Re: BigBird/Barney SUCKS-PBSgate	43
Re: Let Them Eat Block Grants/The GOP's nonexistent	36
Re: *Clinton's Storm Trooper's	1
Re: Comparisons	3
Re: The Constitution of the Untited States (part I	8
Re: $$$ DEFICIT REDUCTION, or TAX CUTS FOR THE RICH	4
Re: "Bubba" Buchanan?	29
Re: Clinton's Storm Trooper's	11
Re: Killing the American Dream	61
Re: Why Shouldn't People EARNING $100,000 get a tax	24
Sen. Exon, Look up Mann Act	1
Re: The Hoax of School Lunches.	35
Re: QRAP #0: change the subject line to include you	19
North Korea and the Right to Technology	3

Figure 6.3 `alt.politics.usa.newt-gingrich`
Discussions of Newt Gingrich's politics are conducted at this UseNet newsgroup.

This chapter looks at three of those politicians. All three believe that government information should be available on the Net, and are doing something about it.

President Bill Clinton

Upon taking office, President Clinton immediately pushed a wide range of issues, many of them controversial. These controversial positions made Clinton a target for the mainly conservative inhabitants of the Net. His status with the online community was further harmed by a series of scandals related to his personal life, his investments, and his appointees.

President Clinton can claim a number of accomplishments. He succeeded in passing his first priority, a federal budget with real deficit reductions. He generated bipartisan support to pass the North American Free Trade Agreement (NAFTA), and he put the Vice President to work on a National Information Infrastructure.

NOTE

President Clinton's e-mail address is:
president@whitehouse.gov

Despite these accomplishments, most of the coverage of the President on the Net is critical. You can find Clinton scandal sites and even a set of Clinton jokes. You can't find a Clinton fan club, or even much sympathetic coverage.

It's unclear whether this is a sign of low regard for Bill Clinton, a general disillusionment with the President as leader of the government, or a combination of both.

Highlights of the Clintons' First 18 Months in the White House

http://www.whitehouse.gov/
White_House/Family/html/
Clintons_First_Year.html

This page is part of the material available at the White House Web site (see fig. 6.4). It lists what the Administration believes are the highlights of the Clinton Presidency. These highlights include achievements such as an economic plan that made real reductions in the deficit; a bipartisan coalition to pass the North American Free Trade Agreement (NAFTA); and the Family and Medical Leave Act, which protects those who must take time from work to care for children or sick relatives.

Accomplishments on other fronts include appointing Ruth Bader Ginsberg to the Supreme Court, only the second woman to serve there; meeting with Pope John Paul II and issuing a joint address; and presiding over the signing of a Mideast Peace agreement.

These and other accomplishments are described on the page. Many of the descriptions are accompanied by small photographs. Clicking these photos causes an enlarged version to appear. A few of the descriptions include links to more details.

6

POLITICAL PEOPLE

Figure 6.4 `http://www.whitehouse.gov/White_House/Family/html/`
`Clintons_First_Year.html`
Highlights of President Clinton's term in office.

 Scandals of the Clinton Administration

`http://www.cs.dartmouth.edu/`
`~crow/whitewater/scandal.html`

Since before the election, President Clinton has been plagued by rumors and insinuations. During much of his time in office, more attention has been focused on rumors and investigations of rumors than on what the Administration is doing for the country. The Scandals of the Clinton Administration Web page is a central location for information on criticisms and rumors involving the President and his Administration (see fig. 6.6).

One major feature of the site is its Whitewater coverage. Whitewater is a tangled tale of alleged financial misconduct involving Mr. and Mrs. Clinton, various Arkansas banks, and the Whitewater Development Company. Although no one has yet proven that the Clintons did anything wrong, continuing allegations and investigations keep Whitewater in the news.

The Whitewater page has extensive coverage of all aspects of the case, from profiles of the people and companies involved to the reports of independent prosecutors and the Justice Department to a timeline of significant events.

President Bill Clinton

In 1992, Bill Clinton won a three-way contest with George Bush and Ross Perot to become President of the United States (see fig. 6.5). He won with 43 percent of the vote. The future President was born in Hope, Arkansas, in 1946. He attended Georgetown University, England's Oxford University as a Rhodes scholar, and the Yale Law School. He avoided being drafted in Vietnam and became Governor of Arkansas in 1978. He lost a reelection attempt in 1980, regained the Governor's Office in 1982, and retained it until 1992.

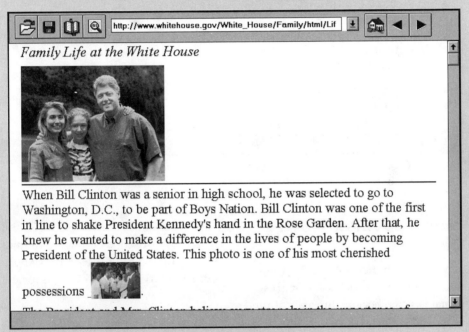

Family Life at the White House

When Bill Clinton was a senior in high school, he was selected to go to Washington, D.C., to be part of Boys Nation. Bill Clinton was one of the first in line to shake President Kennedy's hand in the Rose Garden. After that, he knew he wanted to make a difference in the lives of people by becoming President of the United States. This photo is one of his most cherished possessions

Figure 6.5 http://www.whitehouse.gov/White_House/Family/html/Life.html
President Bill Clinton and his family are featured at this site.

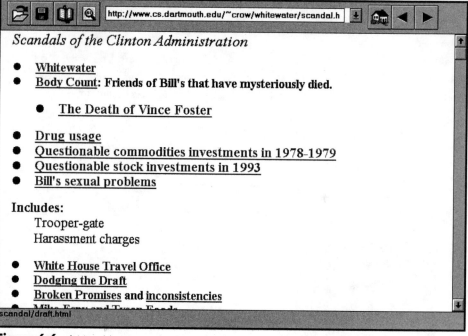

Figure 6.6 http://www.cs.dartmouth.edu/~crow/whitewater/scandal.html
The Scandals of the Clinton Administration page.

House Speaker Newt Gingrich

Newt Gingrich, Republican Representative from Georgia's Sixth Congressional District, became Speaker of the House after the GOP victories in 1994. Gingrich believes that we are entering the Information Age, and that the Net is an important part of it. Speaker Gingrich is the author of the Contract with America, the GOP plan for redefining the role of government. You can find a summary of the Speaker's Congressional record, including the committees he is on and the legislation he has sponsored, by browsing his page in the House of Representatives Member Directory (see fig. 6.7). It is located at:

> WWW address: **http://www.house.gov/mbr_dir/GA06.html**

NOTE

You can send e-mail to Speaker Gingrich at **georgia6@hr.house.gov**.

Newt Gingrich

Newt Gingrich is the son of an army officer. Born in 1943, his childhood was spent moving from one place to the next. Mr. Gingrich earned a Bachelor's degree from Emory University and a Masters and Doctorate from Tulane and is now an adjunct professor at Reinhardt College. He did not serve in the military. He was elected to the House of Representatives in 1978, became minority whip in 1989, and Speaker of the House in 1994.

Speaker Gingrich is a partisan, confrontational politician. But, in my opinion, he is also a future-oriented thinker who has a vision for the country. He frequently speaks of the Third Wave, mankind's transition to an information society.

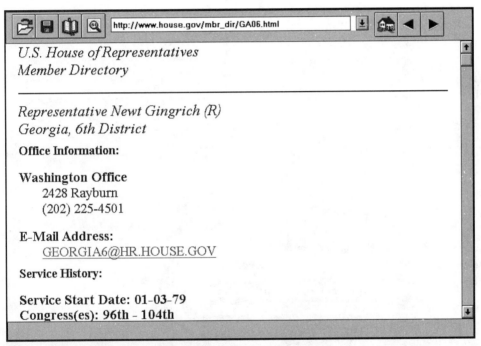

Figure 6.7 `http://www.house.gov/mbr_dir/GA06.html`
Newt Gingrich's page in the House of Representatives Member Directory.

One of his first actions as Speaker was the introduction of the Thomas information service. Named for Thomas Jefferson, this WWW site provides information on Congressional legislation through the services of the Library of Congress (see Chapter 13 for more information about this site). At one point, he suggested—but later backed away from—tax credits for poor people to buy laptop computers and participate in the information revolution.

The three core principles of Gingrich's vision for the country are accountability, responsibility, and opportunity. To achieve these goals, he wants to sharply reduce the size of government, cut taxes and regulations, and eliminate programs that make people dependent on the government. The future he sees is described in detail in the transcripts of his lectures at Reinhardt College. They're available at the Renewing American Civilization Web site (see fig. 6.8).

> **NOTE**
>
> There's also a Newt Gingrich Fan Club on the Web. It's covered in detail in Chapter 2. If you want to go directly to it, set your Web browser to WWW address: `http://www.clark.net/pub/jeffd/mr_newt.html`.

Figure 6.8 `http://www.pff.org/renew`
The Renewing American Civilization home page.

The Renewing American Civilization WWW Home Page

`http://www.pff.org/renew`

Newt Gingrich is not only Speaker of the House, he is an Adjunct Professor at Reinhardt College. He teaches Renewing American Civilization, a 10 week course designed to empower citizens to think about and improve their own and the country's future. The Renewing American Civilization page has links to transcripts of each of the 10 lectures, which were held on consecutive weeks between January 7 and March 11, 1995.

Each lecture combines lessons from America's past and present to help Americans move into the Information Age and world market. Some of the topics covered are entrepreneurial free enterprise, the Third Wave, and creating American jobs in the world market. The Third Wave is futurist Alvin Toffler's term for the Information Age.

However, not everyone agrees with the Gingrich vision of the future, or the tactics he uses to achieve it. The NewtWatch page is one source of criticism.

NewtWatch

`http://www.cais.com/newtwatch/`

NewtWatch is a political action committee (PAC). According to its sponsors, the purpose of NewtWatch is to "raise public awareness and provide a forum for publicly available information on selected public officials, most notably Speaker of the House Newt Gingrich." The NewtWatch page is on the World Wide Web (see fig. 6.9).

To further its mission, the NewtWatch page contains links to a variety of anti-Gingrich documents. Copies of ethics complaints, excerpts from his voting record, and lists of commemorative bills co-sponsored by Gingrich are just part of the material gathered here.

NewtWatch: The First Virtual PAC?

The developers of NewtWatch designed it to be the first virtual political action committee (PAC). NewtWatch exists only on the Web. Its target audience is those Americans who "recognize the Web as an increasingly accessible and quintessentially democratic means to access information about—and participate in—American politics."

As a PAC, NewtWatch can accept contributions, but it will use them in a way that recognizes the essential nature of the Net. NewtWatch will not contribute to candidates for public office, nor will it spend any money for anything other than to expand and maintain its Web page. This PAC deals solely in information. It's a form of political activity perfectly suited for the Information Age.

IN RECESS

6

POLITICAL PEOPLE

One page is a searchable list of individual contributors to Gingrich campaigns. The list covers the period from January 1, 1979, to June 30, 1994, and can be searched alphabetically or by ZIP code. It includes the contributer's name, occupation (if available), city, state, ZIP code, date of contribution, and the amount. The people included in the list are those who contributed $200 or more in a calendar year.

Vice President Al Gore

Vice President Gore is a strong advocate of technology and telecommunications at the White House. He has been an advocate of an Information Superhighway for nearly 20 years.

NOTE

You can send e-mail to the Vice President at this address: `vice-president@whitehouse.gov`.

The Vice President's name appears all over the Net, and where his name appears, it is with regard to his projects and duties as Vice President. With his commitment to making government information more widely available, his major projects have their own Web pages. He is involved in environmental issues, the revitalization of inner cities, space policy, and more. On January 13, 1994, the Vice President made history as the highest ranking U.S. government official ever to participate in a live online discussion.

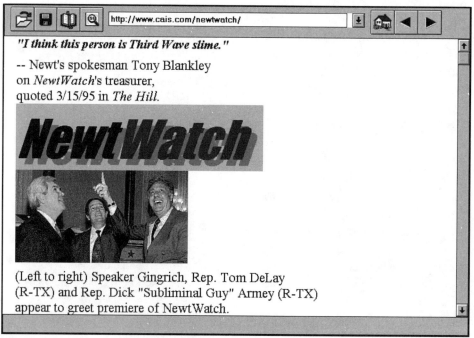

Figure 6.9 `http://www.cais.com/newtwatch/` NewtWatch is a political action committe (PAC).

Vice President Al Gore

The son of former Senator Albert Gore, Sr., Al Gore grew up in Tennessee and Washington D.C., and graduated from Harvard with honors and a degree in government. He volunteered for the Army and served in Vietnam before beginning his political career.

Vice President Gore served eight years as a member of the House of Representatives before being elected to the Senate in 1984. He unsuccessfully sought the Democratic Presidential nomination in 1988 and became Bill Clinton's running mate in 1992. Figure 6.10 shows Al Gore's home page.

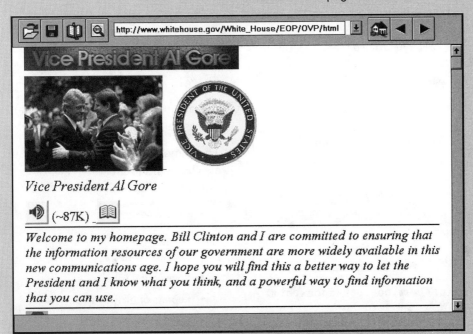

Figure 6.10 `http://www.whitehouse.gov/White_House/EOP/OVP/html/`
`GORE_Home.html`
Vice President Gore's home page.

The Vice President's Electronic Town Meeting

On January 13, 1994, *U.S. News and World Report* magazine hosted an electronic town meeting on CompuServe. The guest of honor was Vice President Gore, the highest ranking U.S. government official ever to participate in such an event. I was one of a limited number of people who was able to attend. While it was somewhat slow and cumbersome, the meeting did allow people to talk directly with the Vice President

without even leaving their homes. Participants with C-SPAN were able to see the Vice President on TV while he answered questions online.

A transcript of the meeting is available at:

FTP address: `ftp://`
`ftp.whitehouse.gov/pub/`
`political-science/internet-`
`related/VP-on-`
`Compuserve-1-13-94`

Two of his projects are particularly relevant to us. The National Performance Review is a program to create a better-working, less-expensive government. The National Information Infrastructure is the Administration's plan for the future of cyberspace.

 ### The National Performance Review

`http://www.npr.gov/index.html`

The National Performance Review is part of the Clinton Administration's attempt at "Creating a Government That Works Better and Costs Less." Vice President Gore leads this effort, which is now working on the new performance review REGO II, short for Reinventing Government Phase 2.

The National Performance Review home page is a complete source for information on the review (see fig. 6.11). The page provides an overview and lets visitors make comments or suggestions via e-mail. When I visited

this site in April of 1995, over 76,000 others had been there before me.

The National Performance Review site also has a unique feature called the Toolkit. The Toolkit is a set of six tools:

- Open Meeting
- Net Results
- Success Stories
- Reinvention Labs
- Reports of NPR
- Library

The Open Meeting is a place where government representatives and the public get together to discuss ideas for improving the government. Unfortunately, the Open Meeting is no longer accepting input from the public. The Net Results, Success Stories, and Reinvention Labs tools are still open to new participants, but they are primarily geared toward government employees and people with certain specific qualifications. Even so, the Toolkit is one way citizens can directly participate in the redesign of the government.

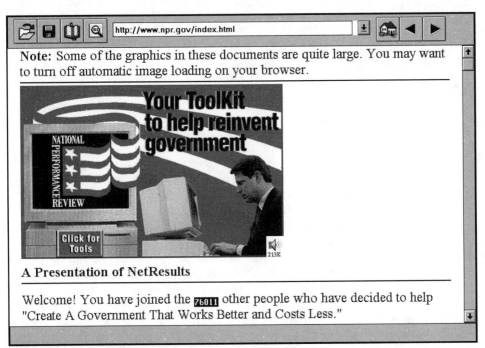

Note: Some of the graphics in these documents are quite large. You may want to turn off automatic image loading on your browser.

Your ToolKit to help reinvent government

NATIONAL PERFORMANCE REVIEW

Click for Tools

213K

A Presentation of NetResults

Welcome! You have joined the ▊▊▊▊ other people who have decided to help "Create A Government That Works Better and Costs Less."

Figure 6.11 `http://www.npr.gov/index.html`
The National Performance Review is an attempt of the Clinton administration to create a government that "works better and costs less."

 The National Information Infrastructure

`http://www.whitehouse.gov/`
`White_House/EOP/OVP/html/`
`nii1.html`

Vice President Gore claims that he coined the term "Information Super-highway" nearly two decades ago. So it should come as no surprise that he is the leader of the Administration's plans to develop a National Informa-tion Infrastructure (NII). The NII would connect every classroom, library, hospital and clinic in the United States, as well as link the U.S. to a Global In-formation Infrastructure.

The National Information Infrastruc-ture Web site is the central source for information on the NII (see fig. 6.12).

It provides a short summary of the Administration's plans, followed by links to five NII-related documents. The most comprehensive of these links is simply called National Information Infrastructure. It contains the complete NII Agenda for Action document in hypertext form. A built-in search tool makes it easy to find particular words or phrases within the body of the document.

The National Information Infrastruc-ture Web site doesn't contain the tradi-tional "links to related documents" section, but the Agenda for Action page does. What you do find on the main NII page is a link to the transcript of the Vice President's electronic town meeting described previously.

POLITICAL PEOPLE

6

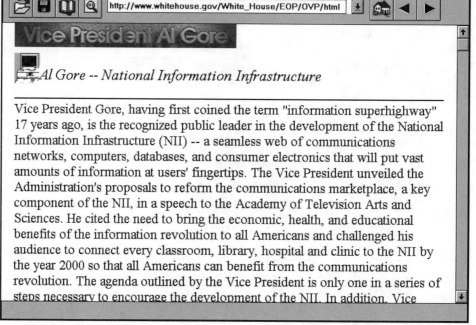

Figure 6.12 `http://www.whitehouse.gov/White_House/EOP/OVP/html/nii1.html`
The National Information Infrastructure page is the central source for NII information.

Influential Citizens

Politicians are not the only people who affect politics on the Net. Every person who participates in a newsgroup or mailing list has an effect, if only a small one. Every person who creates a political site on the Net—whether it's an FTP, Gopher, or WWW site—has an effect, sometimes a significant one. And then there are individuals who, through what they do or the attention they receive, have a real impact.

This part of the chapter looks at two individuals who are not politicians, but who impact online politics. Each does so indirectly: Rush Limbaugh through the actions of his supporters, and John Perry Barlow through his offline activities and the actions of his organization,

the Electronic Frontier Foundation (EFF).

Rush Limbaugh: Radio Talk Show Host

Even though Rush Limbaugh doesn't spend time on the Net, his fans do. He is probably the biggest celebrity on the Net. His name appears all over the place—a WebCrawler search turned up 74 locations. The locations include individual pages, summaries of his radio shows (one archive goes back three years), and at least two Rush Limbaugh home pages on the Web. There are also two Rush Limbaugh newsgroups and a mailing list. All of the sites are unofficial.

Limbaugh is a conservative radio and
TV host, as well as a best-selling author.
His shows are huge hits, with millions
of people listening. His book, *The Way
Things Ought to Be*, reached the top of
some best-seller lists.

Limbaugh is a vocal critic of liberals
and their beliefs. He calls feminists
"feminazis" and creates lists like "The
14 Commandments of the Religious
Left." Commandment number eight on
that list is an example of its content:
"Thou shalt not steal. Unless thou art

disadvantaged or upset with a jury ver-
dict." Limbaugh's fans find him amus-
ing and generally agree with him, but
his views also make him many enemies.

Jeremy Schertzinger's Unofficial Rush Limbaugh Home Page

**http://www.eskimo.com/
~jeremyps/rush**

This page is one of the unofficial Rush
Limbaugh Home Pages on the Web
(see fig. 6.13). Like other Limbaugh
sites, it is primarily a collection of links
to copies of Limbaugh's pronounce-
ments and to other Limbaugh resources. There doesn't seem to be
any online information about Rush
Limbaugh the person; it all focuses on

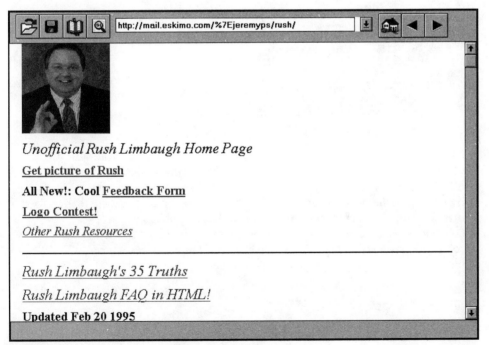

Figure 6.13 http://www.eskimo.com/~jeremyps/rush
An Unofficial Rush Limbaugh Home Page.

6

POLITICAL PEOPLE

what he says or what others say about him.

One pronouncement that's included at this site is the Undeniable Truths list. This is a list of 35 "undeniable truths" published by Limbaugh in a 1988 article for the *Sacramento Union.* This site contains both the original list and an updated one publicly announced on Limbaugh's February 18, 1994, radio show. The truths cover a range of topics from the USSR to morality, liberalism, and the NFL. In the new list—also 35 truths—he removes the references to the USSR and places more emphasis on morality and criticisms of liberalism.

Another link connects the home page to a hypertext version of the Rush Limbaugh Frequently Asked Question (FAQ) and Station List. The List answers questions related to Limbaugh and his Excellence in Broadcasting (EIB) Network, including how to tune in to Rush Limbaugh coverage in your area. In response to a question on Web sites, the list has links to a few pro-Rush sites and also connects to FAIR (Fairness & Accuracy in Reporting), a group that has had a verbal battle with Limbaugh since the summer of 1994.

 FAIR: Fairness & Accuracy in Reporting

`http://www.igc.org/fair/`

FAIR is an organization that looks for bias in the news media. It believes that the national media are biased toward corporate and government interests,

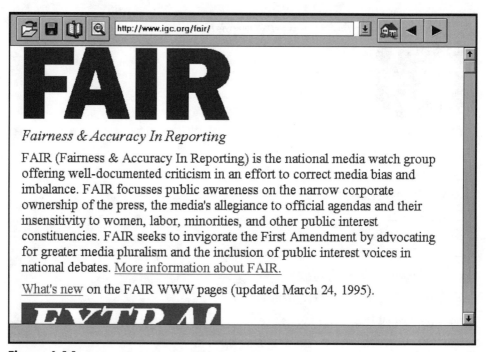

Figure 6.14 `http://www.igc.org/fair/`
The FAIR home page includes links to its verbal battle with Rush Limbaugh.

and ignore or censor progressive and minority voices. It claims to have shown that National Public Radio (NPR) and the Public Broadcasting System (PBS) are also biased against labor and other anti-business groups.

FAIR's Web site provides information about the organization, excerpts from *EXTRA!*, its magazine, and Special Reports (see fig. 6.14). The Special Reports section includes three large files that document FAIR's criticisms of Limbaugh, his response to those criticisms, and FAIR's response to his response.

The conflict between Limbaugh and FAIR began with an article entitled, "The way things aren't: Rush Limbaugh debates reality," that was carried in the July/August '94 edition of *EXTRA!* That article accused Limbaugh of twisting and distorting the facts on his radio show. The article contained numerous specific examples with an analysis of each. Limbaugh responded to the charges a few months later. FAIR then responded to that response. Each side claims to have won the verbal battle. You can decide for yourself by following the links from the FAIR home page.

John Perry Barlow: Founder of the Electronic Frontier Foundation

Many Net veterans have never heard of John Perry Barlow, cofounder of the Electronic Frontier Foundation (EFF). The creation of EFF made Mr. Barlow an important figure on the Net. He and Mitchell Kapor, the founder of Lotus, formed EFF in 1990 to promote freedom of expression in digital media. His online political impact comes from the speeches he gives, the offline writing he does, and EEF activities.

 The Electronic Frontier Foundation

`http://www.eff.org/index.html`

The Electronic Frontier Foundation (EFF) is a nonprofit civil liberties organization. Since its creation, EFF has worked to protect democratic values like the First Amendment right to free speech and the right to privacy. Its aim is to ensure that these rights are protected on all communications systems, including the Internet. The EFF's ultimate goal is the creation of Electronic Democracy.

To support its efforts, EFF has created its own Net sites. It maintains UseNet newsgroups, mailing lists, FTP, Gopher, and Web (see fig. 6.16) sites. Beyond the Internet, EFF is active on bulletin board systems and online services like AOL and CompuServe. Members of EFF receive a variety of benefits, and even non-members can get a lot from EFF sites.

6

POLITICAL PEOPLE

John Perry Barlow

Here's a man who has lived an interesting life. John Perry Barlow was born in Wyoming and educated in a one-room schoolhouse (see fig. 6.15). A graduate of Wesleyan University in Connecticut, he received an honors degree in comparative religion in 1969.

Barlow began two important projects in 1971. One was the operation of the Bar Cross Land and Livestock Company, a Wyoming firm he sold in 1988. The other project was co-writing songs for the Grateful Dead, something he apparently still does from time to time.

While serving as Vice Chairman of EFF, Barlow finds time to write and lecture on subjects related to the "virtualization of society." He is a contributing editor for *Microtimes, Mondo 2000*, and other magazines. His impact on Net politics comes from his activities in the physical world and the actions of his creation, EFF.

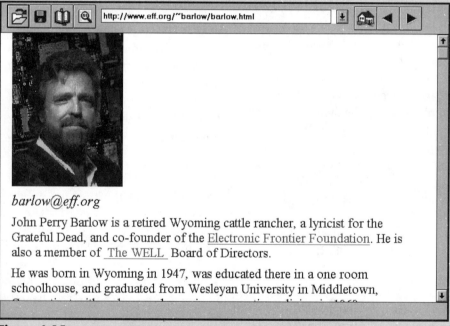

http://www.eff.org/~barlow/barlow.html

barlow@eff.org

John Perry Barlow is a retired Wyoming cattle rancher, a lyricist for the Grateful Dead, and co-founder of the Electronic Frontier Foundation. He is also a member of The WELL Board of Directors.

He was born in Wyoming in 1947, was educated there in a one room schoolhouse, and graduated from Wesleyan University in Middletown,

Figure 6.15 http://www.eff.org/~barlow/barlow.html
The John Perry Barlow home page documents Barlow's interesting background.

One type of service is EFF Action Alerts. The Alerts deal with hot civil liberties issues like current legislation and lawsuits. The hottest of hot issues at the time of this writing is Senator Exon's Communications Decency Act. The EFF Action Alerts contain complete coverage of the situation, including statements against the bill, analysis of the bill's potential effects, and tips on what individuals can do to prevent the bill's passage.

Many other resources are available at the EFF Web site. There's a link to the latest EFF newsletter and an online library accessible by WWW, Gopher, and FTP. There are links to other publications and related Net sites. There are also guides to the Net, including a Virtual World Tour of Cyberspace, featuring the music of Aerosmith.

Political People on the Online Services

The online services have less information about the people in this chapter than the Net does. What you can find depends on which service you are dealing with. All three services cover stories about political people in their respective news areas. Beyond that, it varies.

Note that America Online has no organized area for any of the people featured in this chapter. What it does have is special events, like Republican Presidential candidate Lamar Alexander's

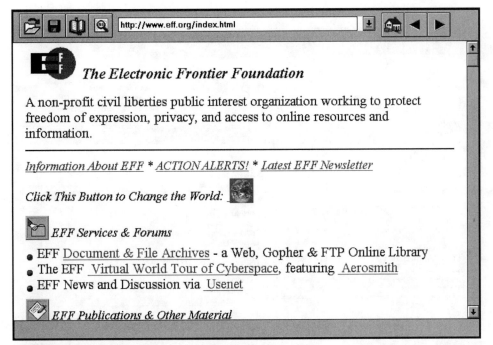

Figure 6.16 `http://www.eff.org/index.html`
The Electronic Frontier Foundation home page.

announcement of his candidacy or C-SPAN's April 3, 1994, online press conference.

 The Issues Forum on CompuServe

Go: CIS:ISSUES

The CompuServe Issues forum is a place to discuss political and social issues (see fig. 6.17). There are message sections devoted to male-female relations, baby boomers, and minorities, as well as several other subjects. But the busiest section is the one devoted to Rush Limbaugh.

The Limbaugh message areas are not only the busiest ones here, they are probably the most acrimonious.

Limbaugh partisans and opponents exchange heated messages in this forum. The Rush Limbaugh library section contains hundreds of files, which are mainly unofficial daily summaries of Limbaugh's shows and texts from the fans that support his positions.

 Prodigy's Political Profiles

Jump: POLITICAL PROFILE

Prodigy has a powerful tool that provides information on every member of Congress. The Political Profile combines information from Congressional Quarterly and the National Library of Money & Politics (NLMP) into a detailed profile of each Senator or Congressman (see fig. 6.18). The

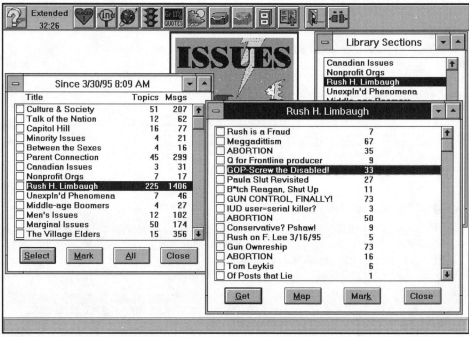

Figure 6.17 Go: CIS:ISSUES
Rush Limbaugh in CompuServe's Issues forum.

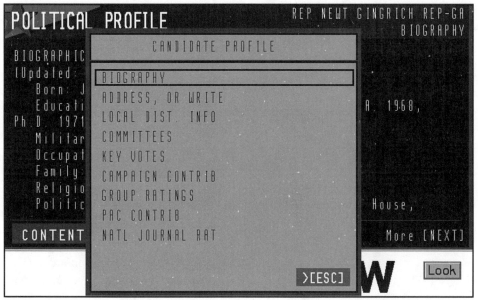

Figure 6.18 Jump: POLITICAL PROFILE
Profiles of Congressmen on Prodigy contains a description of the careers of office holders.

information available includes biographies, committee standings, and voting records on key issues. PAC contributions are listed, as are election results and a description of the Congressman's state or district.

The political profiles contain more than dry numbers and statistics. A narrative description of the office holder's career is available, which can be quite extensive. The narrative for Newt Gingrich runs to nine printed pages.

> **NOTE**
>
> While the information available from this service is thorough, it may not be up-to-date. The biographical data on Gingrich was seven months old when I wrote this; some of the other data was 18 months old.

Recommended Sites to See

This list contains the addresses of the Net sites discussed in this chapter, as well as numerous others that may also be of interest. The list is broken into the same sections as the body of the chapter.

Getting the News

News about U.S. government people.

> UseNet address:
> `clari.news.usa.gov.personalities`

Discussions about Bill Clinton's politics.

> UseNet address:
> `alt.politics.clinton`

Discussions about Newt Gingrich's politics.

UseNet address: `alt.politics.usa.newt-gingrich`

Arguments about Rush Limbaugh's views.

UseNet address: `alt.rush-limbaugh`

President Clinton and his party.

UseNet address: `alt.politics.democrats.clinton`

The Newt Gingrich fan newsgroup.

UseNet address: `alt.fan.newt-gingrich`

The Rush Limbaugh fan newsgroup.

UseNet address: `alt.fan.rush-limbaugh`

President Clinton

Administration plans for the country.

CompuServe address: `Go: CIS:WHITEHOUSE`

President Clinton and his family.

WWW address: `http://www.whitehouse.gov/White_House/Family/html/Life.html`

Clinton Administration accomplishments list.

WWW address: `http://www.whitehouse.gov/White_House/Family/html/Clintons_First_Year.html`

Clinton Administration scandal page.

WWW address: `http://www.cs.dartmouth.edu/~crow/whitewater/scandal.html`

Computer Programmers for Social Responsibility directory of Clinton files.

FTP address: `ftp://cpsr.org/cpsr/government_info/clinton`

Donors to the Clinton Legal Defense Fund.

WWW address: `http://www.clark.net/pub/jeffd/donors.html`

Clinton jokes FTP site.

FTP address: `ftp://cco.caltech.edu/pub/humor/political/clinton.jokes`

Speaker of the House Gingrich

Newt Gingrich's House of Representatives Web page.

WWW address: `http://www.house.gov/mbr_dir/GA06.html`

The Newt Gingrich WWW Fan Club.

WWW address: `http://www.clark.net/pub/jeffd/mr_newt.html`

The Renewing American Civilization
WWW home page.

> WWW address: `http://`
> `www.pff.org/renew`

The NewtWatch virtual PAC Web page.

> WWW address: `http://`
> `www.cais.com/newtwatch/`

Mother Jones anti-Newt article.

> WWW address: `http://`
> `www.mojones.com/089/`
> `beers.3.html`

Working Assets Long Distance (WALD)
Stop Newt telephone calling cards.

> WWW address: `http://`
> `cyberzine.org/html/wald/`
> `newt.html`

What's Newt, an anti-Gingrich page.

> WWW address: `http://`
> `www.cyberquest.com/users/`
> `dans/newt.html`

A collection of Gingrich speeches.

> WWW address: `http://`
> `dolphin.gulf.net/Gingrich/`

Vice President Gore

Vice President Gore's home page.

> WWW address: `http://`
> `www.whitehouse.gov/`
> `White_House/EOP/OVP/html/`
> `GORE_Home.html`

Gore's electronic town meeting on
CompuServe.

> FTP address: `ftp://`
> `ftp.whitehouse.gov/pub/`
> `political-science/internet-`
> `related/VP-on-Compuserve-1-`
> `13-94`

The National Performance Review.

> WWW address: `http://`
> `www.npr.gov/index.html`

The National Information Infrastructure Web page.

> WWW address: `http://`
> `www.whitehouse.gov/`
> `White_House/EOP/OVP/html/`
> `GORE_Home.html`

The National Performance Review at
Sunsite UNC.

> WWW address: `http://`
> `sunsite.unc.edu/npr/`

The 1994 National Information
Infrastructure progress report.

> WWW address: `http://`
> `ftp.arpa.mil/`
> `NII_Report_94.html`

A Global Information Infrastructure
document collection.

> WWW address: `http://`
> `ntiaunix1.ntia.doc.gov:70/0/`
> `papers/documents/`
> `giiagend.html`

Vice President Gore's biography.

> WWW address: `http://`
> `www.whitehouse.gov/`
> `White_House/EOP/OVP/html/`
> `Bio.html`

Rush Limbaugh

An unofficial Rush Limbaugh home page on the Web.

> WWW address: `http://www.eskimo.com/~jeremyps/rush/`

Rush Limbaugh's 35 Undeniable Truths.

> WWW address: `http://www.eskimo.com/~jeremyps/rush/truths.html`

A hypertext version of the Rush Limbaugh FAQ & Station List.

> WWW address: `http://www.eskimo.com/~jeremyps/rush/rush-faq.html`

The FAIR Web page.

> WWW address: `http://www.igc.org/fair/`

FAIR's original criticisms of Limbaugh.

> WWW address: `http://www.igc.org/fair/limbaugh-debates-reality.html`

Limbaugh's reply to the FAIR article.

> WWW address: `http://www.clark.net/pub/jeffd/final.html`

FAIR's response to Limbaugh's response.

> WWW address: `http://www.igc.org/fair/fair-limbaugh-rebuttal.html`

Another unofficial Limbaugh home page.

> WWW address: `http://www.wwwi.com/~jgarzik/rush/`

Yet another Limbaugh page.

> WWW address: `http://www.clark.net/pub/jeffd/rushpage.html`

The 14 Commandments of the Religious Left.

> WWW address: `http://www.clark.net/pub/jeffd/rel_left.html`

More Rush Limbaugh articles and resources on the Net.

> WWW address: `http://www.well.com/www/srhodes/rush.html`

An archive of messages from alt.fan.rush-limbaugh.

> Gopher address: `gopher://gopher.cs.uregina.ca`
>
> > Select the following directories: `Online Information Various UseNet Group frequently asked Questions alt.fan.rush-limbaugh`

A page on Limbaugh-mania from the online version of the book *Aether Madness*.

> WWW address: `http://www.aether.com/Aether/limbaugh.html`

An FTP location for Limbaugh's response to FAIR.

FTP address: `ftp://wuarchive.wustl.edu:/pub/MSDOS_UPLOADS/eIB-Rush/rushfair.zip`

John Perry Barlow

John Perry Barlow's home page.

WWW address: `http://www.eff.org/~barlow/barlow.html`

The Electronic Frontier Foundation's home page.

WWW address: `http://www.eff.org/index.html`

The WELL, where Mr. Barlow is on the Board of Directors.

WWW address: `http://www.well.com`

Wired magazine, where Mr. Barlow is a contributing editor.

WWW address: `www.wired.com`

Chapter 7

Issues Related to the Bill of Rights

Our rights, from free speech to privacy, are debated and fought over on the Net. This chapter shows you where.

In this chapter

- *Newsgroups and mailing lists*
- *Freedom of speech, firearms, and privacy issues*
- *Equality under the law*
- *Other Bill of Rights issues*

In other chapters

← *Jim Warren is a privacy advocate. You can find out more about Jim in Chapter 1.*

← *The Electronic Frontier Foundation defends the Bill of Rights on the Net and elsewhere. The EFF Web site is examined in Chapter 6.*

← *John Perry Barlow founded the EFF and opposes the Clipper Chip. Find out more about him in Chapter 6.*

The Constitution of the United States contains the principles by which the country is governed. Originally ratified in 1788, the Constitution defined the structure of the government and outlined the basic laws, but did not contain guarantees of individual rights. To remedy that, the first 10 Amendments to the Constitution, collectively know as the Bill of Rights, were added in 1791. The Amendments contained in the Bill of Rights, together with some others, provide the legal basis for the rights addressed in this chapter.

Newsgroups and Mailing Lists

Many of the Amendments to the Constitution involve the definition and protection of individual rights in America. Some of the supporters of those rights use the Net to discuss the issues, organize political activities, and promote their views. This section examines some of the newsgroups and mailing lists that discuss the Bill of Rights and other Constitutional Amendments.

 **The Militia Activism Newsgroup**

`misc.activism.militia`

The Militia Activism newsgroup is a place for discussion of militias and militia activities. In the aftermath of the Oklahoma City bombing, this newsgroup has become a very busy place, with many threads related to the bombing (see fig. 7.1).

The threads I read had their share of rude comments. Perhaps that is only to be expected with a subject that raises such strong emotions as militias.

 **Discussions on Free Speech**

LISTSERV address: `amend1-l`

The Amend1 free speech mailing list is maintained by the American Communication Association and is dedicated to the discussion of free speech issues. Anything to do with freedom of speech is fair game for discussion here. To subscribe, send an e-mail message to `listserv@uafsysb.uark.edu`, with the message **SUBSCRIBE AMEND1-L**, followed by your name.

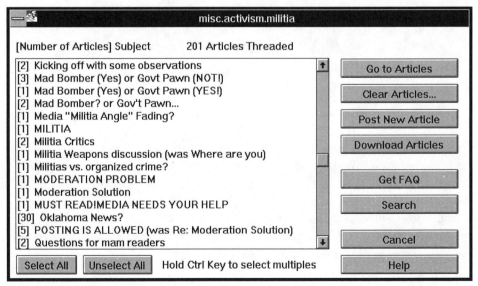

Figure 7.1 `misc.activism.militia`
The Militia Activism newsgroup is a place to discuss anything related to militias.

The Privacy Newsgroup

`alt.privacy`

The Privacy newsgroup covers a wide variety of privacy-related topics. Some, like pointers to new security software, or discussions of calls for online censorship in the wake of the bombing of the federal building in Oklahoma City, deal with computer privacy. Others, like tips on ending telemarketing calls, or discussions of FBI subpoena activity, deal with the world beyond the Net.

 Abortion Discussion Newsgroup

`talk.abortion`

Here's a place for people to talk about abortion. In reality, it's a place where pro- and anti-abortion people scream at each other. Most of the threads are flames, with each side calling the other whatever names they can think of. Interspersed among all the noise you can find some reasonable discussions of the abortion issue.

Freedom of Speech Issues—First Amendment

The First Amendment guarantees several rights, one of which is the right of free speech. Whenever a new communications medium appears, it stimulates a national debate about freedom of speech. The Internet is no exception.

On one side of the debate are those who wish to limit free speech rights on the Net. On the other side are those who oppose censorship, and argue for broad freedom of speech on the Net.

> **NOTE**
>
> The Communications Decency Act, one effort to censor the Internet, is addressed in Chapter 6.

 The American Communication Association Page

`http://cavern.uark.edu/depts/comminfo/www/ACA.html`

The American Communication Association (ACA) is a nonprofit corporation designed to deal with all aspects of communication. Its membership is comprised of scholars, students, and others interested in the field of communication studies. The Association's Web page consists of links to dozens of other communication-related resources, including a free speech link that takes you to a page with over 160 links to freedom-of-speech resources (see fig. 7.2).

> **NOTE**
>
> The Political Communication link on the ACA home page takes you to a list of more than 300 political Net sites, including most of the sites covered in this book.

The AMERICAN COMMUNICATION ASSOCIATION is the national professional organization of scholars, students, and practitioners in the field of communication studies. This site provides information about the ACA, a collection of materials on communication law and First Amendment issues, resources for teaching and research in communication studies, and an extensive reference resource page for scholars and activists. To learn more about the American Communication Association, its programs and activities, and becoming a member, click here.

ACA CENTER FOR COMMUNICATION LAW

Figure 7.2 http://cavern.uark.edu/depts/comminfo/www/ACA.html
The American Communication Association home page leads to many free speech resources.

The Net and the Oklahoma City Bombing

IN RECESS

On April 19, a bomb destroyed the Alfred P. Murrah Federal Office Building—the worst act of terrorism in U.S. history, claimed 167 lives and it injured hundreds more. Net users responded to the attack by getting online to get the latest news, provide information on the victims and the perpetrators, and offer their condolences and support.

According to an April 27 story carried on the New York Times News Service, human rights groups reported a sharp increase in newsgroup discussions of bomb-making on the Net several weeks before the Oklahoma City bombing. The report stated that one message posted in March included instructions for creating the same kind of bomb used in Oklahoma. The messages were found in newsgroups dealing with White Supremacy and paramilitary organizations. Additionally, within days after the bombing, many more messages explaining how to make bombs appeared. Events such as these provide more ammunition for those who wish to censor the Internet.

One of the Free Speech links on the American Communication Association home page connects you to a search tool for the ACA's free speech mailing list, **amend1-1**. You can search for specific topics discussed in the mailing list, or see an index of the approximately 800 topic threads—everything from academic freedom to Phil Zimmermann.

Another link in the Free Speech list takes you to the *Vocal Point,* a hypertext newsletter by students, grades kindergarten through 12, in the Boulder Valley School District. The Free Speech list points to an issue that features censorship from the student's perspective. Some of the specific issues covered include school dress codes, book-banning, and the media.

Other Free Speech links connect you to documents that provide the basis for free speech throughout the world, reports on censorship on the Net and in the "real" world, and anti-censorship and freedom of speech organizations.

The Right to Keep and Bear Arms—Second Amendment Issues

The Second Amendment guarantees the right to keep and bear arms. Some American organizations take their Second Amendment rights very seriously and actively oppose efforts that would limit the right to keep and bear arms. The National Rifle Association (NRA) is one organization that uses the legal system to battle limitations on Second Amendment rights.

Militias are another type of organization that is strongly focused on defending the right to keep and bear arms. They prefer to arm themselves and prepare in case anyone tries to take their guns away from them. They often cite the siege and subsequent destruction of the Branch Davidian compound as an example of the kind of government action they fear.

The Church of Scientology vs. the Net

One recent example of alleged censorship of the Net involves the Church of Scientology and the postings of several individuals in the UseNet newsgroup **alt.religion.scientology**. The Church claims that its copyrighted secrets are being stolen and posted in the newsgroup. Church members allegedly tried to delete the offending messages, and they were accused of harassing the people who posted them. The individuals claim that they are exercising their right to freedom of speech. You can find the pro-Internet view of the situation at:

> WWW address: **http://www.mit.edu:8001/people/rnewman/scientology/home.html**

In this section, we examine firearms sites. One site is the NRA's Web page. I planned to include a militia's site along with the NRA site. However, since the bombing in Oklahoma City, the militia sites on the Net have disappeared. Because of the current lack of militia sites, I went to The Left Side of the Web, an anti-militia site, for information.

 The National Rifle Association

`http://www.nra.org/`

The National Rifle Association (NRA) is an ardent defender of the right to keep and bear arms. The NRA home page contains links to a lot of information on guns and gun control (see fig.

7.3). Some of the links on this page include:

- The Electronic Version of the 1995 Firearms Fact Card
- Current News
- A database search tool
- Information on state and federal firearms laws
- Educational programs

One of the options from the NRA home page is to search for information. You can search the NRA's archives and those of the Second Amendment Foundation (SAF) and the Citizens Committee for the Right to Keep and Bear Arms (CCRKBA). You can also search an archive of books maintained by the SAF and CCRKBA.

IN RECESS

Where Did All the Militia Sites Go?

Prior to the bombing in Oklahoma City, it was easy to find militia sites on the Net. The day after the bombing, my militia search generated several sites. However, within a week, similar searches generated nothing—all of the militia Web and Gopher sites were gone.

During my quest, I did find sites that weren't militia sites, but had links to militia sites. When I tried those links, the target system wasn't responding, or the URL wasn't valid.

During an extensive search, I found one site that was compiling information about

state militias. Unfortunately, the person compiling the list had abandoned the effort due to an overwhelming amount of e-mail accusing him of gathering militia information for the federal government.

About the only militia information left on the Net when I wrote this chapter was the `misc.activism.militia` newsgroup and the **Militia** directory in the Patriot Archives (an FTP site). Both sites are covered in this chapter.

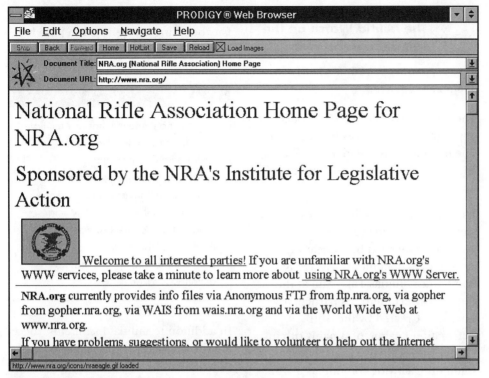

Figure 7.3. `http://www.nra.org/`
The National Rifle Association's home page links you to a variety of pro-gun resources.

Other links take you to the Federal Affairs or the State-specific Affairs directories. They are collections of documents describing federal or state legislation affecting Second Amendment rights.

The NRA home page also has links to several gun-related programs run by the NRA. There are educational and competitive programs for women, youth, and other groups. Since the majority of gun owners are adult men, the programs are designed to get other groups involved in pro-gun issues and activities.

> **NOTE**
>
> The NRA page makes it easy to get involved with gun control and Second Amendment issues. The information in the Federal and State-specific Affairs directories—as well as the information in the archives discussed previously—gives you the background to act. The Congress link on this same page provides the contact information to make your voice heard. Whether you are pro- or anti-gun control, the NRA page is a useful resource.

The Militia Watch on the Left Side of the Web

`http://paul.spu.edu/~sinnfein/`
`progressive.html`

The Left Side of the Web is a collection of progressive resources (see fig. 7.4). The main topic is called Militia Watch, and consists of links to documents and sites dealing with militias.

The Watch contains links to nine documents with information on militias, primarily published by left-leaning groups. One document, "Armed & Dangerous: Militias Take Aim at the Federal Government," is particularly extensive. Created by the Anti-Defamation League of B'nai B'rith in October 1994, this 30-page report examines the activities of militias in 13 states. One of those states is Michigan,

where the suspects in the Oklahoma City bombing are believed to have had some contact with militia units.

> **NOTE**
>
> There is no evidence that any militia was in any way involved in the Oklahoma City bombing.
> In fact, some messages in the **misc.activism.militia** newsgroup indicate that the Michigan Militia reported one of the suspects to authorities as potentially dangerous well before the bombing, but that no action was taken.

In addition to militia documents, there are three links that connect to far-Right sites. The unofficial John Birch Society home page is represented here, as is

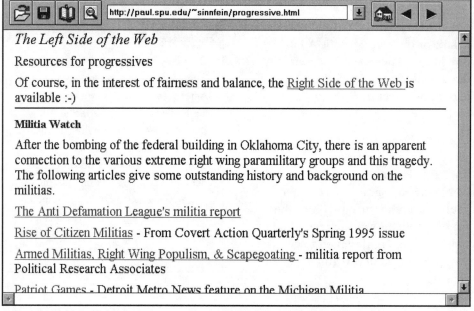

Figure 7.4 `http://paul.spu.edu/~sinnfein/progressive.html`
The Left Side of the Web links to nine documents critical of militias.

the BeastNet Archive, an FTP site full of conspiracy theories. One other far-Right link takes you to the Patriot Archives, an FTP site with militia and conservative material.

The Patriot Archives Militia Directory

`ftp://tezcat.com/patriot/Militia/`

While the militia sites seem to have disappeared from the Web, there is still militia material on the Net. The Militia directory at the Patriot Archives is one of those places (see fig. 7.5). The Militia directory contains 27 pro-militia files gathered from all over the Net. The site administrator claims no responsibility for the contents of the files.

Some of the primary themes in these documents include:

- Alleged federal abuses of power
- Laws governing militias
- Background material on militias

One document claiming federal abuses of power is **Fed_Power.txt**. The author of this document, J.B. Weaver, has previously called for militias to rise against the goverernment, and believes he is being closely monitored by the government.

The document itself contains allegations of federal harassment of militia members, reported sightings of foreign military vehicles in the United States, and rumors of United Nations or other foreign troops operating within the

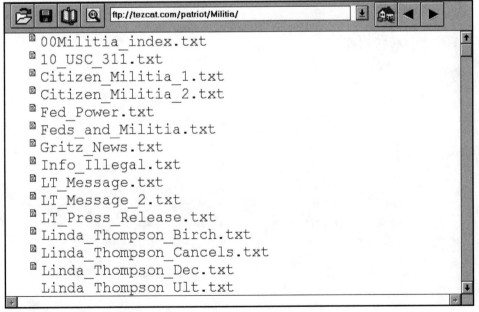

Figure 7.5 `ftp://tezcat.com/patriot/Militia/`
The Patriot Archives Militia Directory contains a number of militia-related documents.

country. It ends with calls for militias to establish radio communication systems and to initiate patrols of their areas to protect against expected government assaults. The other documents included here seem to have similar sentiments.

Privacy Issues— Fourth Amendment

The Fourth Amendment has been interpreted by the Supreme Court as a guarantee of privacy. Like other rights, the right to privacy is not absolute, and is subject to reinterpretation to adapt to changing conditions. As more personal information is stored on computers, and as more communication traverses the Net, the issue of privacy becomes more urgent.

 The Privacy Rights Clearinghouse

`http://www.manymedia.com/prc/`
`index.html`

The Privacy Rights Clearinghouse is a California organization dedicated to helping consumers deal with the effect of technology on their privacy. It informs the public about privacy issues, provides tips on protecting privacy, responds to privacy complaints, and makes Californian's privacy concerns known to policy makers.

The Privacy Rights Clearinghouse Web pages describe the organization, its purpose, and the services it provides (see fig. 7.6). A primary service of the organization is the publication and distribution of privacy Fact Sheets.

IN RECESS

The BlackNet

In my opinion, The BlackNet is an example of a way the right to privacy can be used irresponsibly. BlackNet buys and sells information, specifically other people's secrets. BlackNet will consider purchasing any secret information, but is particularly interested in trade secrets, semiconductor manufacturing techniques, and nanotechnology. It also uses PGP encryption and other techniques to effectively hide its location and the

identity of its members. BlackNet considers export laws, patent laws, national security, and even nation-states to be obsolete.

BlackNet can pay for secrets several ways, including: anonymous bank deposits, direct mailing of cash to a specified location, or CryptoCredits, which can be used to buy other secrets.

Selecting the Publication link from the home page leads you to a list of the Fact Sheets. When I wrote this chapter, there were 15 sheets listed, covering subjects like ending harassing phone calls and determining how private your medical information is. Anyone can request copies of Fact Sheets, although people outside California may have to pay a small fee.

> **NOTE**
>
> By the time you read this chapter, a new Fact Sheet should be available from the Privacy Rights Clearinghouse. It will address privacy in cyberspace.

The Privacy Rights Clearinghouse can be reached by mail, phone, fax, e-mail, Gopher, FTP, or direct dial. You can get the contact information by selecting the How to Contact Us link on any page.

> **NOTE**
>
> While the Privacy Rights Clearinghouse exists to serve the needs of California consumers, it will respond to questions from out of state. If you contact the Clearinghouse, keep in mind that while Federal privacy laws apply everywhere, state laws vary, and the Clearinghouse cannot guarantee that the information it gives you will apply in your state.

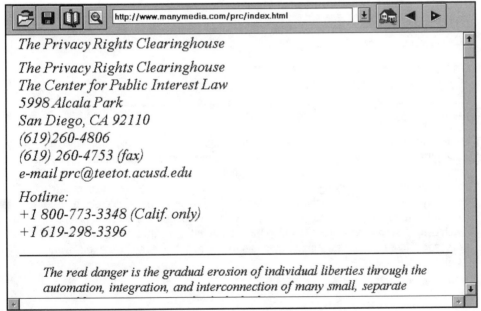

Figure 7.6 `http://www.manymedia.com/prc/index.html`
The Privacy Rights Clearinghouse can help with many privacy issues.

The Cryptography and PGP Page

`http://rschp2.anu.edu.au:8080/crypt.html`

One effort to ensure the privacy of digital communication and information is known as Pretty Good Privacy, or PGP. PGP is a free encryption program that can be used to render text unreadable by anyone who does not have the correct key. PGP is widely available on the Net, but its developer, Phil Zimmermann, is involved in legal trouble with the government over the program (see the sidebar "Phil Zimmermann—Privacy Advocate," for more information).

At the Cryptography and PGP page, you can find an essay from Zimmermann on why PGP is necessary (see fig. 7.7). In addition, there is a list of organizations and groups that are interested in promoting individual privacy on the Net. The three main organizations listed are the Electronic Frontier Foundation, Computer Professionals for Social Responsibility, and the League for Programming Freedom.

The Cryptography and PGP page also maintains instructions on getting a copy of PGP. There are several versions of the program available—some are legal worldwide and others are for U.S. use only. You also can find versions for MS-DOS, OS/2, Macintosh, UNIX, and systems running VMS.

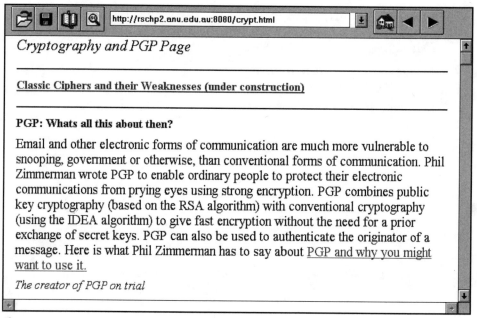

Figure 7.7 `http://rschp2.anu.edu.au:8080/crypt.html`
The Cryptography and PGP page is a great place to find online privacy material.

Phil Zimmermann—Privacy Advocate

Phil Zimmermann developed the popular encryption program PGP. He is also the target of a Federal investigation for possible violation of munitions export laws. What are the munitions he allegedly exported—PGP.

Prior to the government's investigation, Zimmermann was already well known for creating PGP and making it available for free—he became a hero to Net users who value the privacy of their information. PGP is available at hundreds of sites around the Net.

With the investigation, Zimmermann is even more popular online. He won the 1995 Electronic Frontier Foundation's Pioneer prize. Online activists like Jim Warren—who is also peripherally involved in the PGP case—are speaking out on Zimmerman's behalf. Support for Zimmermann appears in FTP and Gopher sites, in newsgroups and mailing lists, and on Web pages like the one in figure 7.8.

Zimmermann has spent much of his time over the last several years improving PGP, giving speeches on cryptography, and testifying before Congress. With the investigation underway, hundreds of publications have featured him in articles, including the *Wall Street Journal*, *New York Times*, and *U.S. News and World Report*.

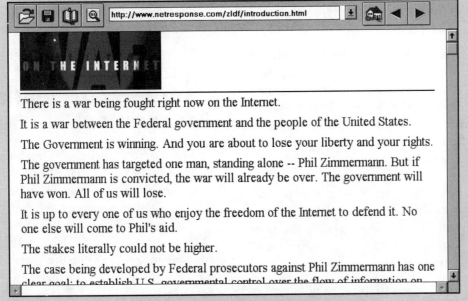

There is a war being fought right now on the Internet.

It is a war between the Federal government and the people of the United States.

The Government is winning. And you are about to lose your liberty and your rights.

The government has targeted one man, standing alone -- Phil Zimmermann. But if Phil Zimmermann is convicted, the war will already be over. The government will have won. All of us will lose.

It is up to every one of us who enjoy the freedom of the Internet to defend it. No one else will come to Phil's aid.

The stakes literally could not be higher.

The case being developed by Federal prosecutors against Phil Zimmermann has one clear goal: to establish U.S. governmental control over the flow of information on

Figure 7.8 `http://www.netresponse.com/zldf/introduction.html`
The Zimmermann Legal Defense Fund page solicits support for Zimmermann's legal battle with the government.

The Clipper Chip

`http://www.quadralay.com/www/Crypt/Clipper/Clipper.html`

The government has been pushing its own privacy solution—the Clipper Chip. This chip would function similarly to PGP, but would also make it easy for law enforcement agencies to get the information needed to decode messages on the basis of a valid warrant. When the Clipper Chip was announced, it triggered widespread opposition from pro-privacy groups and Net users in general. At this writing, it is still unclear how this issue will be resolved.

The Clipper Chip page pulls together information about the chip the government wants Americans to use to encrypt electronic communication (see fig. 7.9).

For users who want an overview of the Clipper Chip, and the Net's reaction to it, the Non-Technical Overview link on The Clipper Chip page is a fine starting place. It leads to pro-Clipper announcements from the White House and AT&T, and anti-Clipper announcements from the Electronic Frontier Foundation and the Computer Professionals for Social Responsibility. It also has a number of news articles about the Clipper Chip. This link provides a good overview of the pros and cons of the chip.

Another view of the Clipper controversy is available through the Denning-Barlow Debate link. It leads to a transcript of a debate between Dr. Dorothy Denning, chairperson of the Computer Science Department at Georgetown University, who favors Clipper, and John Perry Barlow of the EFF, who opposes the chip.

Equal Protection Issues—Fourteenth Amendment

The Fourteenth Amendment has been interpreted by the Supreme Court as a guarantee of equal protection under the law. This Amendment has been interpreted in different ways at different times (see the sidebar entitled "Reevaluating—'Separate But Equal'," for a historical perspective on one aspect of the changing interpretation of this Amendment).

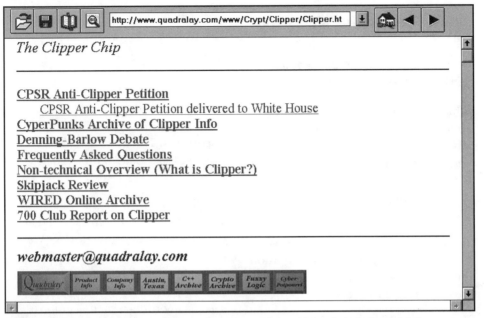

Figure 7.9 `http://www.quadralay.com/www/Crypt/Clipper/Clipper.html`
The Clipper Chip page has technical and non-technical information about the chip.

Reevaluating—"Separate But Equal"

In the 1896 *Plessy vs. Ferguson* case, the Supreme Court ruled that Louisiana's racially segregated "separate but equal" railway cars were constitutional. The Court held that the Fourteenth Amendment's equal protection clause required political equality, but not social equality. This ruling cleared the way for a variety of segregation laws.

In the 1954 *Brown vs. Board of Education* case, the Supreme Court ruled that racially segregated "separate but equal" schools were unconstitutional. The Court held that such segregation violated the Fourteenth Amendment's equal protection clause. This ruling led to the elimination of segregation laws.

The Abortion Rights Web

`http://192.231.221.9/~lmann/`
`feminist/abortion.html`

While the Fourteenth Amendment is applicable to many rights issues, the most controversial right protected under this Amendment is a women's right to an abortion. This right was decided in the 1973 Supreme Court case *Roe vs. Wade.*

The Abortion Rights Web page is devoted to providing links to pro-abortion information (see fig. 7.10). The links are divided into five sections:

- Abortion-Related Web Sites
- Supreme Court Decisions About Abortion
- Responding to…
- Anti-Abortion Terrorism
- Birth Control Resources

The first and last sections on the page consist of pointers to other resources while the middle three link to specific documents. The next section on the page looks at some of those documents.

The links on the Supreme Court Decisions page take you to files stored at the Cornell Law School or Case Western Reserve University. Both places maintain copies of Supreme Court decisions and the links take you to specific abortion-related decisions. The articles in the Responding to… section are essays by the author of this page and others.

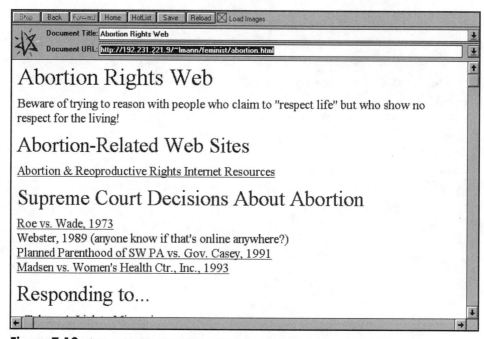

Figure 7.10 `http://192.231.221.9/~lmann/feminist/abortion.html`
The Abortion Rights Web page links you to pro-abortion sites and resources.

The documents in the Anti-Abortion Terrorism section also come from a variety of sources and deal with the violence and threats directed at abortion clinics and abortion doctors. One document, Abortion Clinic Violence— What Can *You* Do?, is a set of ideas for combating the problem, and for making abortion a benefit under any national health care reform.

 The ProLife News

`http://www.pitt.edu/~stfst/pln/AboutPLN.html`

The ProLife News is a free electronic newsletter that covers abortion and euthanasia, as well as other pro-life issues. The content is primarily composed of stories contributed by readers, and summaries of articles found in other publications. The ProLife News home page provides access to current and back issues of the newsletter, and to other pro-life resources (see fig. 7.11).

As of 1995, new issues of the ProLife News became available as hypertext documents on the Web. Previous editions are also available, but not in hypertext form. The ProLife News home page contains links to subject indexes for 1994 and 1995 issues of the newsletter. From the indexes, you can jump directly to the issue with the information you want.

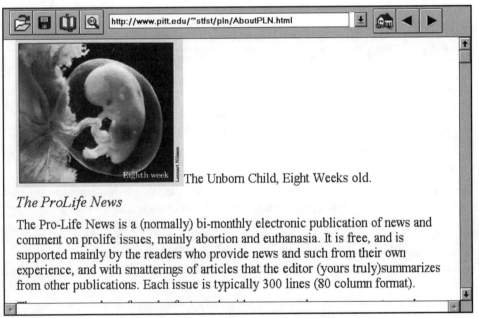

The Unborn Child, Eight Weeks old.

The ProLife News

The Pro-Life News is a (normally) bi-monthly electronic publication of news and comment on prolife issues, mainly abortion and euthanasia. It is free, and is supported mainly by the readers who provide news and such from their own experience, and with smatterings of articles that the editor (yours truly)summarizes from other publications. Each issue is typically 300 lines (80 column format).

Figure 7.11 `http://www.pitt.edu.~stfst/pln/AboutPLN.html`
The ProLife News opposes abortion and euthanasia.

Fighting Environmental Racism: A Selected Annotated Bibliography

http://
drseuss.lib.uidaho.edu:70/docs/
egj01/weint01.html

The Fourteenth Amendment was used in 1954 to strike down segregation laws. Although segregation and discrimination are now illegal, the battle over racial equality continues today.

With overt discrimination, segregation, and racism illegal, much of the debate about discrimination and racism has moved into less obvious realms. One area that has received attention in recent years is known as environmental racism. Environmental racism is described as the alleged practice of intentionally siting toxic waste dumps, landfills, and other hazardous facilities in or near minority communities. "Fighting Environmental Racism: A Selected Annotated Bibliography" is a valuable resource for information on the subject (see fig. 7.12).

The file is taken from the June 1994 Electronic Green Journal and contains dozens of sources of information on environmental racism. The introduction of the document describes the perceived threat and cites studies (from organizations like the Commission for Racial Justice) that report a problem. The rest of the document is a bibliography of reference material. Each newsletter, magazine, or report cited is accompanied by text that describes the content of the source.

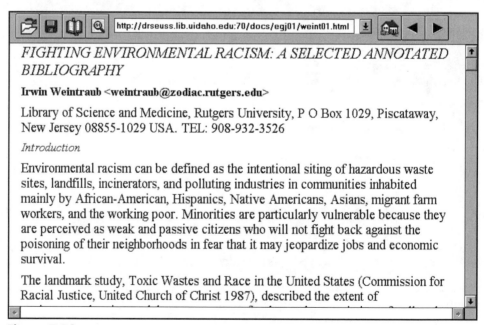

Figure 7.12 http://drseuss.lib.uidaho.edu:70/docs/egj01/weint01.html
This file contains historical information and references on environmental racism.

The California Civil Rights Initiative (CCRI)

`http://theforecast.com/`
`forecast/affirm.html`

Affirmative Action is another battleground in race relations. It goes beyond preventing discrimination, and requires positive action to help groups that have been discriminated against. The California Civil Rights Initiative (CCRI), which was expected to be on the ballot in California in 1996, is designed to stop the use of race and gender as criteria for discrimination or preferential treatment. The document in figure 7.13 provides a summary and analysis of the history leading to the creation of CCRI.

The essay begins with a description of the CCRI and the specific incident that stimulated it. This was the enactment by the state legislature of a bill that would have required the state's public colleges and universities to admit *and* graduate students in the same racial proportions that exist in the community. The bill was vetoed by the Governor of California, but the fact that it passed the legislature was enough to drive opponents of the bill to create CCRI.

The rest of the essay describes the historical basis for race-based laws and policies. It discusses relevant decisions of the Supreme Court, and provides a background for understanding the legal wrangling that is likely to occur if the CCRI is passed.

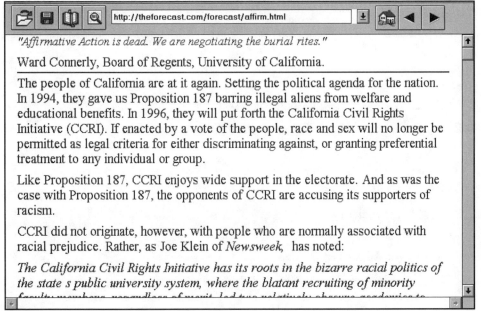

Figure 7.13 `http://theforecast.com/forecast/affirm.html`
An essay on Affirmative Action and the CCRI.

Useful Bill of Rights Resources

Many of the sites on the Net deal with Bill of Rights issues in general. This section examines some of those sites.

 The Constitution of the United States

`http://www.law.cornell.edu/`
`constitution/`
`constitution.overview.html`

When debating Bill of Rights issues, many people refer to the specific amendments to make their point. The Constitution of the United States of America site, which was created by the Legal Information Institute at Cornell Law School, is a complete hypertext version of the U.S. Constitution and all its amendments. The site makes it easy for Net users to see exactly what the Constitution or an amendment says (see fig. 7.14).

The Constitution home page consists of links to four elements of the Constitution. They are:

- The Preamble
- Each Article of the original Constitution
- The Signers of the Constitution
- The Amendments

The Amendments section begins with a page of links to each of the 27 amendments to the Constitution. The first 10

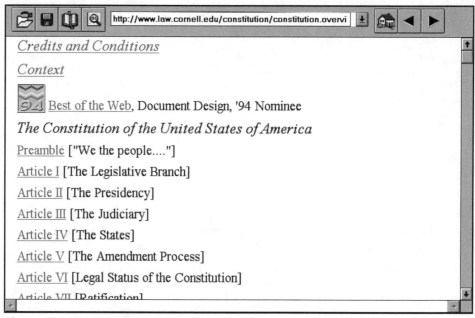

Figure 7.14 `http://www.law.cornell.edu/constitution/`
`constitution.overview.html`
A hypertext version of the U.S. Constitution and its Amendments.

amendments comprise the Bill of Rights. Any of the links to the first 10 amendments take you to the Bill of Rights page. The Bill of Rights page lists the complete text of each amendment in the bill. Each of the other amendments has its own small page.

There are no links from the Bill of Rights or other amendment pages into the Articles of the Constitution, but links do go from the Article that was amended to the relevant amendment.

 A Citizen's Guide to Individual Rights in America

`http://asa.ugl.lib.umich.edu/chdocs/rights/Citizen.html`

A Citizen's Guide to Individual Rights in America is a guide to Net resources that deal with individual rights, whether those rights are guaranteed by the Constitution, Federal law, or other national legal principles (see fig. 7.15). The links from this page are divided into five main categories. They are:

- Rights Under the Constitution and Bill of Rights
- Rights Under Select Federal Statutes
- Rights of Americans By Status or Group

- Rights Arising Under Various Federal Programs
- General Legal Resources

While all of the sections have useful information, I have highlighted the Rights Under the Constitution and Bill of Rights category found on this page.

The Rights Under the Constitution and Bill of Rights is itself comprised of links to more detailed information, primarily divided by each Constitutional Amendment.

The First Amendment page is populated primarily with documents from the American Civil Liberties Union (ACLU). The First Amendment page addresses topics like artistic freedom, hate speech on campus, and pornography.

The Second Amendment page contains links to pro-gun groups like the Right to Keep and Bear Arms (RKBA) and the National Rifle Association (NRA). The NRA Web page is covered in the Second Amendment section of this chapter.

The remaining sections of the Rights Under the Constitution and Bill of Rights page are similarly composed of links to documents and other Net sites.

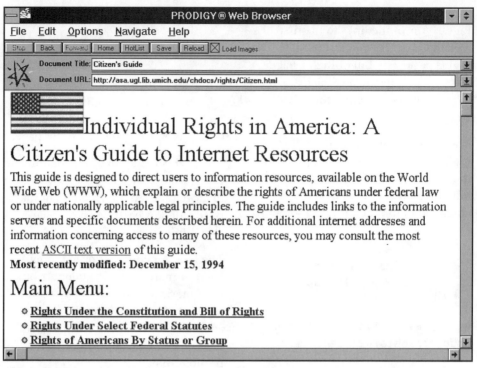

Figure 7.15 `http://asa.ugl.lib.umich.edu/chdocs/rights/Citizen.html`
A Citizen's Guide to Individual Rights in America includes links to five key areas.

Bill of Rights Issues on the Online Services

The online services cover some of the rights and responsibilities topics addressed earlier in this chapter.

The Electronic Frontier Foundation on AOL

Keyword: EFF

The Electronic Frontier Foundation (EFF) is an organization dedicated to ensuring that the rights guaranteed by the Constitution and the Bill of Rights would be applied to all digital media, including the Internet. The Foundation's forum on AOL is one of EFF's outposts in cyberspace (see fig. 7.16).

One thing you can do in this forum is read back issues of the *EFFector,* the EFF's newsletter. Unfortunately, the most recent newsletter included in this forum is dated 1993. Fortunately, that newsletter contains the answers to common questions about the Clipper Chip, and reviews what is known about the Skipjack algorithm that forms the basis of the Clipper Chip.

The EFF forum provides a discussion area where visitors can talk with the

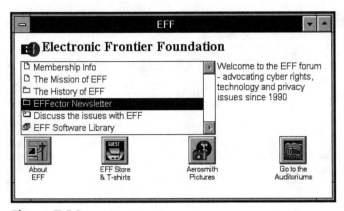

Figure 7.16 Keyword: EFF
The Electronic Frontier Foundation maintains an outpost on AOL.

EFF about rights, technology, and privacy. There are 49 folders in this area, each dealing with a different subject. Civil Liberties Online, Digital Privacy, and Clipper Chip are just three of the topics discussed here.

 The Issues Forum on CompuServe

Go: CIS:ISSUES

The Issues Forum on CompuServe is the place where rights and responsibilities are discussed. Some of the human rights issues discussed include basic human rights, men's rights, women's rights, and the rights of lesbians, gays, and bisexuals. Figure 7.17 shows one of the hottest issues discussed in this forum—abortion. You can go to the discussion area and the library at this site to find out what other human rights issues are discussed.

 Prodigy

I was unable to find any real coverage of Bill of Rights issues on Prodigy.

Recommended Sites to See

The rest of this chapter is a list that contains the information you need to reach the sites listed in this chapter, as well as other sites we didn't cover.

Newsgroups and Mailing Lists

The militia discussion newsgroup.

UseNet address:
`misc.activism.militia`

Discussions of the First Amendment.

LISTSERV address:
`listserv@uafsysb.uark.edu`
subscribe `amend1-l`

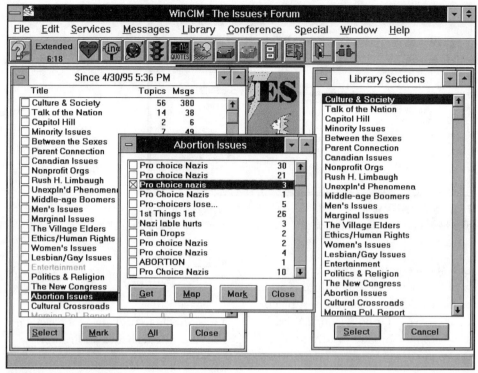

Figure 7.17 `Go: CIS:ISSUES`
Messages in the Issues Forum on CompuServe address many Bill of Rights topics.

General privacy discussions.

UseNet address: `alt.privacy`

Talk about abortion.

UseNet address: `talk.abortion`

The Church of Scientology.

UseNet address:
`alt.religion.scientology`

Talk about guns.

UseNet address: `rec.guns`

Discussions about the encryption program PGP.

UseNet address:
`alt.security.pgp`

Discussions about the Clipper chip and privacy.

UseNet address:
`alt.privacy.clipper`

Freedom of Speech Issues—First Amendment

The American Communication Association.

WWW address: `http://cavern.uark.edu/depts/comminfo/www/ACA.html`

The Church of Scientology vs. the Net.

WWW address: `http://rnewman.www.media.mit.edu/people/rnewman/scientology/`

The Right to Keep and Bear Arms—Second Amendment

The National Rifle Association's Web page.

> WWW address: `http://www.nra.org/`

The Left Side of the Web.

> WWW address: `http://paul.spu.edu/~sinnfein/progressive.html`

The NRA's Gopher site.

> Gopher address: `gopher://gopher.nra.org`

The NRA by FTP.

> FTP address: `ftp://ftp.nra.org`

The Patriot Archives (FTP).

> FTP address: `ftp://tezcat.com/patriot`

Privacy Issues—Fourth Amendment

The Privacy Rights Clearinghouse Web page.

> WWW address: `http://www.manymedia.com/prc/index.html`

The Privacy Rights Clearinghouse by Gopher.

> Gopher address: `gopher://pwa.acusd.edu`

Select the following directories:

```
USD Campus-Wide Information
   System
Privacy Rights Clearinghouse
```

The Privacy Rights Clearinghouse by FTP.

> FTP address: `ftp://ftp.acusd.edu/pub/privacy`

The Cryptography and PGP Page.

> WWW address: `http://rschp2.anu.edu.au:8080/crypt.html`

Information on the Zimmermann Legal Defense Fund.

> WWW address: `http://sunsite.oit.unc.edu/zimmermann-defense.html`

More on the Zimmermann Legal Defense Fund.

> WWW address: `http://www.netresponse.com/zldf/introduction.html`

Jim Warren on the Zimmermann case.

> WWW address: `http://draco.centerline.com:8080/~franl/pgp/warren.html`

Zimmermann fund information by Gopher.

> Gopher address: `gopher://gopher.well.sf.ca.us`

Select the following directories:

```
Hacking
Phil Zimmermann Legal Defense
   Fund Appeal
```

7

BILL OF RIGHTS

Clipper chip information at Quadralay.

WWW address: `http://www.quadralay.com/www/Crypt/Clipper/Clipper.html`

The Cryptography, PGP, and Privacy page.

WWW address: `http://draco.centerline.com:8080/~franl/crypto.html`

Descriptions of the versions of PGP.

WWW address: `http://www.ifi.uio.no/~staalesc/PGP/versions.html`

Equal Protection Issues— Fourteenth Amendment

The Abortion Rights Web.

WWW address: `http://192.231.221.9/~lmann/feminist/abortion.html`

The ProLife News Web page.

WWW address: `http://www.pitt.edu/~stfst/pln/AboutPLN.html`

The CHOICE-NET report.

Gopher address: `gopher://gopher.well.sf.ca.us/`

Select the following directories:
`Politics`
`Abortion and Reproductive`
`   Rights`

An essay on environmental racism.

WWW address: `http://drseuss.lib.uidaho.edu:70/docs/egj01/weint01.html`

About the California Civil Rights Initiative.

WWW address: `http://theforecast.com/forecast/affirm.html`

Other Sites

The U.S. Constitution and its amendments

WWW address: `http://www.law.cornell.edu/constitution/constitution.overview.html`

A Citizen's Guide to Individual Rights in America.

WWW address: `http://asa.ugl.lib.umich.edu/chdocs/rights/Citizen.html`

The Bill of Rights Journal.

Gopher address: `gopher://eagle.birds.wm.edu/`

Select the following directories:
`School of Law`
`Publications`
`The William and Mary Bill of`
`   Rights Journal`

The Constitution.

WWW address: `http://www.house.gov/Constitution/Constitution.html`

The Bill of Rights.

WWW address: `http://www.law.cornell.edu/constitution/constitution.billofrights.html`

The Meanderings newsletter.

WWW address: `http://www.webcom.com/~sppg/meanderings/me204/me204_00.shtml`

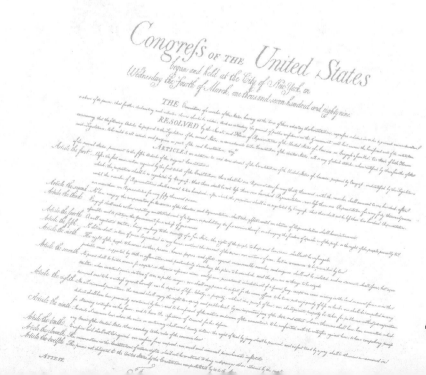

Chapter 8
Policies and Programs

Use the Net to get the latest on government policies and programs.

In this chapter

- *Social security and welfare*
- *Health care reform*
- *AIDS*
- *Illegal immigration*
- *Education reform*

In other chapters

→ *Economic security issues are covered in Chapter 9.*

→ *The system that generates policies and programs is covered in Chapter 11.*

→ *Some of the same issues as this chapter, but at a more local level, are covered in Chapter 12.*

→ *The documents that codify programs are examined in Chapter 13.*

→ *How the Net facilitates international AIDS activism is included in Chapter 14.*

Whenever the government forms a policy or creates a program, it impacts people. A tougher immigration policy affects not only immigrants but those who employ them, or provide services to them. A new crime program affects not only police officers and criminals, but victims, taxpayers, and of course lawyers. A new health care policy can affect every single person in the country.

The effect of policies and programs is different for different groups. More stringent environmental standards might improve the quality of life for most people, but they can hurt businesses and the people who work for them. Reforming our educational system might help our children, but it can harm the teachers' unions.

Because policies and programs have such an impact on our lives, it's no surprise that they get a lot of attention on the Net. Plenty of information is available, usually covering both sides of the issue. Some sites provide non-partisan coverage, but most take sides. The level of discussion can get pretty low in some locations, with name-calling and outright lying. As always with the Net, you need to remember that not everything you see is unbiased, or even close to true.

This chapter examines some of the policies and programs being debated on the Net today. The topics covered here are some of the hottest on and off the Net, so you should certainly find at least one policy or program of direct concern to you.

Like most political topics, government policies and programs get discussed in a number of newsgroups. Unfortunately, there aren't any newsgroups dedicated specifically to policies and programs, so you have to find information in other, more general newsgroups. Two newsgroups that frequently contain discussions of policies and programs are described next.

 ## ClariNet's Miscellaneous U.S. Government Newsgroup

`clari.news.usa.gov.misc`

This newsgroup is created by the ClariNet e-News service. It contains news stories from major sources like the Associated Press and Reuters. As you can see in figure 8.1, there are no message threads here. Instead, the newsgroup contains single messages, each with the contents of a news story. Readers cannot post messages to this newsgroup.

The newsgroup covers any stories related to the U.S. government that don't fit in one of ClariNet's other newsgroups. These stories frequently cover policies and programs.

 ## Miscellaneous Political Talk

`talk.politics.misc`

This newsgroup is a place for anyone to discuss politics in general. It is a much more chaotic place than a ClariNet newsgroup, with people from all over the place commenting on, and screaming about, any political topic. Figure 8.2 shows some typical headings for message threads in this newsgroup.

While many threads have nothing to do with policies and programs, you can usually find some that do. Within the threads, you can find anything from irrational ranting through flaming

```
┌─────────────────────────────────────────────────────────────────────────┐
│ [icons]  [ clari.news.usa.gov.misc          ] ↧ ⟩∎∎⟨ ▶ ∎▸∎ ▶            │
├─────────────────────────────────────────────────────────────────────────┤
│ FTC, Dating Service To Settle   8546   C-ap@clarinet.com (AP)          ↑ │
│ Future Unclear For Water Law     8538   C-ap@clarinet.com (AP)           │
│ GAO: Some Firms Dodge US Taxes   8448   C-ap@clarinet.com (AP)           │
│ Genetic Patenting Opposed        8577   C-ap@clarinet.com (AP)           │
│ Gingrich: Self Promotion's OK    8416   C-ap@clarinet.com (AP)           │
│ GOP At Odds Over Waco Hearings   8415   C-ap@clarinet.com (AP)           │
│ GOP Defend Medicare Plan         8565   C-ap@clarinet.com (AP)           │
│ GOP Rallies Against Foster       8540   C-ap@clarinet.com (AP)           │
│ GOP Seeks Combining Agencies     8534   C-ap@clarinet.com (AP)           │
│ GOP To Dems: Produce Cuts Plan   8484   C-ap@clarinet.com (AP)           │
│ Government Foes Find Voice        8506   C-ap@clarinet.com (AP)           │
│ Govt. Negotiates Safety Rules    8589   C-ap@clarinet.com (AP)         ↓ │
├─────────────────────────────────────────────────────────────────────────┤
│ Article: 8565                                                          ↑ │
│ Newsgroups: clari.news.usa.gov.white_house,clari.biz.industry.health,clari.news.usa.go│
│ From: C-ap@clarinet.com (AP)                                             │
│ Subject: GOP Defend Medicare Plan                                       │
│ Date: Fri, 19 May 95 12:00:19 PDT                                       │
│                                                                         │
│     WASHINGTON (AP) -- Republicans threw President Clinton's own        │
│ words back at him Friday in support of their argument that they are     │
│ just slowing Medicare's growth, not cutting it.                         │
│     But they didn't note that when the president sought to slow         │
│ Medicare spending, he also promised big spending increases on drugs     │
│ and long-term care for the elderly.                                   ↓ │
│ ←                                                                      → │
└─────────────────────────────────────────────────────────────────────────┘
```

Figure 8.1 `clari.news.usa.gov.misc`
Miscellaneous U.S. Government News from ClariNet.

attacks on other users, to reasoned analysis and commentary on policy issues.

Social Security and Welfare

The United States has numerous programs that are designed to provide economic assistance to people. Welfare programs, such as Aid to Families with Dependent Children (AFDC) and Medicaid, are provided by the federal or state government to those in need of financial assistance.

Unfortunately, the cost of economic security programs is ballooning, taking an ever larger share of the total budget.

Reforms are a must if these programs are to be contained within a finite budget. The programs that come up most often when this reform is discussed are Social Security and Welfare.

 **Catalog of Federal Domestic Assistance**

`marvel.loc.gov`

Select the following directories:

```
Government Information
Federal Information
   Resources
Information by Branch of
   Federal Government
```

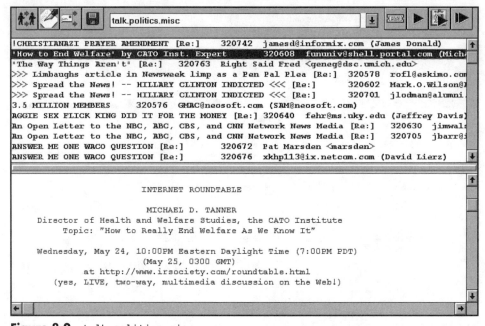

Figure 8.2 `talk.politics.misc`
This newsgroup is the place to talk about anything related to politics.

```
General Information
     Resources
Catalog of Federal Domestic
     Assistance
```

The Federal Government provides an online catalog of information about domestic programs, including welfare and Social Security. The information is maintained at the Marvel Gopher site and is accessed through a simple search program (see fig. 8.3).

The search program scans the catalog based on keywords you supply. A search on the word **welfare** turned up over 70 documents, each describing a welfare-related policy or program. If you want to find information about economic security programs and other forms of domestic assistance, this site is the place to start.

The Bipartisan Commission on Entitlements and Tax Reform Web Page

`http://www.charm.net/~dcarolco/`

The Bipartisan Commission on Entitlements and Tax Reform maintains a Web page where the public can monitor the commission's activities and recommendations (see fig. 8.4). The commission was created by President Clinton in 1993 to recommend bipartisan changes to the nation's entitlement programs.

The Bipartisan Commission on Entitlements and Tax Reform's Web page has links to six sections, four of which contain useful or interesting material. The Entitlements Challenge section contains the commission's interim progress report, as well as related documents and charts. The Search for Solutions section contains the commission's final letter to the President and options for reforming the existing system.

The For more information... section is full of information on other groups involved in the debate about entitlements, and links to other entitlement and budget information on the Net. The other interesting link takes you to

a game called Budget Shadows. A Lotus 1-2-3 for Windows spreadsheet, it lets you try your hand at controlling runaway entitlement costs and balancing the budget.

Social Security

A vast amount of information on the American Social Security system—and even foreign ones—is available through the Social Security Administration's Net sites.

The Social Security Administration (SSA) Home Page

`http://www.ssa.gov/`

The Social Security Administration provides a home page of benefit

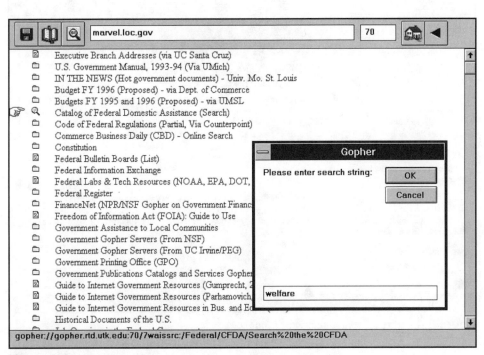

Figure 8.3 `marvel.loc.gov`
Searching the Catalog of Federal Domestic Assistance at LC Marvel.

information, policies, and statistics about Social Security. Figure 8.5 shows the page and its Quick Index of major topics.

If you want to know what your Social Security benefits are likely to be when you retire, you can download form SSA-7004, the succinctly titled "Request for Earnings and Benefit Estimate Statement." After you print out this form, you can send it to the SSA and receive a personalized estimate of your future benefits.

The SSA page is rich in online information. There are links to a growing list of online services provided by the SSA. A search program can track down information on specific Social Security topics. There are links to the SSA's Gopher and FTP servers. There's even a link to a page of other servers with information related to Social Security.

Welfare Reform

Here's something both the Democrats and Republicans agree on: the welfare system is broken and needs to be fixed. Welfare programs, such as Aid to Families with Dependent Children (AFDC), food stamps, and Medicaid are a large and growing portion of the federal budget.

This section profiles two Net sites where you can find more about how politicians plan to fix welfare.

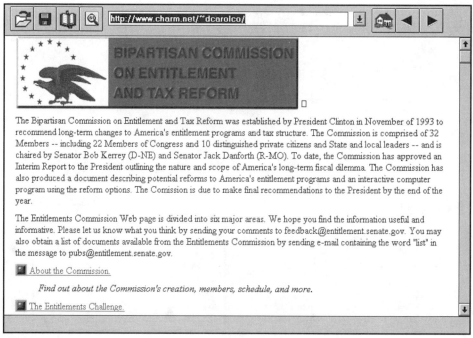

Figure 8.4 `http://www.charm.net/~dcarolco/`
The Bipartisan Commission on Entitlements and Tax Reform's Web page.

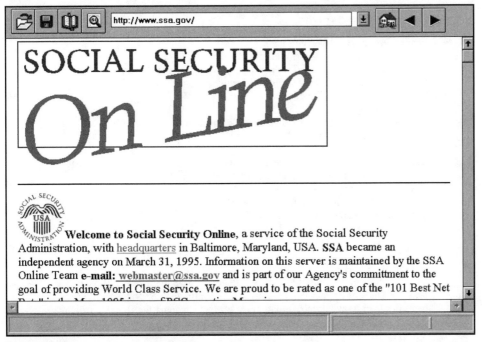

Figure 8.5 `http://www.ssa.gov/`
The SSA online has a search program to help you track down information on Social Security issues.

 ## Department of Health and Human Services Abstracts

`gopher://gopher.os.dhhs.gov`

Select the following directories:

> **DHHS Resources by**
> **Organization**
> **Office of the Secretary**
> **Office of the Assistant**
> **Secretary for Planning**
> **and Evaluation**

The Department of Health and Human Services maintains a database of abstracts related to welfare and welfare reform. The database contains hundreds of abstracts from reports and other documents, all accessible through a simple search program. Entering a keyword like **welfare** or **AFDC** will bring up a list of up to 50 resources related to that word. Figure 8.6 shows the results of a search on the keyword **welfare**.

The search returned all sorts of documents including the word welfare. They range from high-level, long-term topics like Family: Preserving America's Future, and the International Roundtable on Child Welfare, to statistical reports like Welfare Research and Statistics. Because this database is continuously updated, the specific reports you find might differ from those shown in the figure.

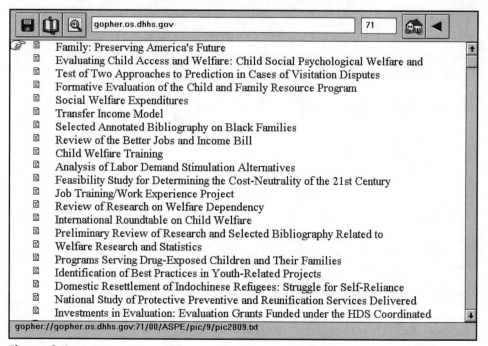

gopher://gopher.os.dhhs.gov:71/00/ASPE/pic/9/pic2809.txt

Figure 8.6 gopher.os.dhhs.gov
Welfare-related abstracts from a search at the DHHS Gopher.

Health Care Reform

The 1993 National Health Security Plan was to be one of the most sweeping changes in national policy ever attempted. In the name of ensuring universal medical coverage for all Americans, it called for a complete reorganization of the U.S. health care industry. That industry is a collection of providers, insurers, and consumers that amounts to one-seventh of the total economy. With so much at stake, a heated political battle was inevitable.

President Clinton committed his administration to ensuring the passage of this plan. A huge amount of effort went into developing the plan, but much of it went on behind closed doors. The plan included features like a Health Security Card for every American, and promised less paperwork, better coverage, and reduced costs.

Many questioned the plan's assumptions, and opposition to almost every part of the plan appeared immediately. When the dust settled, the President's plan was scrapped, and health care reform was shelved until after the 1994 elections.

 The National Health Security Plan Page

http://sunsite.unc.edu/nhs/ NHS-T-o-C.html

This page provides complete information on the National Health Security

Plan proposed by President Clinton in 1993. Figure 8.7 shows some of what is available here. The site includes the full text of the plan, and a number of supporting documents.

The supporting documents include the text of the President's address to a joint session of Congress, where he formally announced his plan. Both the text of the address as written, and a transcript of it as it was actually delivered, are available. The Administration's beliefs on the need for reform are also here, and provide a basis for understanding why the Administration proposed the plan it did.

One unusual element of the Administration's health care reform effort was the high-level involvement of the First Lady, Hillary Rodham Clinton. The profile on Hillary Rodham Clinton has more information on this powerful woman and her role in the Administration's proposed health care plan.

> *One unusual element of the Administration's health care reform effort was the high-level involvement of the First Lady, Hillary Rodham Clinton.*

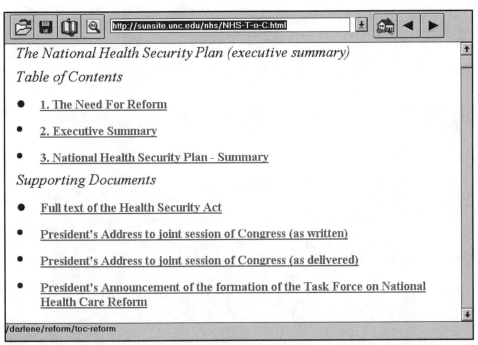

Figure 8.7 `http://sunsite.unc.edu/nhs/NHS-T-o-C.html`
The National Health Security Plan was proposed by Clinton in 1993.

Hillary Rodham Clinton

One of the first things Bill Clinton did as President was to name Hillary Rodham Clinton the Chairperson of the Task Force on National Health Care Reform. Wielding more official power than any First Lady before her, Mrs. Clinton was charged with developing the Administration's health care plan. To get transcripts of the First Lady's speeches on health care and other subjects, as well as a more detailed biography, set your Web browser to take you to the following address:

. WWW address: **http:/ www.whitehouse.gov/ White_House/EOP/First_Lady/ html/HILLARY_Home.html**

This address brings you to Mrs. Clinton's personal Web page at the White House. Figure 8.8 shows the opening image on this page.

Hillary Rodham Clinton is a newsmaker. You'll find her name throughout the Net and online services. Articles about her current activities appear anywhere on the Net that current events are discussed. Just about any site that covers health care will also have at least excerpts from her policy speeches. A Veronica search using the keywords **Hillary Clinton** will turn up hundreds of articles.

Like most famous people, Mrs. Clinton attracts controversy. Her relationship with the Children's Defense Fund, and the content of some papers she wrote for them in the 1970s is an online discussion topic. For a short, sympathetic summary of this flap, set your Web browser to:

WWW address: **http:// www.ai.mit.edu/people/ellens/ NCRA/horton.html**

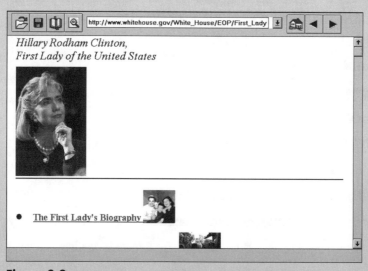

Figure 8.8 http:/www.whitehouse.gov/White_House/EOP/First_Lady/html/ HILLARY_Home.html
Hillary Rodham Clinton's page on the White House Web site.

AIDS

AIDS policy is another controversial health care issue. While no one disputes that AIDS is a horrible disease, there is much disagreement on what to do about it. AIDS activists want more money, more prevention programs, and a national focus on AIDS as our primary health care problem. Other groups, particularly conservatives and some religious groups, are either silent on the issues or actively opposed.

A vast amount of AIDS-related information is available on the Net. Databases full of statistics, mortality reports, press releases, and more are available at numerous sites. The rest of this section looks at one particularly interesting page, and then covers a couple of other pages that are collections of links to AIDS and AIDS-related sites.

> **NOTE**
>
> AIDS activism is an international activity. The Net gives groups unprecedented power to work globally, coordinating their efforts with others around the world. Chapter 14, "Political Hot Spots," looks at this phenomenon.

A vast amount of AIDS-related information is available on the Net.

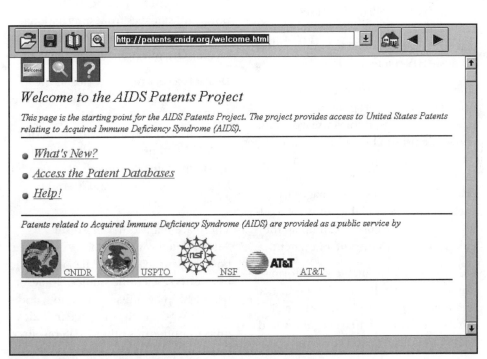

Figure 8.9 `http://patents.cnidr.org/welcome.html`
The AIDS Patents Project Web page.

The AIDS/HIV Information page contains links to a number of online AIDS reports.

 The AIDS Patents Project

`http://patents.cnidr.org/`
`welcome.html`

One of the most innovative AIDS-related sites on the Net is the AIDS Patent Project. This site is an extensive database of AIDS-related patent information (see fig. 8.9). Within seconds, researchers or other interested parties can query the database for information on any AIDS-related patent.

The AIDS Patents Project Web page provides a search program that does free-text searches, Boolean searches, or allows the user to browse the entire database. Once a patent is found, the user can view the abstract, front page, or the full text. All of the images from each patent are available for downloading. It's even possible to call up all the patents related to the current patent.

Other resources available are information on the AIDS Patent Mailing List, a link to a FAQ file, and even one leading to ArtAIDS, a virtual art gallery and AIDS fund-raising project.

 The QRD AIDS/HIV Information Page

`http://www.qrd.org/qrd/www/`
`AIDS.html`

The Queer Resources Directory (QRD) is an electronic research library dedicated to groups that have been traditionally labeled as "queer." The goal of the QRD is to gather as much information as possible on discrimination against lesbians, gays, and bisexuals. It is also a treasure trove of information on AIDS and HIV.

The AIDS/HIV Information page contains links to a number of online AIDS reports, many of them from official U.S. Government sources like the Center for Disease Control, and the U.S. Surgeon General (see fig. 8.10). Reports and statistics from international organizations, such as the World Health Organization, are available too.

Death is a very real presence in the AIDS community as you can see on the QRD AIDS/HIV Information page, where links are available to obituaries of AIDS victims, and to morbidity and mortality statistics. There's also a direct link to the Morbidity and Mortality Weekly Report.

There are many other interesting AIDS-related resources here, including book reviews, copies of AIDS-related newsletters, scientific studies, domestic partnership benefits information, and a set of FAQs. Finally, the page includes links to numerous other AIDS resource lists.

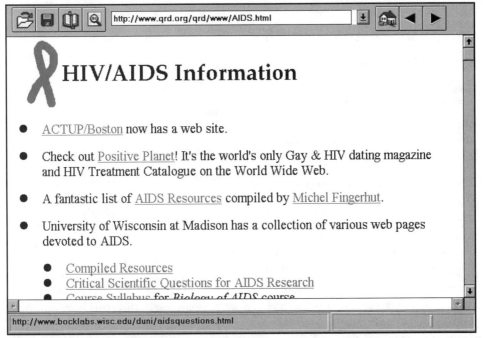

Figure 8.10 `http://www.qrd.org/qrd/www/AIDS.html`
The QRD AIDS/HIV Information page.

Illegal Immigration

Immigration policy has always been a sensitive issue in the United States. At certain times in history, our borders were like open gates, letting virtually anyone enter freely. At other times, strict restrictions have been in place, limiting the flow of immigrants to a trickle. Regardless of the rules, some people have always entered the country illegally.

The flow of illegal immigrants has now become a flood, and is causing some Americans to turn against immigration—illegal or legal. The impact of America's hardening attitude toward immigration is already beginning to result in changing policies, starting with Proposition 187.

 Proposition 187

`http://www.oclc.org/VoteSmart/`
`lwv/prop187.htm`

Depending on who you listen to, Proposition 187 is either a racist attempt to blame Hispanics for California's problems, or a sensible response to the social and economic costs of illegal immigrants. The proposition basically cuts off all non-emergency aid and benefits for illegal immigrants and their children. If it ever goes into effect—it was voted into law in the November 1994 election but is on hold awaiting legal appeals—it would ban approximately 300,000 children from the state's schools, and deny

There are also concise arguments for and against Proposition 187.

There are also concise arguments for and against the proposition.

 **The 187Resist Gopher**

`gopher://`
`garnet.berkeley.edu:1870`

non-emergency medical care to as many as 1.6 million people.

The League of Women Voters provides non-partisan analyses of propositions and other political issues. There is a VoteSmart Web site for California that contains an analysis of various propositions from the November '94 California elections. For Proposition 187, the page gives a description of the illegal immigrant situation in the state, a summary of the proposition, and an estimate of its fiscal impact (see fig. 8.11).

Opponents of Proposition 187 used sites on the Net to organize their activities to try to defeat this referendum. One such site is the 187Resist Gopher at the University of California at Berkeley (see fig. 8.12). The politics here are rather liberal, as are most of the groups opposed to Proposition 187.

There are eight directories within the 187Resist site. The Key 187 Resistance Documents directory contains the text of the ACLU's suit against the proposition,

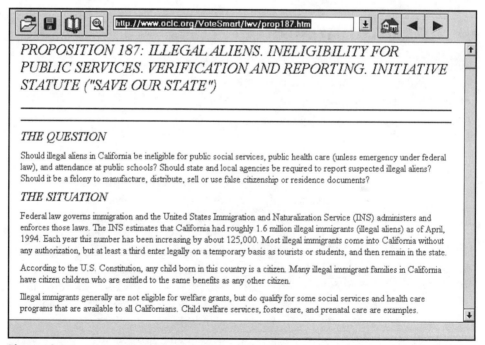

Figure 8.11 `http://www.oclc.org/VoteSmart/lwv/prop187.htm`
Non-Partisan Information on Proposition 187 is available here.

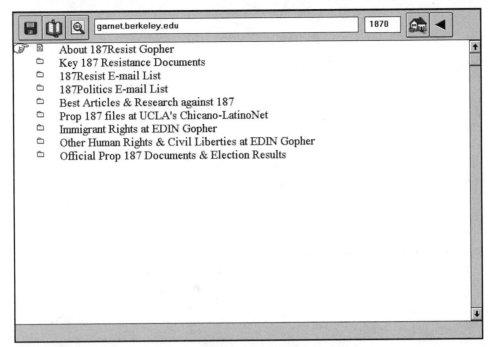

Figure 8.12 `gopher://garnet.berkeley.edu:1870`
There are eight directories in the 187Resist Gopher site.

as well as anti-proposition 187 statements from groups like the California Library Association. The directory also contains the text of magazine articles on the subject.

Two of the directories at the 187Resist Gopher address mailing lists about the proposition. They provide instructions on subscribing to the lists, and selecting messages from them. Other directories contain additional anti-187 material, information on other human rights, immigration rights material, and official Proposition 187 documents and election results.

Education Reform

There seems to be a consensus in this country that we need to reform our educational system. Unfortunately, there isn't a consensus on exactly what to do. Some people advocate integrating multimedia PCs and edutainment software into the school experience. Others want longer school years. The concept of school choice is popular, as are national standards. It all adds up to a lot of action and confusion, especially when you consider that the schools themselves are locally controlled. School districts across the country are trying all of the ideas listed above with varying results.

This section looks at two Net sites related to education and education reform in the United States. The first is the Department of Education's Web page, an ideal place to get background information on education across the country. The second Net site addresses the use of computers to enhance the educational experience.

 The U.S. Department of Education Page

`http://www.ed.gov/`

If you want to find out more about education in the United States, start at the U.S. Department of Education's Web page (see fig. 8.13). This site is a huge repository of data on federal education policy and programs. Among its resources, it lists national educational goals, education-related press releases, and the text of speeches and Congressional testimony on education.

The table of contents for this page lists 14 major topics. When you select a topic, you receive a short introduction to the material, including links to more detailed information on the topic. Choosing National Educational Goals, for example, leads to a list of eight goals to be achieved by the year 2000. Selecting the Summary Guide to the third annual National Education Goals Report link takes you to a hypertext version of the Summary Guide.

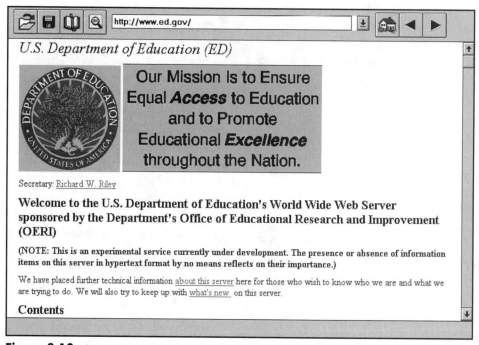

Figure 8.13 `http://www.ed.gov/`
The U.S. Department of Education's Web site has 14 major topics in its table of contents.

Some other topics included at this site are newsletters and press releases on education, Congressional testimony by the Secretary of Education, and department-wide initiatives. The page is also linked to the Department of Education Gopher, where even more material can be found.

 Engines for Education

`http://www.ils.nwu.edu/`
`~e_for_e/`

The Net is a good way to keep up with educational reform activity. Many educational organizations and reformers make their ideas and results available online. The Engines for Education page is one such site (see fig. 8.14).

Engines for Education is a hypertext document dealing with many aspects of education and education reform. One focus of the site is the value of computers in improving education. There is a mass of material at this site; the detailed Table of Contents is six pages, so Engines for Education uses an unusual interface to make the material more accessible to visitors. It offers four areas of interest that visitors can pursue. Just Curious… is for people with no specific agenda. Media Maven… is for people who are interested in innovations in media. Business Person… is for those concerned with education in business and industry. Educator… focuses on education and learning.

Each area of interest offers different starting points for exploring Engines

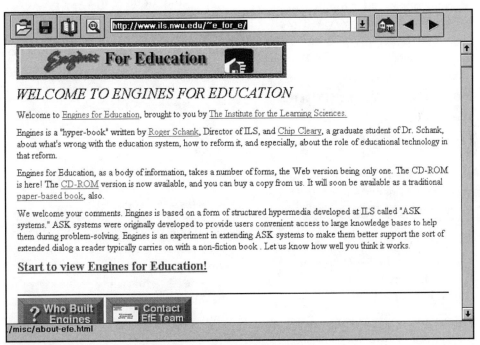

Figure 8.14 `http://www.ils.nwu.edu/~e_for_e/`
The Engines for Education page addresses education reform.

for Education. These starting points are selected to lead you directly to areas you will find interesting. Just Curious... leads to information about the document and the facility that produced it, as well as some educational and software material. Education... leads to material on how children learn and mistakes in current educational practices.

Policies and Programs on the Online Services

Government policies and programs are well represented on the online services. As always, each service has its own emphasis in coverage and resources, making one better than the other for coverage of particular topics. In this section, I've tried to give you a good idea of the policy and program information on each service.

Policies and Programs on AOL

America Online provides excellent coverage of government policies and programs. There are a number of useful sources of policy and program information, including the National news service (**Keyword: US News**), the Educational area (**Keyword: Education**) and clubs like the AARP Online and the Environmental forum (**Keyword: Clubs**).

Two locations on AOL are prime sources for information on Policies and Programs. The most useful of these is the Capital Connection.

 AOL

Keywords: **POLITICS, CAPITAL**

The Capital Connection is AOL's focus for most things political. Here, you can find everything from libraries of documents, to digitized Sound bites on political topics to message boards where you can put your own two cents in. Integrating the Net into the online service, the forum contains links to a number of Gopher sites, including the National Rifle Association's site.

 AOL

Keyword: **WELFARE**

One feature of the Capital Connection that is particularly relevant is AOL's Special Report on Welfare Reform. This site pulls together a mass of material on welfare and what Washington wants to do about the current welfare system (see fig. 8.15).

 AOL

Keyword: **WHITE HOUSE**

The White House forum is the other prime source for policy and program coverage. This area contains the text of speeches, briefings, and remarks by the President, and others in the Executive Branch. The material is divided into topics, including education, the environment, health care, and law and order.

Policies and Programs on CompuServe

CompuServe's coverage of policies is mainly individual subjects distributed within related forums.

A non-political forum that touches on policies and programs is the Education forum (**Go: CIS:EDFORUM**). At this site, where the focus is all aspects of education, the message area is devoted to reform. Social Security and Medicare have their own area in the Retirement Living forum (**Go: CIS:RETIREMENT**).

 CompuServe

Go: **CIS:REPUBLICAN**

The Republican forum primarily gives the Republican view on policies and programs. There are specific message sections for health care and crime, and the domestic issues area often includes discussions on welfare and gun control.

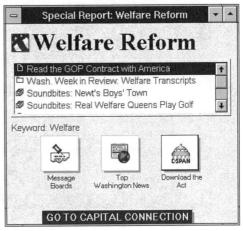

Figure 8.15 Keyword: WELFARE *AOL's Special Report on Welfare Reform at AOL.*

Library sections contain information on legislative activities and the Contract with America.

As will happen when free speech is involved, some of the posts found in this forum go beyond the bounds of acceptable behavior. Figure 8.16 shows an excerpt from a message thread that I doubt the Republican party is very happy about.

Keep Your Eyes Open!

Like the other services, AOL invites celebrities onto the system to discuss topical issues. Sometimes the celebrity is a politician, and the issue is a policy or program.

The day before I wrote this sidebar, AOL had Senator Bob Kerrey in its Center Stage Spotlight to discuss entitlement reform. And I was out getting a haircut! This incident provides a good lesson. Even though all the services have specific areas for political topics, they often have special events or features that might have just the information you need. The moral of the story is to log onto the services regularly, and keep your eyes open.

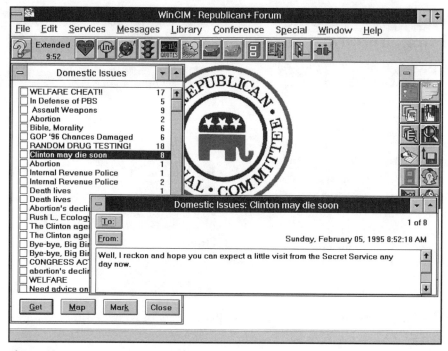

Figure 8.16 Go: CIS:REPUBLICAN
A nasty message thread in CompuServe's Republican forum.

 CompuServe

Go: CIS:POLITICS

The Political Debate forum is exactly that—a place to debate, discuss, and argue over political issues. This forum has message sections specifically addressing health care, education, and guns.

 CompuServe

Go: CIS:DEMOCRATS

The Democratic forum covers policies and programs too. This forum has a number of paired message sections and libraries that cover topics such as health care, guns and crime, education, the environment, and welfare. An interesting feature here is specific coverage of political reform, which touches on policies and programs, and on reinventing government.

Policies and Programs on Prodigy

Of the three online services, Prodigy provides the least coverage of policies and programs; even so, there is still information available. This section features one good place to search for general information, and one of the locations where information is dispersed throughout.

Prodigy

Jump: WHITE HOUSE

As it says in the banner for this section, the White House memo area consists of the texts of "...unedited briefings, speeches, transcripts, and more...." Within the area, the topics are divided into sections like health care, social security, and more. Each section has a search program that lets you scan the text for specific words or phrases.

 Prodigy

Jump: AARP

Much of Prodigy's policy and program coverage is found within non-political areas like the AARP forum. As the forum for the American Association of Retired Persons, some of the discussions and material in this forum focus on Social Security and other government programs.

Recommended Sites to See

The following list contains addresses of Net sites discussed in this chapter, as well as numerous others that might be of interest. The list is broken up into the same sections as the body of the chapter.

Newsgroups and Mailing Lists

Press coverage of domestic policy.
  UseNet address:
  `clari.news.usa.gov.misc`

Political activist announcements.
  UseNet address: `alt.activism`

Political activist discussion.
  UseNet address: `alt.activism.d`

Messages to the White House.
  UseNet address:
  `alt.dear.whitehouse`

General political discussions.
  UseNet address:
  `talk.politics.misc`

Education reform newsletter.
  LISTSERVE address:
  `ukeral@ukcc.uky.edu`

New approaches to learning.
  LISTSERVE address:
  `altlearn@sjuvm.stjohns.edu`

Educational policy analysis.
  LISTSERVE address:
  `edpolyan@asuvm.inre.asu.edu`

General education discussions.
  UseNet address:
  `misc.education`

Health care politics.

UseNet address:
`talk.politics.medicine`

The AIDS Patent Mailing List.

LISTSERVE address:
`listserv@cnidr.org`

New and politics about AIDS.

UseNet address:
`clari.tw.health.aids`

Immigration issues.

UseNet address:
`misc.immigration.usa`

Social Security and Welfare

Search program for domestic assistance programs.

Gopher address:
`marvel.loc.gov`

Once connected, navigate through the following directories:

```
Government Information
Federal Information
   Resources
Information by Branch of
   Federal Government
General Information
   Resources
Catalog of Federal Domestic
   Assistance
```

Welfare and poverty resources.

Gopher address:
`garnet.berkeley.edu`

Once connected, navigate through the following directories:

```
Housing, Health & Poverty
Poverty and Welfare
```

The Bipartisan Commission on Entitlements and Tax Reform.

WWW address: `http://www.charm.net/~dcarolco/`

The Social Security Administration.

WWW address: `http://www.ssa.gov/`

A search program for the Department of Health and Human Services.

Gopher address:
`gopher.os.dhhs.gov`

Once connected, navigate through the following directories:

```
DHHS Resources by
   Organization
Office of the Secretary
Office of the Assistant
   Secretary for Planning
   and Evaluation
```

The Thomas Legislative Information system.

WWW address: `http://thomas.loc.gov/`

Health Care Reform

The National Health Security Plan.

WWW address: `http://sunsite.unc.edu/nhs/NHS-T-o-C.html`

Hillary Clinton's home page.

WWW address: `http://www.whitehouse.gov/White_House/EOP/First_Lady/html/HILLARY_Home.html`

Hillary and the Children's Defense Fund.

WWW address: `http://www.ai.mit.edu/people/ellens/NCRA/horton.html`

Liberal health care newsletter.

Gopher address: `info.umd.edu`

Once connected, navigate through the following directories:
```
Computing Resources
Network Information
Newsletters
The American Health
   Security News
```

AIDS

The AIDS Patent Project.

WWW address: `http://patents.cnidr.org/welcome.html`

The QRD home page.

WWW address:
`http:''www.qrd.org/`

The QRD AIDS/HIV Information page.

WWW address: `http://vector.castri.com/QRD/.html/AIDS.html`

The AIDS/HIV page on Yahoo.

WWW address: `http://akebono.stanford.edu/yahoo/Health/Medicine/AIDS_HIV/`

AIDS information at the NIH.

Gopher address:
`odie.niaid.nih.gov`

Once connected, navigate through the following directory:
`AIDS Related Information`

Illegal Immigration

Information on Proposition 187.

WWW address: `http://www.oclc.org/VoteSmart/lwv/prop187.html`

Anti-Proposition 187 activists.

Gopher address:
`garnet.berkeley.edu 1870`

Another anti-187 site.

Gopher address:
`latino.sscnet.ucla.edu`

Education Reform

The U.S. Department of Education.

WWW address: `http://www.ed.gov/`

The Engines for Education page.

WWW address: `http://www.ils.nwu.edu/~e_for_e/`

U.S. Department of Education.

FTP address: `ftp://ftp.ed.gov/gopher/*`

Sorted list of educational resources.

FTP address: `ftp://nic.umass.edu /pub/ednet/edusenet.gde`

Gopher address: `info.umd.edu`

Once connected, select the following directories:

```
Computing Resources
Network Information
Newsletters
EDU Page
```

A daily educational issue newsletter.

Gopher address: `nysernet.org`

Once connected, select the following directories:

```
Special Collections  Empire
  Internet Schoolhouse
  (K-12)
School Reform and Technol-
  ogy Planning Center
Daily Report Card News
  Service
```

Chapter 9

The Economy and Trade

Use the Net to explore the politics of the economy and trade.

In this chapter ·

- *General information about the economy*
- *Government cash flow: taxing & spending*
- *Concerns about the state of the economy*
- *Trade-related issues*
- *Economy and trade on the online services*

In other chapters

← *The Administration's economic plan included the Reinventing Government effort. See VP Gore in Chapter 6 for more information.*

← *Some UAW members recommend labor support leftist political parties like the New Party, which is covered in Chapter 5.*

→ *USAID, a federal agency that promotes American interests overseas, is covered in Chapter 10.*

→ *GATT and NAFTA, two major trade agreements, are covered in Chapter 10.*

The U.S. economy is the largest and most complex in the world. Almost every citizen makes multiple economic decisions every day. Understanding how the whole thing works seems like an impossible task. The Gross Domestic Product (GDP) for 1993, the value of goods and services produced in the country in that year, exceeded 6.3 trillion dollars. It is, however, possible to get some feel for the economy as a whole through statistics like the GDP. This chapter looks at some sources for this kind of information.

While no one, including the President, can control the economy, the actions of government do affect it. And the economy, of course, affects every citizen. Sections in this chapter address some of the parts of the government that influence the economy, and some of the concerns people have about it.

Another economic area influenced by politics is international trade. The U.S. economy isn't closed; Americans trade with over 100 countries. Since this trade exceeds a trillion dollars a year, it has a significant impact on the rest of the economy. A positive balance of trade, one where the value of exports exceeds that of imports, can help make up for other weaknesses in the economy. The trade section of this chapter looks at some government resources dedicated to stimulating international trade.

Newsgroups and Mailing Lists

There are a number of newsgroups that cover the economy and trade. This section looks at some that are closely related to topics discussed in this chapter.

 The Politics and Economics Newsgroup

`alt.politics.economics`

A wide range of issues is discussed in this newsgroup; most stick close to political economic issues. Figure 9.1 shows the titles of some recent threads in this newsgroup.

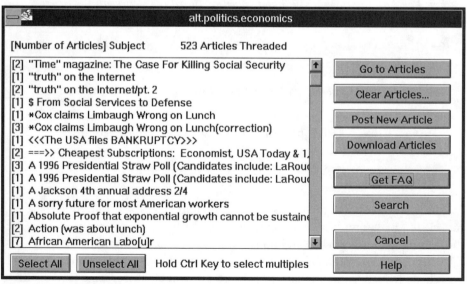

Figure 9.1 `alt.politics.economics`
This newsgroup includes UseNet discussions of political economics.

The discussions here are generally polite, with few of the really rabid posts you see in other newsgroups. Even so, the discussions do sometimes get heated. There's plenty of room for disagreement, with subjects like Social Security, Rush Limbaugh, and racial economic issues being covered.

 ## Government Financial News Stories

`clari.news.usa.gov.financial`

This newsgroup, provided by the ClariNet e.News service, consists of articles from mainstream news services, primarily the Associated Press. Figure 9.2 shows recent articles in this newsgroup.

Any article concerned with U.S. government finances may appear in this newsgroup. Like other ClariNet newsgroups, the only thing you will find is news. You won't find any flame wars or blatantly biased articles. You also won't find any discussions of the articles. If you keep in mind the strengths and weaknesses of this newsgroup, it is an easy way to stay up to date on the government's financial situation.

 ## The Labor Union Issues Newsgroup

`alt.society.labor-unions`

This newsgroup is for discussing issues that are important to organized labor.

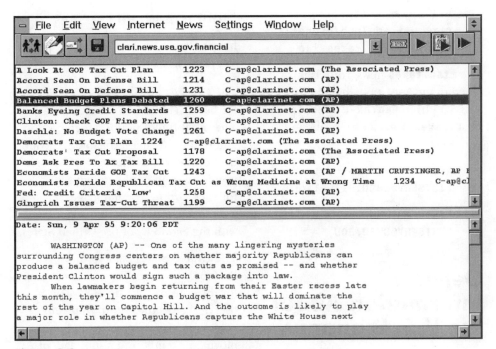

Figure 9.2 `clari.news.usa.gov.financial`
This newsgroup consists of articles about U.S. government finances.

Many of the postings deal with political issues. Recent threads covered labor law, labor-oriented political movements, and organized protests against conservative legislation.

 Discussions of U.S. Taxes

`misc.taxes`

This unmoderated newsgroup is for discussing tax law and getting tax advice. Before posting to this newsgroup, you should read its Frequently Asked Questions (FAQ) file. The FAQ contains guidance on proper posting techniques, lists of common abbreviations and notation, and alternate sources for tax advice. The FAQ is available by anonymous FTP at:

> FTP address: `ftp://rtfm.mit.edu/pub/usenet/news.answers/taxes-faq`

The `misc.taxes` newsgroup is mirrored to the **FedTax-L** mailing list, and messages from **FedTax-L** appear in `misc.taxes`. You can subscribe to **FedTax-L** at:

> LISTSERV address:
> **LISTSERV@SHSU.BITNET**, or

> LISTSERV address:
> **LISTSERV@SHSU.EDU**

General Information About the U.S. Economy

Many organizations gather information about the economy, allowing the development of some broad statistical measures. The Central Intelligence Agency has gathered this kind of information for the United States and the other countries of the world and put it into the CIA World Factbook. The Factbook section on the United States is a quick way to get a high-level view of the state of the U.S. economy.

Other government agencies gather detailed information related to their areas of responsibility. The Bureau of Labor Statistics develops detailed reports on factors that affect labor, both in the U.S. and abroad. The United States section of the World Factbook, and the Bureau of Labor Statistics, is examined next.

 The U.S. in the CIA World Factbook

`http://www.ic.gov/94fact/country/249.html`

The CIA World Factbook is produced for use by U.S. Government officials. The site is full of political, geographic, and other information about the countries of the world. There is also an economic overview and detailed statistics for each country, which makes it a good place to start getting acquainted with the economy of the United States.

The United States page in the World Factbook also contains economic data for the country (see fig. 9.3). The overview gives the country's recent economic history, growth, and unemployment trends, and a summary of economic problems, all in one big paragraph.

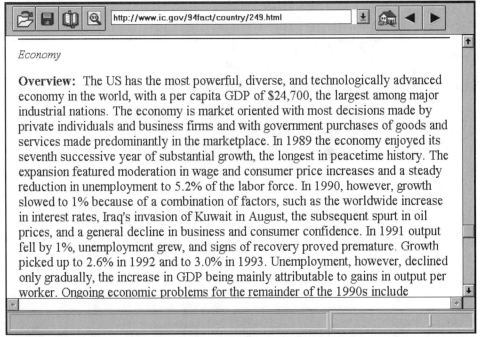

Economy

Overview: The US has the most powerful, diverse, and technologically advanced economy in the world, with a per capita GDP of $24,700, the largest among major industrial nations. The economy is market oriented with most decisions made by private individuals and business firms and with government purchases of goods and services made predominantly in the marketplace. In 1989 the economy enjoyed its seventh successive year of substantial growth, the longest in peacetime history. The expansion featured moderation in wage and consumer price increases and a steady reduction in unemployment to 5.2% of the labor force. In 1990, however, growth slowed to 1% because of a combination of factors, such as the worldwide increase in interest rates, Iraq's invasion of Kuwait in August, the subsequent spurt in oil prices, and a general decline in business and consumer confidence. In 1991 output fell by 1%, unemployment grew, and signs of recovery proved premature. Growth picked up to 2.6% in 1992 and to 3.0% in 1993. Unemployment, however, declined only gradually, the increase in GDP being mainly attributable to gains in output per worker. Ongoing economic problems for the remainder of the 1990s include

Figure 9.3 `http://www.ic.gov/94fact/country/249.html`
The CIA World Factbook includes plenty of information about the U.S.

NOTE
Other facets of CIA World Factbook are covered in Chapter 10, "Foreign Affairs."

Trade is also addressed in the economy section of this page. There's a concise summary for both imports and exports that includes the dollar value of trade, the primary products traded, and the major trading partners.

To better understand the U.S. economy, you can use the Factbook to compare our economy to those of other major nations like Japan, Germany, and China.

 The Bureau of Labor Statistics Home Page

`http://stats.bls.gov/blshome.html`

The Bureau of Labor Statistics (BLS) is a branch of the U.S. Department of Labor. It serves as the statistical arm of that department, as well as an independent agency that collects, analyzes, and distributes economic and statistical data. The data it distributes is required to be timely, relevant, accurate, and impartial.

The BLS home page is the Net community's gateway to BLS resources (see fig. 9.4). The page has links to five topics, including Major BLS Programs and the BLS Data (LABSTAT) database.

9

THE ECONOMY AND TRADE

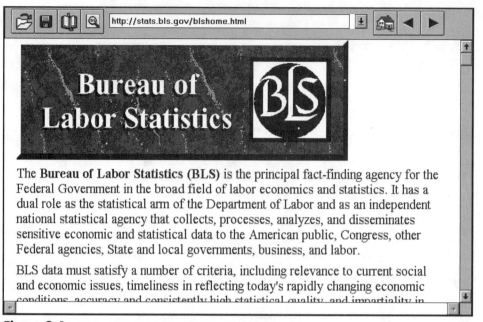

The address bar reads: http://stats.bls.gov/blshome.html

Bureau of Labor Statistics **BLS**

The **Bureau of Labor Statistics (BLS)** is the principal fact-finding agency for the Federal Government in the broad field of labor economics and statistics. It has a dual role as the statistical arm of the Department of Labor and as an independent national statistical agency that collects, processes, analyzes, and disseminates sensitive economic and statistical data to the American public, Congress, other Federal agencies, State and local governments, business, and labor.

BLS data must satisfy a number of criteria, including relevance to current social and economic issues, timeliness in reflecting today's rapidly changing economic conditions, accuracy and consistently high statistical quality, and impartiality in

Figure 9.4 http://stats.bls.gov/blshome.html
The Bureau of Labor Statistics home page is the gateway to BLS resources.

The Major BLS Programs link connects to 23 programs divided into five categories:

- Employment & Unemployment
- Statistics, Prices, and Living Conditions
- Compensation and Working Conditions
- Productivity and Technology
- Employment Projections

All are useful for examining the current state of, and prospect for, American workers.

NOTE

The BLS page shown here is only temporary. By the time you read this, the BLS's new Web site should be up and running.

The BLS Data (LABSTAT) page is actually an interface to the bureau's Gopher-based database. The bulk of the page contains an explanation of the 26 surveys contained in the database. The reports include collective bargaining data, unemployment statistics, producer price trends, and more. Once you are comfortable with the available information and the way it is stored, you can click a link that takes you to the database itself.

Taxing and Spending

Government spending, and the taxes that fund it, have a major impact on the economy. So does the persistent Federal budget deficit, recently held down to only $140,000,000,000 or so.

 President Clinton's Economic Plan

`gopher://wiretap.spies.com`

Select the following directories:

> **Government Docs (US & World)**
> **Clinton's Economic Plan**

Recent Presidents have manipulated taxes and spending to affect the course of the economy, and President Clinton is no exception. Upon taking office, he proposed an economic plan that addressed his goals for the economy. The text of President Clinton's 1993 Economic Plan is available at this Gopher site (see fig. 9.5). Although the President has changed directions numerous times to respond to changing circumstances, it forms the basis for what he planned to do when he came into office.

President Clinton's First Economic Plan is comprised of nine files. The first is the Letter of Transmittal that accompanied the Plan when it was delivered to Congress. The other eight cover the major points of the President's Plan. Parts 1 and 2 are particularly interesting because they describe the ideological basis for the Clinton Presidency.

The remaining sections outline specific policies and programs that the President wanted to enact. Some, like the economic stimulus plan, were defeated, while others were passed. Still other aspects, like the plan to make government work better—described in Part 7—are still in progress.

The Federal Budget

The Federal Budget is the document that defines spending by the government. If you want to take a look at a copy of the proposed 1996 Federal Budget, you can find it at this address:

> Gopher address: `gopher://sunny.stat-usa.gov`

Once you're connected, navigate through the following directories:

> **Budget of the United States Government**
> **Fiscal Year 1996**

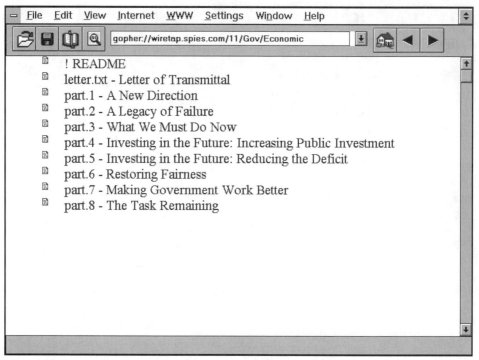

Figure 9.5 `gopher://wiretap.spies.com/11/Gov/Economic`
President Clinton's First Economic Plan is comprised of nine files.

 The Department of the Treasury

`http://www.ustreas.gov/`
`Welcome.html`

The Department of Treasury's most well-known purpose is to manufacture the money used in the economy. But that's just one of its multi-faceted missions. Other responsibilities include collecting taxes, recommending tax and economic policies, and protecting the President. The Department of the Treasury Web site provides information on these and other areas of the Department's mission (see fig. 9.6).

The Treasury Department's World Wide Web site has links to information on the 12 bureaus within the Department, the services provided by the Department, and the Department's Reinventing Government efforts. In addition, you will find biographies of Department officials and a collection of links to other government information servers.

> **NOTE**
>
> At the time of this writing, the Treasury Department's Web site was still under construction. You may find some differences in the particular resources available.

One bureau of the Treasury Department is the Internal Revenue Service (IRS). The mission of the IRS is to "collect the proper amount of revenue at the least cost to the public…." The purpose of the IRS presence on the Net is to provide online access to tax information and services. The page has links to four resources, including downloadable copies of tax forms, a Frequently Asked Questions (FAQ) file, tips on where to file your tax return, and sources of tax help.

Another bureau is the U.S. Mint. For over 200 years, the Mint has manufactured the coins used in America.

Besides conventional coins, the Mint produces and sells various special coins and medals. The Mint also runs Fort Knox, the repository for the gold reserves of the United States.

Economic Concerns

The performance of the economy impacts the life of every American. When economic growth slows, standards of living grow more slowly, or even decline. A combination of factors has slowed economic growth in recent years.

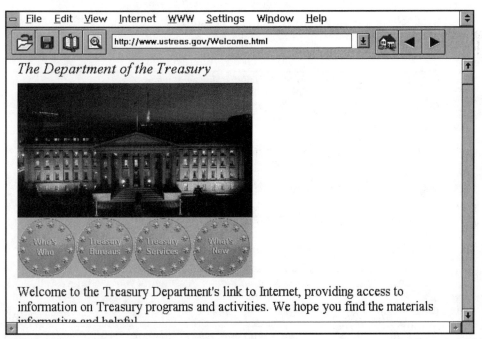

Figure 9.6 http://www.ustreas.gov/Welcome.html
The Treasury Department's World Wide Web site provides all kinds of information.

Retrieving White House Documents

`http://www1.ai.mit.edu/`
`retrieve-documents.html`

Reading press releases and other documents is a good way to see what the government thinks about the economy. This Web page, part of the Intelligent Information Infrastructure Project at the Massachusetts Institute of Technology, lets users search over 4000 White House publications (see fig. 9.7). Searches are conducted by date of publication and category.

There are 10 categories under which documents fall. The content of a document can include one or more of seven categories, including the Economy.

The types include Executive Acts, Presentations by Staff, and Presentations by Principals—principals being the President, Vice-President, or First Lady.

You use the search tool by selecting categories to include or exclude from the search, and specifying a date. To search for economic documents from March of 1995, for example, you would set an earliest publication date of 03/01/95 and a most recent publication date of 03/31/95. The Economy category would be set to Include, and the other categories included, excluded, or ignored as suits your purpose.

You can also search the documents manually by selecting the Taxonomy of Categories link. It breaks the 10 categories on the home page into 174

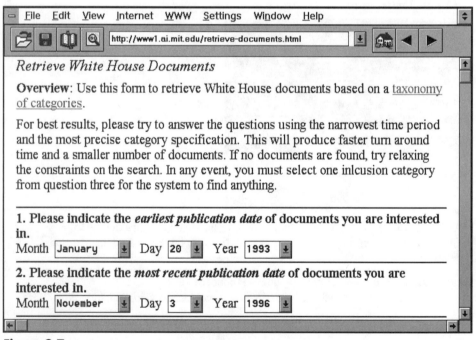

Figure 9.7 `http://www1.ai.mit.edu/retrieve-documents.html`
Retrieving White House Documents allows access to the government's latest press releases and more.

subcategories like Proclamations, Agriculture, or publications dealing with Idaho. Selecting one of these subcategories gives you links to the documents of that subcategory that are available.

 ### The UAW New Directions Movement

`gopher://gopher.igc.apc.org`

Select the following directories:

```
LaborNet-Labor
Unions & Organizations
United Auto workers New
    Directions
```

American performance in international markets has been improving for the last several years. In 1994, the United States was recognized by several different organizations as the world's most competitive economy. But this competitiveness has come at a price.

Organized labor has taken its share of the pain, with unions forced to compromise on traditional principles like work rules and seniority. While these adjustments may lead to improved productivity and economic growth for the companies, many union members aren't happy about them. Some members of the United Auto Workers (UAW) want to do something about it.

The UAW New Directions Gopher directory contains the text of the movement's pamphlet on restructuring union-management relations (see fig. 9.8). The files describe the current situation, outline its problems, and

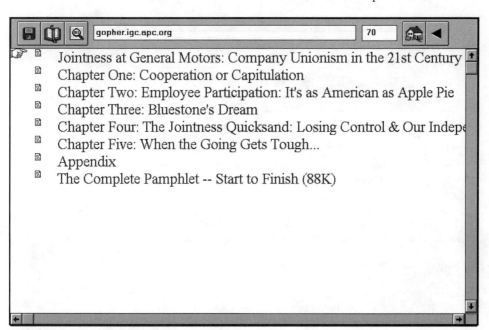

Figure 9.8 `gopher://gopher.igc.apc.org`
This site features the United Auto Workers New Directions plan.

Patrick Buchanan

One candidate who generates a lot of controversy is Patrick Buchanan. He is a pro-life conservative whose views are influenced by the Bible. Buchanan pursued the Republican Presidential nomination in 1992—and gave George Bush a scare in New Hampshire, winning 37 percent of the vote.

Besides his pro-life views, Buchanan opposes affirmative action and wants new limits on immigration. On economic issues, he is a protectionist, arguing for policies that would shield American workers from the effects of foreign competition. Such views have earned him much criticism from sources like Mother Jones magazine (see the article at

WWW address: `http://www.mojones.com/JF94/klein.html`, or Time-Warner's profile of him, accessible through the Republican Primary page at WWW address: `http://www.umr.edu/~sears/primary/main.html`).

Buchanan's views do resonate with some portion of the electorate. A poll conducted for TIME/CNN between February 23 and March 1, 1995 (available through the Republican Primary page) shows Buchanan running a distant third behind Bob Dole and Phil Gramm for the Republican nomination. And the Right Side of the Web includes Buchanan on its list of candidates whom they would like to see on the Republican Presidential ticket in 1996 (see fig. 9.9).

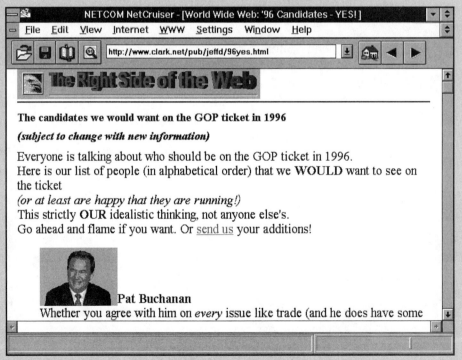

Figure 9.9 `http://www.clark.net/pub/jeffd/96yes.html`
An endorsement of Pat Buchanan for President.

propose a solution. That solution calls for a return to more adversarial relations with management. They also call for changes to labor laws that would make unionizing easier, and suggest that workers support left-leaning third parties like the New Party. They hope these changes will lead to shorter work hours and better pay.

Trade

Trade is a vital component of the American economy. It's also controversial right now. The United States has traditionally maintained fewer tariffs and trade barriers than its trading partners. With public concern about the economy, those policies are under attack. Populists like Patrick Buchanan are proposing protectionist policies to shield workers against foreign competition or tariffs on countries that won't allow American imports. See the profile on Buchanan for more on his policies.

One alternative to protectionism is increasing exports. The U.S. government has programs to help businesses by providing trade-related information.

> **NOTE**
>
> The two big treaties covering international trade are the General Agreement on Tariffs and Trade (GATT) and the North American Free Trade Agreement (NAFTA). You can find out more about them in Chapter 10.

The United States has traditionally maintained fewer tariffs and trade barriers than its trading partners.

 The International Trade Administration

`http://www.doc.gov/resources/ITA_info.html`

The International Trade Administration (ITA) is the branch of the U.S. government responsible for promoting non-agricultural exports. The ITA maintains a Web site as a source of information on its organization and activities (see fig. 9.10).

The ITA page has links to a range of information and resources. One of these links takes you to its Frequently Asked Trade Questions file. The file answers export questions such as "Where are the best countries to export my product?" and "Is there a tariff or quota that applies to my product in country X?"

Some of the other links here take you to trade-related speeches and press releases, the international trade advocacy center, and the National Trade Data Bank.

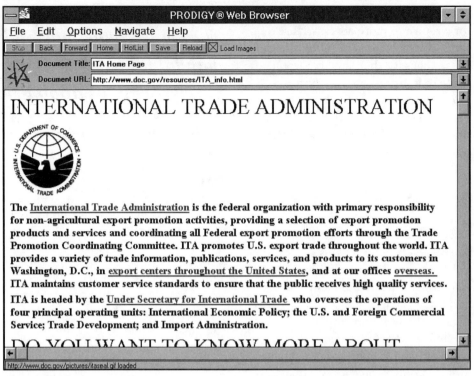

Figure 9.10 `http://www.doc.gov/resources/ITA_info.html`
The International Trade Administration site is a source of information on its organization and activities.

 ## The National Trade Data Bank Gopher

`gopher://sunny.stat-usa.gov`

Select the following directories:

```
STAT-USA: A Source...
National Trade Data Bank
    (NTDB)
```

The National Trade Data Bank (NTDB) is the U.S. Government's most complete collection of world trade data. Covering topics like export opportunities, how to market overseas, and socio-economic conditions in other countries, the NTDB is a compre-

hensive resource for any exporter. The NTDB has been available by subscription on CD-ROM, and is now found on the Net. The NTDB is available on the Web, where a fee is charged for its use. It's also available for free by anonymous FTP, or at the STAT-USA Gopher site covered here (see fig. 9.11).

The NTDB Gopher directory structure is enormous. In all, there are over 160,000 documents and over one gigabyte of data. This mass of material is distributed across 134 subdirectories. Two subdirectories are particularly helpful if you have a question about U.S. economic policy.

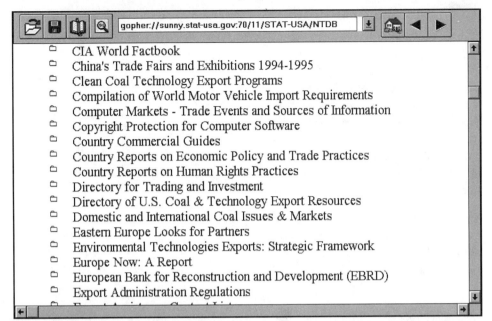

Figure 9.11 `gopher://sunny.stat-usa.gov`
The National Trade Data Bank Gopher has over 160,000 documents and over one gigabyte of data.

The State Department generates yearly reports on the economic policies and trade practices of over 100 nations. The Country Reports on Economic Policy and Trade Practices subdirectory contains copies of these reports. There are nine sections in each report, detailing topics like Significant Barriers to U.S. Exports and Investment, and Workers Rights. The data is gathered by U.S. Embassies, and represents the best information available to the U.S. Government.

The International Labor Statistics subdirectory contains reports from the Bureau of Labor Statistics that analyze labor conditions and developments in the U.S. and other countries. The statistical information used to generate the reports is provided by international agencies to the country in the report.

There are five sets of reports here: Unemployment and related measures, productivity and related measures, consumer price indexes, work stoppage statistics, and capital investment ratios.

The Economy and Trade on the Online Services

Each online service covers topics that are addressed in this chapter. AOL and CompuServe have extensive coverage of taxes. CompuServe also has an International Prodigy's Careers Bulletin Board which deals with jobs and includes a section dedicated to union issues (Trade Forum). All three services talk about general economic issues in various sections.

America Online's Tax Forum

Keyword: **TAX FORUM**

The Tax Forum on America Online is the main tax resource on the service (see fig. 9.12). It includes information and services from government and private sources, and gives AOL members a single place to go for all their tax needs.

One major component of the forum is its Tax Software Libraries. The libraries contain IRS tax forms and the instructions for them. Other libraries include software that may be useful in preparing your taxes—things like spreadsheets and accounting packages.

Other features here include timely tax news, and services from several groups. The NAEA Tax Channel is a source for tax advice from the National Association of Enrolled Agents. Publisher John Wiley & Sons makes available a copy of the best-selling Ernst & Young tax guide, with graphics and an online search tool. Finally, Intuit and Kiplinger Tax Software provide support for their popular tax programs, TurboTax and Kiplinger TaxCut.

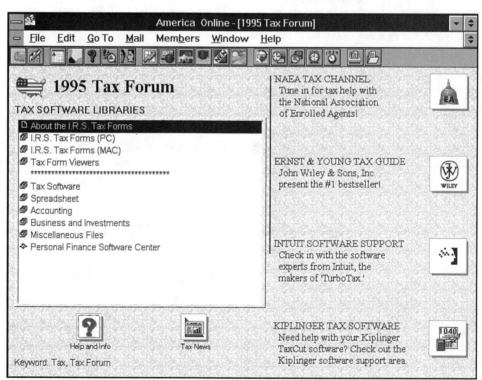

Figure 9.12 Keyword: TAX FORUM
AOL's primary tax resource is this Tax Forum.

CompuServe's International Trade Forum

Go: `CIS:TRADE`

CompuServe's International Trade forum is a place to share information, find leads, and get help on international trade (see fig. 9.13).

NOTE

The forum administrator reminds visitors to verify the information you find here; the forum accepts no responsibility for the content.

Like other CompuServe forums, this one is divided into three areas: message sections, libraries, and conferences. The message areas deal with topics such as Services, Business Travel, and general discussions of trade with different regions of the world. The discussions here are virtually free of the flaming you find in some other forums; this is a place for serious business.

The libraries contain documents that address similar subjects to the message areas. The conferences are divided into the Informal Discussion room, which is available at any time, and the Formal Conferences room, which is reserved for use with guest speakers.

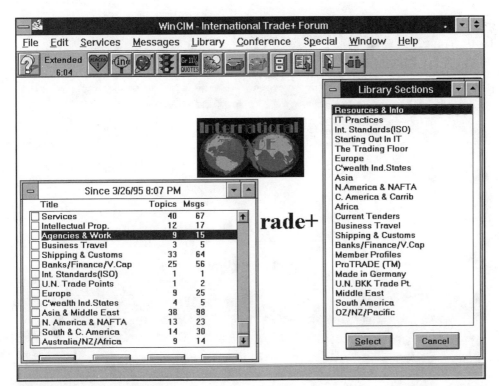

Figure 9.13   Go: `CIS:TRADE`
CompuServe's International Trade Forum.

Prodigy's Careers BB

Jump: **CAREERS BB**

Prodigy's Careers Bulletin Board is a place to discuss many different careers (see fig. 9.14). One of the topics on this bulletin board is called Union Trades. It's a place where union members get to sound off about issues that concern them.

All sorts of issues are discussed in this topic, everything from replacement scabs to strike tactics to politics. The threads that I read were all civil and supportive of union causes. There weren't many non-union or anti-union messages.

Recommended Sites to See

The remainder of this chapter is a list of the addresses for Net resources dealing with the economy and trade. The addresses are divided into sections that correspond to the major sections of this chapter.

Newsgroups and Mailing Lists

Politics and economics discussions.

UseNet address:
`alt.politics.economics`

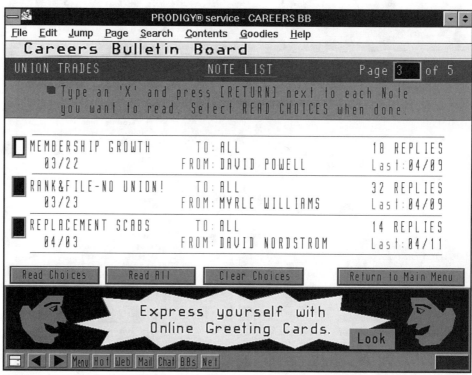

Figure 9.14 Jump: CAREERS BB
Prodigy's Careers Bulletin Board.

News stories dealing with U.S. government finances.

> UseNet address:
> `clari.news.usa.gov.financial`

Issues of importance to labor unions.

> UseNet address:
> `alt.society.labor-unions`

Discussions of tax laws and tax advice.

> UseNet address: `misc.taxes`

`FedTax-L`, the mailing list mirror of `misc.taxes`.

> LISTSERV address:
> `LISTSERV@SHSU.BITNET` or

> LISTSERV address:
> `LISTSERV@SHSU.EDU`

News stories about strikes.

> UseNet address:
> `clari.news.labor.strike`

News stories about layoffs.

> UseNet address:
> `clari.news.labor.layoff`

General Information about the U.S. Economy

The United States in the CIA World Factbook.

> WWW address: `http://www.ic.gov/94fact/country/249.html`

A search tool for White House publications.

> WWW address: `http://www1.ai.mit.edu/retrieve-documents.html`

The Census Bureau's Economic Programs page.

> WWW address: `http://www.census.gov/org/econ/economic.html`

The National Bureau of Economic Research Gopher site.

> Gopher address: `gopher://nber.harvard.edu/`

Taxing and Spending

The 1995 Federal Budget.

> Gopher address: `gopher://cyfer.esusda.gov`

>> Select the following directories:

>> `Americans Communicating Electronically`
>> `Shortcuts to Hot Topics on Agendas`
>> `Proposed 1995 U.S. Budget`

President Clinton's 1993 Economic Plan.

> Gopher address: `gopher://wiretap.spies.com`

>> Select the following directories:

>> `Government Docs (US & World)`
>> `Clinton's Economic Plan`

The Department of the Treasury's home page.

WWW address: `http://www.ustreas.gov/Welcome.html`

Information relating to the U.S. Federal Budget.

FTP address: `ftp://sun1.hep.anl.gov/pub/federal-government/federal.html`

Economic Concerns

The Bureau of Labor Statistics home page.

WWW address: `http://stats.bls.gov/`

The UAW's New Directions Gopher directory.

Gopher address: `gopher://sunsite.unc.edu`

Select the following directories:
`LaborNet-Labor Unions & Organizations United Auto workers New Directions`

National Consumers Week Web site.

WWW address: `http://idi.net/release.html`

Trade

The International Trade Administration (ITA).

WWW address: `http://www.doc.gov/resources/ITA_info.html`

The National Trade Data Bank (NTDB).

Gopher address: `gopher://sunny.stat-usa.gov`

Select the following directories:
`STAT-USA: A Source... National Trade Data Bank (NTDB)`

The United Nation's Global Trade Point Network.

WWW address: `http://www.unicc.org/untpdc/gtpnet/gtpnet.html`

Consumers for World Trade on protectionism.

FTP address: `ftp://ftp.digex.net/pub/access/web/cwt01.html`

An International Trade page.

WWW address: `http://www.helsinki.fi/~lsaarine/internat.html`

Mother Jones on Pat Buchanan.

WWW address: `http://www.mojones.com/JF94/klein.html`

Chapter 10

Foreign Affairs

The Net is a rich source of information on how the United States interacts with the rest of the world. This chapter shows some of the best sites.

In this chapter

- *Foreign affairs newsgroups and mailing lists*
- *The U.S. Department of State*
- *The United Nations and some of its agencies*
- *Intelligence agencies and resources*
- *Major International Treaties*
- *Propaganda in Foreign Affairs*
- *Space Exploration as the Ultimate in Foreign Affairs*

Other chapters have material related to foreign affairs. The following list points to some locations you might find useful.

In other chapters

← *Ross Perot and United We Stand America, opponents of NAFTA, are discussed in Chapter 5.*

← *Socialist parties that have connections to parties in other countries are discussed in Chapter 5.*

← *Immigration is covered in Chapter 8.*

→ *Some places where documents, including treaties, are stored online are examined in Chapter 13.*

→ *International hot spots are covered in Chapter 14.*

→ *Other interesting international Net sites are examined in Chapter 15.*

This chapter is a whirlwind tour of an incredibly complex, information-rich topic: foreign affairs. There is no way to give in-depth coverage of foreign affairs on the Net in a single chapter; there is so much foreign affairs information on the Internet that it could occupy an entire book.

Newsgroups and Mailing Lists

Newsgroups and mailing lists are useful ways to keep up with foreign affairs. Some of the organizations covered in this chapter have their own newsgroup or mailing list to keep readers up to date on activities by posting announcements and answering questions.

The Foreign Policy News Story Newsgroup

clari.news.usa.gov.foreign_policy

This newsgroup is the best single source for foreign policy news—if your Internet provider subscribes to the ClariNet **e.News** service. This newsgroup is nothing but news stories on foreign policy. Figure 10.1 shows the names of some typical articles, and the beginning of one.

Any newsworthy event regarding U.S. foreign policy is likely to appear in this newsgroup. For more information on ClariNet's **e.News** service, turn to the "What is ClariNet?" section in Chapter 12, "State and Local Politics."

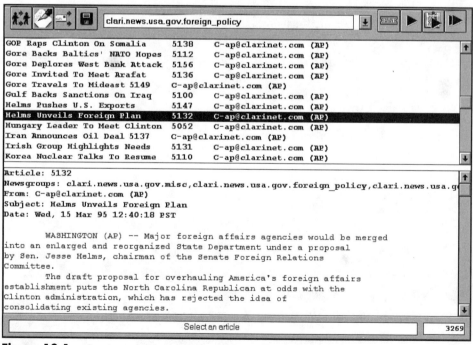

Figure 10.1 clari.news.usa.gov.foreign_policy
U.S. government foreign affairs news stories can be found in this newsgroup.

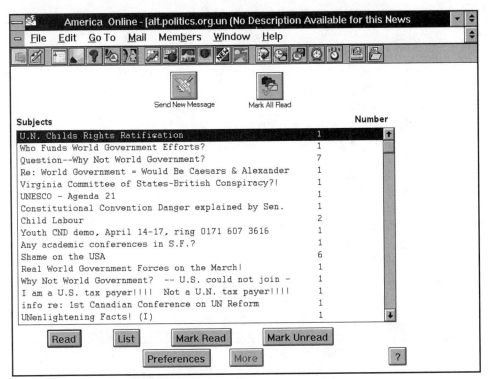

Figure 10.2 `alt.politics.org.un`
Some typical message threads in the UN politics newsgroup.

The Politics and the United Nations Newsgroup

`alt.politics.org.un`

This newsgroup covers the United Nations (see fig. 10.2). The topics cover a wide range of subjects. Some threads deal with the function and activities of the UN or its constituent parts; some are more philosophical, discussing the UN's proper place in world society. These threads are usually pretty civilized, with coherent positions and discussions.

Unfortunately, a large number of the threads in this newsgroup are not constructive. Some messages say little more than "the UN stinks" or "it should be disbanded." A larger group of threads could best be described as conspiracy theory. They accuse the UN of secretly setting up some sort of world government. These theories, and the arguments about them, comprise a significant percentage of the messages in this newsgroup.

The Politics and the CIA Newsgroup

`alt.politics.org.cia`

This newsgroup covers anything related to the CIA. Some threads discuss CIA activities or public information it

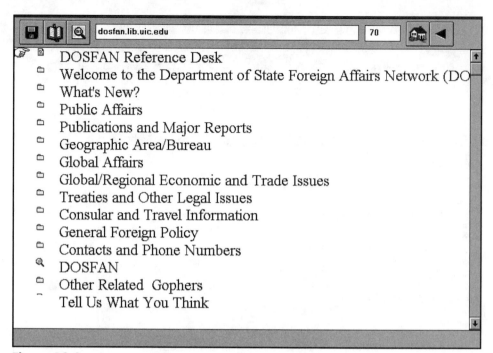

Figure 10.3 `gopher://dosfan.lib.uic.edu`
The Department of State Foreign Affairs Network Gopher site.

provides. Others consist of speculations about secret projects or jobs with the CIA.

Some threads are downright hostile to the Agency (CIA). One person posts excerpts from the magazine *Covert Action Quarterly*, an anti-CIA magazine that accuses the Agency of all sorts of nasty things. Another post asks if alleged CIA cocaine imports are included in the U.S. Balance of Trade figures.

The U.S. Department of State Foreign Affairs Network (DOSFAN)

`gopher://dosfan.lib.uic.edu`

The U.S. Department of State (commonly known as the State Department), handles foreign affairs for the country. It provides much of the information used by other parts of the government, and is responsible for implementing U.S. foreign policy. The State Department runs over 250 embassies, consulates and missions, in over 170 countries. The State Department was created by Congress in 1789.

State Department information is available on the Net through the Department of State Foreign Affairs Network (DOSFAN) Gopher. DOSFAN is a joint creation of the State Department and the University of Illinois at Chicago. Figure 10.3 shows the top level of the Gopher menu. There's a lot of material here, but there's also a search program, represented by the

DOSFAN menu option, that makes it easier to find what you need. Each of the directories in this menu contains one or more subdirectories, and most have their own search programs. DOSFAN has information on most of the groups discussed in this chapter, often as part of a daily State Department briefing.

> **NOTE**
>
> There is a Web page for DOSFAN, but all it contains is a visual tour of the State Department and a link to the DOSFAN Gopher. All the good stuff is at the Gopher site.

 Overseas Travel Advisories

`gopher://dosfan.lib.uic.edu`

Once connected, select the directory:
    Consular and Travel Information.

A well-known service of the State Department is its overseas travel advisories. These reports warn travelers about dangerous situations in various countries, and are produced by the State Department's Bureaus of Consular Affairs. Other reports from these bureaus cover things like travel tips, visa requirements, and international child abductions. You can get the current travel advisories and other reports at the address shown at the start of this section.

The United Nations (UN)

The United Nations (UN) was formed in 1945 to maintain peace and security after World War II. It was designed as a place where the nations of the world could come to discuss grievances and work together on social, economic, and other problems. Most of the nations in the world are now members.

International Service Agencies

International Service Agencies (ISA) is a federation of 55 groups that helps disaster victims and the poor throughout the world. The ISA raises funds through workplace giving campaigns. The money is divided between member agencies, or delivered directly to a designated agency.

The Agencies under the ISA umbrella can be divided into six categories. They are Children, Medical Care, Education, Refugees/Disaster Relief, Hunger Relief, and Job Creation/Economic Support. Some of the better-known members of ISA include: CARE, Doctors without Borders, the Boy and Girl Scouts, and Save the Children. You can find out more about the International Service Agencies by browsing their Web page at:

    WWW Address: `http://www.charity.org/`

IN RECESS

The UN presence on the Net is as sprawling and confusing as the organization.

The UN is composed of six major organs that includes the General Assembly, the Security Council, and the Secretariat, which is headed by the Secretary General. Beyond that, there are a myriad of agencies with familiar names, such as the International Monetary Fund (IMF); the World Health Organization (WHO); and less familiar ones, like United Nations Relief, and Works Agency for Palestinian Refugees (UNRWA).

 The United Nations Home Page

`http://www.unicc.org/`

The UN presence on the Net is as sprawling and confusing as the

The World Citizen Web

IN RECESS

As you saw in the `alt.politics.org.un` newsgroup, some people feel that the UN is trying to impose a world government. Whether that is true or not, there's one organization on the Net that *is* in favor of a world government. In fact, you can send them money to become a World Citizen. The organization is the World Service Authority, and its home on the Net is the World Citizen Web.

I had never heard of it before stumbling across this site, and I don't follow all of its reasoning. Even so, it's an interesting site. Check it out for yourself at:

WWW Address: `http://www.together.org/orgs/wcw/`

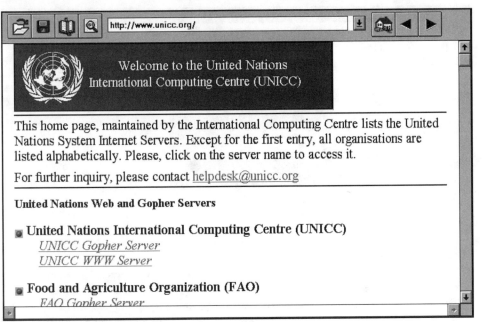

Figure 10.4 http://www.unicc.org/
The UN home page on the Web.

organization. The UN home page is maintained by the UN's International Computing Centre (see fig. 10.4). It consists of links to the UN's other Gopher and Web servers. There are 28 UN organizations included in the list, most of which have more than one server. Some of the UN organizations with their own servers are:

- The International Monetary Fund
- The UN Conference on Trade and Development
- The United Nations Environment Programme (UNEP)
- The World Health Organization (WHO)
- The World Trade Organization (WTO)

The UN home page also includes a search program that lets users find out which servers contain information on which topics.

 The World Health Organization (WHO)

http://www.who.ch/

The World Health Organization (WHO) is the United Nations organization charged with ensuring the highest possible level of health for all the people of the world. The WHO Web page is one method of making WHO information and resources available to the world (see fig. 10.5).

The search program lets users find out which servers contain information on which topics.

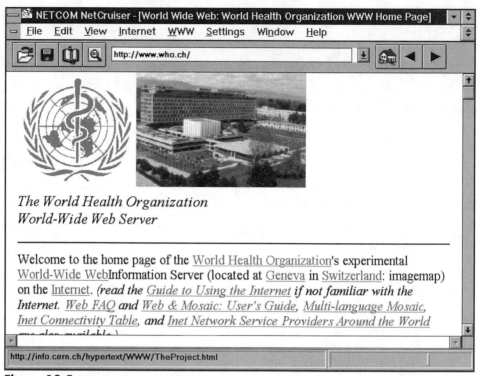

The World Health Organization
World-Wide Web Server

Welcome to the home page of the World Health Organization's experimental World-Wide WebInformation Server (located at Geneva in Switzerland: imagemap) on the Internet. *(read the Guide to Using the Internet if not familiar with the Internet. Web FAQ and Web & Mosaic: User's Guide, Multi-language Mosaic, Inet Connectivity Table, and Inet Network Service Providers Around the World*

http://info.cern.ch/hypertext/WWW/TheProject.html

Figure 10.5 `http://www.who.ch/`
The World Health Organization's home page provides health information to the world.

More than 30 links take you from the WHO home page to specific health resources. Some of those links include:

- Ebola Virus Outbreak
- International Travel and Health—Vaccination Requirements and Advice
- WHO Publications
- Other Health-related Web Servers

A large part of dealing with other countries is intelligence gathering.

The Ebola Virus Outbreak provides information on the latest international health crisis, the Ebola virus outbreak in Zaire. The page contains WHO's latest press releases on the subject. There is also travelers advice, an information sheet, and links to other Ebola resources on the Net.

Intelligence Gathering

A large part of dealing with other countries is intelligence gathering. The country that knows the most about the other's plans and capabilities has a distinct advantage in negotiations or other foreign relations. The United States has many intelligence gathering organizations, some of which make information available on the Net.

 ### The Central Intelligence Agency (CIA)

`http://www.ic.gov/index.html`

The CIA. This three-letter acronym for America's foreign intelligence agency is known throughout the world. With its reputation for secrecy, you would expect an organization like the CIA to have little or no information on the Net—surprisingly, it does.

The CIA has a large Web site of its own. The home page lists the Agency's mission, and links visitors to two impressive resources: the World Factbook 1994,

and the Factbook on Intelligence (see fig. 10.6).

 ### CIA World Factbook

`http://www.ic.gov/94fact/`
`fb94toc/fb94toc.html`

The World Factbook 1994 is a comprehensive reference to the entire world, covering nations, oceans, and other locations (see fig. 10.7). The material is drawn from the CIA, Census Bureau, DIA, and many other sources. Each entry contains a variety of detailed information; for example, geography, government, and communications. Some entries include maps.

Figure 10.6 `http://www.ic.gov/index.html`
The Central Intelligence Agency's home page on the WWW is full of useful information.

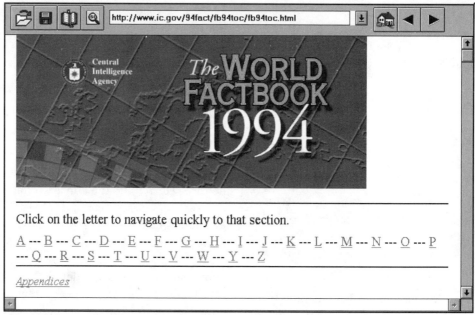

Figure 10.7 `http://www.ic.gov/94fact/fb94toc/fb94toc.html`
The 1994 World Factbook has information on every country.

The supplemental information in the 1994 World Factbook is also impressive. A collection of reference maps covers geographical and political regions in much greater detail than the maps included with individual entries. The Appendixes contain lists of International Organizations, standard Weights and Measures, and so on. A Notes, Definitions, and Abbreviations page completes the Factbook.

CIA Factbook on Intelligence

`http://www.ic.gov/facttell/`
`toc.html`

The Factbook on Intelligence tells you anything you might want to know about the CIA—except its current or past operations. It contains the history

of the CIA, information about the people who are part of it, and general information about the Agency. Descriptions of the intelligence community and intelligence gathering help you understand how the CIA operates, while information on executive and legislative oversight explains how the organization is controlled.

Real Time Support for the Warrior

`http://www.ait.nrl.navy.mil/`
`rts/warrior.html`

The Naval Research Laboratory (NRL) created this Web page as a clearing-house for the kind of information needed to fight a war (see fig. 10.8) It is full of relevant information on subjects like:

- Climate and Weather
- Disasters
- Information and Intelligence
- Maps and Imagery
- News
- Social and Political documents
- Weapon Systems

For each subject there are several links to specific resources located around the Net.

Information and Intelligence

The links in this section of Real Time Support for the Warrior connect to a half-dozen resources. Each comes from a different place on the Net, so they vary in depth of coverage and style. They are:

- The Central Intelligence Agency (covered in detail in the previous section)
- The Journal of Electronic Defense
- The Terrorist Profile Weekly
- The Nuclear Information WWW Server
- Events in Afghanistan and the Asian Sub Continent
- Brittanica Online

Aside from the CIA's pages, the most interesting link in this section takes you to The Terrorist Profile Weekly. It is an electronic newsletter dedicated to spreading information about terrorism. It contains profiles of 16 terrorist groups, from the 15 May Organization to Hizbalah. The profile for each group contains a description of the group, its ideals, where it gets its

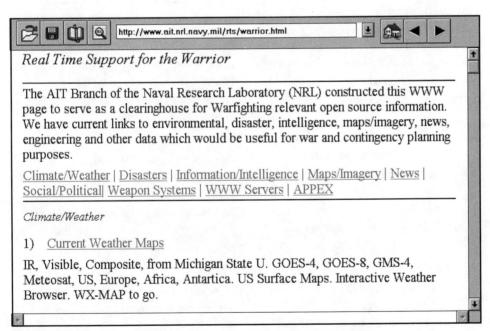

Figure 10.8 http://www.ait.nrl.navy.mil/rts/warrior.html
Real Time Support for the Warrior is full of war-fighting information and intelligence.

funding, where it operates, and more. The information in these profiles comes from *The Profiles of Global Terrorism,* a State Department publication.

Treaties

Nations that don't fight often negotiate treaties instead. Treaties can be bilateral, agreements between two parties (or multilateral agreements between three or more parties). The General Agreement on Tariffs and Trade (GATT) and the North American Free Trade Agreement (NAFTA) are two multilateral treaties that have received a lot of press recently. Both of these treaties will affect the lives of Americans in the near future; fortunately, the Internet provides information and discussion on these agreements.

The North Atlantic Treaty Organization (NATO) has been in operation since the end of World War II. With the collapse of the Soviet threat, NATO is being reevaluated by each of its member countries.

 ### The North American Free Trade Agreement (NAFTA)

`gopher://cyfer.esusda.gov`

Once connected, navigate through the following directories:

```
Americans Communicating
   Electronically
National Policy Issues...
North American Free Trade
   Agreement (NAFTA)
```

NAFTA, the North American Free Trade Agreement, was one of the hottest issues of the early 1990s. The debate over signing the treaty was long and loud, and created some unusual alliances. Ross Perot and most unions opposed the treaty; Bill Clinton and most Republicans supported it. You can use the Net to see what people were fighting about.

> **NOTE**
>
> The Gopher site at `cyfer.esusda.gov` is maintained by the United States Department of Agriculture and the National Agricultural Library. Given the importance of food exports to American agriculture, it makes sense that this is the place to find the most detailed information on trade issues.

The NAFTA Gopher site is the source that many other sites on the Net point to. The site includes the 1992 and 1993 NAFTA documents, as well as press releases and daily updates from the White House (see fig. 10.9).

The 1992 and 1993 NAFTA Documents directories contain the entire text of the treaty, with each section as its own file. The White House press releases and daily updates show you how much effort the Administration put into winning approval of the treaty.

Another item on NAFTA's main Gopher menu is the Executive Summary for the General Agreement on Tariffs and Trade.

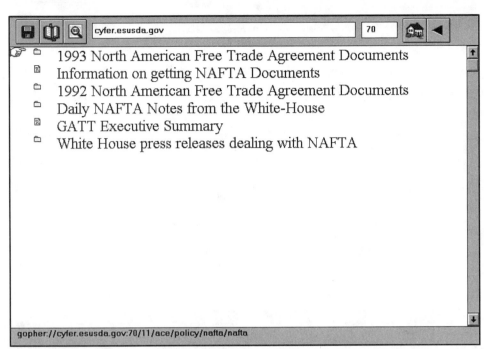

Figure 10.9 `gopher://cyfer.esusda.gov`
The NAFTA Gopher contains the text of the North American Free Trade Agreement.

 The General Agreement on Tariffs and Trade (GATT)

gopher://cyfer.esusda.gov

Once connected, navigate through the following directories:

```
Americans Communicating
    Electronically
National Policy Issues...
General Agreement on
    Tariffs and Trade (GATT)
```

The General Agreement on Tariffs and Trade (GATT) is the latest in a series of international trade agreements. It defines the rules for the international trade of most products and services. Specifically, it defines the subsidies, tariffs, and trade barriers that can be used by nations to protect their industries and aid their exports. Figure 10.10 shows the main menu for the GATT Gopher site.

> **NOTE**
>
> The acronym GATT is used to refer to two different things. It is used for the treaty governing tariffs and trade, but it also refers to a Special Agency of the United Nations with the confusing name of General Agreement on Tariffs and Trade (the same as the treaty).

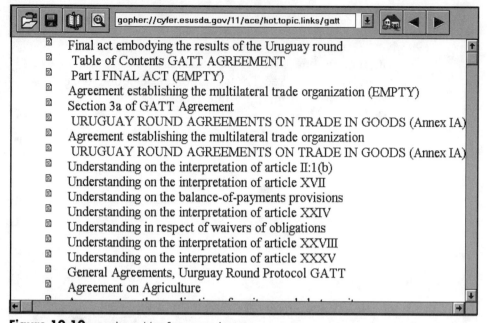

Figure 10.10 `gopher://cyfer.esusda.gov`
The GATT Gopher site contains the text of the General Agreement on Tariffs and Trade.

One decision that came out of the 1994 round of GATT—often referred to as the Uruguay Round because of the location of the negotiations—is a new international body, the World Trade Organization (WTO). The WTO is now the primary organization governing world trade, and it is a Specialized Agency of the United Nations.

> **NOTE**
>
> You can find the agreement establishing the World Trade Organization at:
>
> `http://heiwww.unige.ch/gatt/`
> `final_act/04-wto.html.`

The North Atlantic Treaty Organization (NATO)

`www.saclant.nato.int/nato.html`

In 1949, 14 European nations, along with the United States and Canada, signed the North Atlantic Treaty, a collective defense agreement. The North Atlantic Treaty Organization (NATO) is the organization that implements the agreement.

Historically, NATO served to deter the Soviet Union from attacks on Europe. Since the collapse of the Soviet Union, NATO has been trying to find a new focus. The NATO Web site is a starting point for finding out what's going on in NATO (see fig. 10.11).

NATO's page serves two purposes. First, it provides an overview of NATO, touching on the organization's history and purpose. Second, it is the index to NATO and NATO-related resources on the Net.

The most important link takes you to the NATO Gopher site. It seems that anything about NATO that isn't classified is available here—for example, basic information and biographies, fact sheets and fellowships, press releases and partnerships, and even the text of *NATO Review* magazine.

Other links from the NATO home page are also useful. One link goes to the NATO Handbook, which is a complete guide to the structure and workings of the organization. Another group of links takes you to information on each member country. The rest of the links take you to military and defense research Net sites.

Propaganda

Propaganda can take many forms—in recent years radio has been a very popular medium for it. The Voice of America is one organization that reports for the United States Government. Another is the United States Agency for International Development.

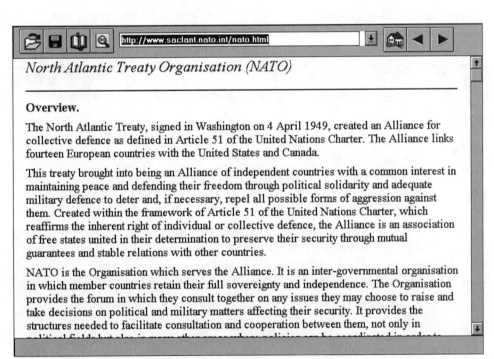

North Atlantic Treaty Organisation (NATO)

Overview.

The North Atlantic Treaty, signed in Washington on 4 April 1949, created an Alliance for collective defence as defined in Article 51 of the United Nations Charter. The Alliance links fourteen European countries with the United States and Canada.

This treaty brought into being an Alliance of independent countries with a common interest in maintaining peace and defending their freedom through political solidarity and adequate military defence to deter and, if necessary, repel all possible forms of aggression against them. Created within the framework of Article 51 of the United Nations Charter, which reaffirms the inherent right of individual or collective defence, the Alliance is an association of free states united in their determination to preserve their security through mutual guarantees and stable relations with other countries.

NATO is the Organisation which serves the Alliance. It is an inter-governmental organisation in which member countries retain their full sovereignty and independence. The Organisation provides the forum in which they consult together on any issues they may choose to raise and take decisions on political and military matters affecting their security. It provides the structures needed to facilitate consultation and cooperation between them, not only in

Figure 10.11 `http://www.saclant.nato.int/nato.html`
The NATO Web page provides all kinds of information on NATO.

The VOA is on the air 24 hours a day, 365 days a year, and reaches an estimated 92 million people, in 47 languages.

 The Voice of America

`gopher://gopher.voa.gov`

The Voice of America (VOA) was founded in 1942, less than three months after the United states entered World War II. Its mission is to provide timely, balanced, and accurate news and features to audiences around the world. The VOA is on the air 24 hours a day, 365 days a year, and reaches an estimated 92 million people, in 47 languages.

The VOA makes much of its material available on the Net. Figure 10.12 shows its Gopher site. Some of the material lists non-Internet activities. For example, programming and

NOTE

Propaganda doesn't have to be lies. Propaganda is also the systematic propagation of information reflecting the views and interests of people advocating a doctrine. Organizations like the Voice of America serve this purpose for the United States.

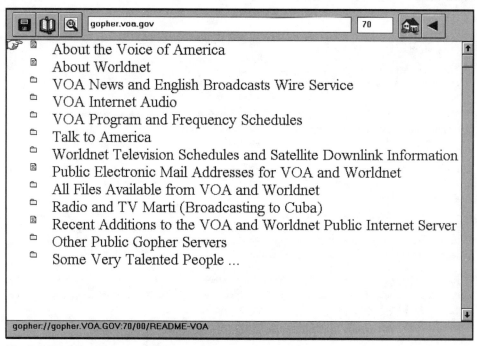

Figure 10.12 `gopher://gopher.voa.gov`
The Voice of America Gopher includes the innovative VOA Internet Audio.

frequency schedules for the VOA and Talk to America radio shows, and WorldNet TV broadcasts help visitors tune in to these primary VOA activities.

Other material at this site is designed specifically for the Net audience. File and e-mail addresses are listed, but the most innovative thing about this site is the VOA Internet Audio directory. This directory contains digitized audio from VOA broadcasts and program segments. Stored in four formats, these huge files—often several megabytes in size—are updated several times every day.

NOTE

The file formats used to store the VOA Internet Audio files are: AU, and AU Compressed; and 8-bit and 16-bit WAVE, zipped. The AU files work on many Sun workstations, while the WAVE files will play under Microsoft Windows once they are unzipped.

The United States Agency for International Development

`http://www.info.usaid.gov/`

President John F. Kennedy established the United States Agency for International Development (USAID) in 1961 to provide humanitarian aid and

foreign assistance to promote American political and economic interests. USAID focuses on four areas:

- Improving health and population conditions
- Promoting economic growth
- Protecting the environment
- Supporting democracy

The USAID Web site addresses each of these four areas, as well as the Agency's disaster relief efforts (see fig. 10.13). For each area there is a document describing the problems, and USAID's efforts to combat the problems.

The International Development Page link takes you to an index of international development Web sites. Some of these deal with USAID activities, but most of them are links to related pages and groups. For visitors interested in USAID activities in specific regions, there is a link to the USAID Regional Bureaus.

President John F. Kennedy established the United States Agency for International Development (USAID) in 1961 to provide humanitarian aid and foreign assistance to promote American political and economic interests.

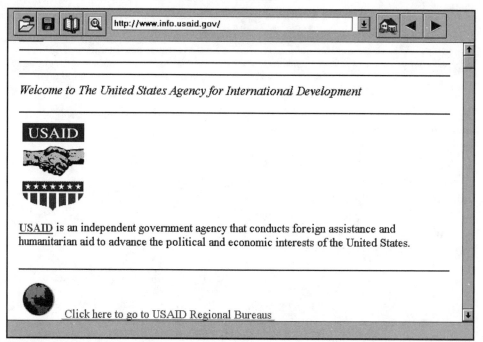

Figure 10.13 `http://www.info.usaid.gov/`
The USAID page addresses each of USAID's four main focuses and its disaster relief efforts.

Foreign Affairs in Space

"Space. The final frontier." To me, those are the most memorable words spoken on television. They are also very important. The future of developed nations leads to space, and it is where international cooperation is both necessary and vital. The benefits of space development ensure that nations will do it, either together in cooperation, or separately in competition. In either case, our foreign affairs will increasingly involve space.

The following sections look at international space resources on the Net: NASA, which has moved from competing with the rest of the world to cooperating with it; the other is the Space Activism home page, a link to the space programs of the world.

 The National Aeronautics and Space Administration (NASA)

`http://www.gsfc.nasa.gov/NASA_homepage.html`

NASA is the National Aeronautics and Space Administration, America's space agency. Once, NASA was one of the prime competitors in the Space Race, battling the Soviets for leadership. Those days are gone. The Soviet Union has disintegrated, and NASA finds itself in a new political environment. The NASA Strategic Plan states that, "In the post-Cold War era...the civil space program will focus on a spirit of expanded cooperation with our traditional international partners and the forging of new partnerships." By doing so, NASA is revitalizing itself and becoming a major participant in foreign affairs.

The NASA home page links users to the Strategic Plan and to many other NASA resources (see fig. 10.14). Visitors can look up technical information, check into specific NASA Centers, or see what's hot today. Throughout, you see signs of NASA's commitment to work with the international community.

The Public Affairs link is particularly valuable for the layperson. It takes you to a large collection of information that is organized for easy use. Major topics covered here include:

- *The Newsroom.* A source of press release, fact sheets, and similar documents.

- *Questions & Answers.* A collection of the answers to questions most commonly asked of NASA.

- *Welcome.* A collection of general information.

- *This is NASA.* Information about the space agency.

- *History.* The story of space exploration.

- *The Library.* A collection of documents and articles.

- *Events.* Describes upcoming events.

- *Education.* Other educational resources.

- A rotating display currently covering Apollo 11.

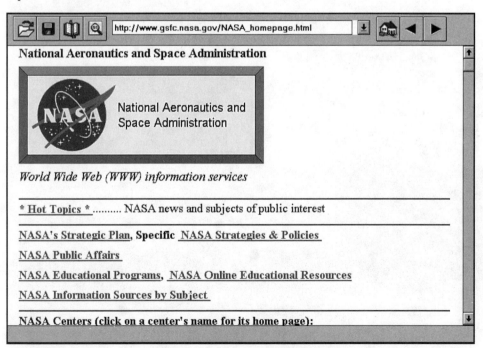

Figure 10.14 `http://www.gsfc.nasa.gov/NASA_homepage.html`
The NASA home page links users to NASA's Strategic Plan among other information.

There is a lot of material available at the NASA Web site, including photo archives, audio clips, and movies. Plan to visit for awhile if you decide to check out the site.

Foreign Affairs on the Online Services

All three services have some material related to foreign affairs, but the levels of coverage vary greatly.

America Online

America Online includes foreign policy and military directories in its White House forum (Keyword: **WHITE HOUSE**), national profiles in the Traveler's Corner (Keyword: **TRAVELER'S CORNER**), and the State Department's Travel Advisories (keyword: **REFERENCE**).

 AOL Travel Advisories

Keyword: **REFERENCE**

Travel advisories from the U.S. Department of State are posted in the State Department Warnings directory of the Reference Desk. State Department Warnings identify dangerous situations

International Space Station Alpha

IN RECESS

International Space Station Alpha (ISSA) is an example of multinational cooperation in space. The space station is a joint project of the United States, the European Space Agency (ESA), the Japanese, the Canadians, and the Russians.

Figure 10.15 http://issa-www. jsc.nasa.gov/ss/prgview/prgview.html *The International Space Station Alpha site.*

ISSA is the descendent of Space Station Alpha, itself the descendent of the planned Freedom Space Station. ISSA is larger and more capable than its predecessors, making it a more valuable resource for the nations building it. The ISSA team has created a Web site that provides both public access and Program Team access. The home page for the ISSA site is at:

> WWW Address: **http:// issa-www.jsc.nasa.gov/ss/ SpaceStation_homepage.html**

One exciting feature of the ISSA page is the large, clickable photograph of Space Station Alpha (see fig. 10.15). Click on any element of the station to find out what it is, and get a short background report.

Figure 10.16 Keyword: REFERENCE
AOL's State Department Warnings directory is part of the Reference Desk.

around the world. They're produced by the State Department's Bureaus of Consular Affairs, and distributed as a service to travelers.

These warnings are the same as those on the Department of State Foreign Affairs Network. Figure 10.16 shows some of the warnings in force when this was written.

CompuServe

CompuServe has the most extensive coverage of the foreign affairs information in this chapter, including:

- *State Department Reports.*
  Go: **CIS:STATE**

- *White House Forum.*
  Go: **CIS:WHITEH**

- *International Trade Forum.*
  Go: **CIS:TRADE**

- *Space Flight Forum.*
  Go: **CIS:SPACEF**

 CompuServe's Space Flight Forum

Go: **CIS:SPACEF**

CompuServe's Space Flight Forum covers all aspects of the subject, from technical discussions of spacecraft to the politics of space travel (see fig. 10.17). The forum is truly international in scope, with coverage of the American, European, Japanese, and Russian space agencies.

Visitors will find lots of space information at Go: **CIS:SPACEF**. The Issues/Politics library alone contains over 50 files. Add the rest of the libraries and all the messages sections, and this turns out to be a great resource.

> **NOTE**
>
> The Space Flight Forum is only one of the space forums on CompuServe. These forums, and related materials, are gathered into a larger group, the Space/Astronomy Forum. The address for this forum is
> Go: **CIS:SPACE**.

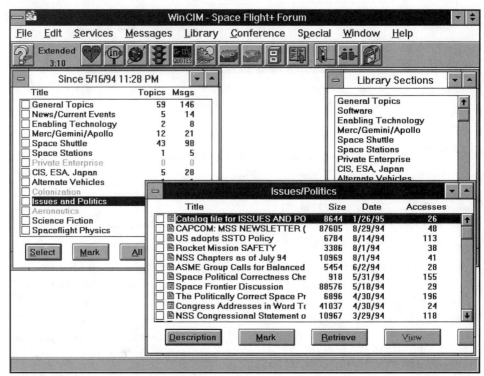

Figure 10.17 Go: CIS:SPACEF
CompuServe's Space Flight Forum.

Prodigy

Prodigy only has the limited foreign affairs coverage you get in news services (Jump: **News**) and the White House Memo area (Jump: **White House**).

Recommended Sites to See

The following lists contain the addresses of the foreign affairs sites covered in the chapter. There is one list for each major section of the chapter. A number of related addresses are included at the end of each list.

Newsgroups and Mailing Lists

News stories about disasters around the world.

> UseNet Address:
> clari.news.disaster

News stories relating to the military.

> UseNet Address:
> clari.news.military

Top news stories from around the world.

> UseNet Address:
> clari.news.top.world

U.S. foreign policy news.

UseNet Address:
`clari.news.usa.gov.foreign_policy`

United Nations politics discussions.

UseNet Address:
`alt.politics.org.un`

The Central Intelligence Agency.

UseNet Address:
`alt.politics.org.cia`

U.S. State Department travel advisories.

LISTSERV Address:
`TRAVEL-ADVISORIES`
subscribe at `STOLAF.EDU`

The National Security Agency.

UseNet Address:
`alt.politics.org.nsa`

NASA information.

UseNet Address: `dod.pb.nasa`

Information from the NATODATA mailing list.

UseNet Address: `list.natodata`

UN Children's rights list.

LISTSERV Address: `CHILDRI-L`
subscribe at `NIC.SURFNET.NL`

Public opinion on foreign policy.

LISTSERV Address: `POFP-L`
subscribe at `UGA.CC.UGA.EDU`

The U.S. Department of State

The U.S. Department of State Foreign Affairs Network.

Gopher Address: `gopher://`
`dosfan.lib.uic.edu`

The International Service Agencies.

WWW Address: `http://`
`www.charity.org/`

The International Federation of Red Cross and Red Crescent Societies

WWW Address: `http://`
`www.ifrc.org/`

CARE, an ISA organization.

WWW Address: `http://`
`www.netmarket.com/isa/html/`
`care.html`

The United Nations

The UN home page.

WWW Address: `http://`
`www.unicc.org/`

The World Citizen Web.

WWW Address: `http://`
`www.together.org/orgs/wcw/`

The UN Charter.

WWW Address: `http://`
`www.undcp.org/charter.html`

The UN Development Program.

WWW Address: `http://`
`www.undp.org/`

The UN Offices at Vienna.

WWW Address: `http://`
`www.un.or.at/`

The UN Volunteers Gopher

Gopher Address: `gopher://`
`gopher.unv.ch`

The International Atomic Energy
Agency.

Gopher Address: `gopher://`
`nesirs01.iaea.or.at`

The International Telecommunication
Union (ITU).

Gopher Address: `gopher://`
`info.itu.ch`

The United Nations Children's Fund
(UNICEF).

Gopher Address: `gopher://`
`hqfaus01.unicef.org`

The World Bank.

WWW Address: `http://`
`www.worldbank.org`

The World Bank Gopher.

Gopher Address: `gopher://`
`ftp.worldbank.org 70`

The World Health Organization
(WHO)

WWW Address: `http://`
`www.who.ch/`

Intelligence

The CIA page.

WWW Address: `http://`
`www.ic.gov/index.html`

Real Time Support for the Warrior

WWW Address: `http://`
`www.ait.nrl.navy.mil/rts/`
`warrior.html`

The CIA Factbook on Intelligence.

WWW Address: `http://`
`www.ic.gov/facttell/toc.html`

The 1994 CIA World Factbook.

WWW Address: `http://`
`www.ic.gov/94fact/fb94toc/`
`ft94toc.html`

The Terrorist Profile Weekly.

WWW Address: `http://`
`www.site.gmu.edu/~cdibona`

The Journal of Electronic Defense.

WWW Address: `http://`
`www.jedefense.com/jed.html`

The Brittanica Online Web page.

WWW Address: `http://`
`www.eb.com/`

Treaties

The NAFTA Gopher.

Gopher Address: `gopher://`
`cyfer.esusda.gov`

> Once connected, select the fol-
> lowing directories:
> `Americans Communicating`
> `  Electronically`
> `National Policy Issues...`
> `North American Free Trade`
> `  Agreement (NAFTA)`

The General Agreement on Tariffs and
Trade.

Gopher Address: `gopher://`
`cyfer.esusda.gov`

> Once connected, select the fol-
> lowing directories:
> `Americans Communicating`
> `  Electronically`
> `National Policy Issues...`
> `General Agreement on Tar-`
> `  iffs and Trade (GATT)`

The NATO home page.

WWW Address:
`www.saclant.nato.int/`
`nato.html`

The NAFTA treaty on the Web.

WWW Address: `http://the-`
`tech.mit.edu/Bulletins/`
`nafta.html`

Another source for the NAFTA treaty.

Gopher Address: `gopher://`
`134.124.1.2`

Once connected, navigate
through the following directories:

`The Library`
`Government Information`
`NAFTA—North American Free`
`   Trade Agreement (Final`
`   Treaty)`

The Trade/Globalization page at
Charlotte's Web.

WWW Address: `http://`
`www.emf.net/~cr/trade.html`

The NATO Handbook.

WWW Address: `http://`
`www.saclant.nato.int/nato/`
`handbook/index.html`

The NATO Gopher site.

Gopher Address: `gopher://`
`gopher.nato.int`

Once connected, select the following directory:

`North Atlantic Treaty`
`   Organization`

Propaganda

The Voice of America.

Gopher Address: `gopher://`
`gopher.voa.gov`

The U.S. Agency for International
Development.

WWW Address: `http://`
`www.info.usaid.gov/`

Digitized audio from VOA broadcasts.

WWW Address: `http://`
`pmwww.cs.vu.nl:8080/htbin/`
`voa_radio`

USAID's mission to promote democracy.

WWW Address: `http://`
`www.info.usaid.gov/welcome/`
`bur/democ.html`

USAID's Europe and Newly Independent States Bureau.

WWW Address: `http://`
`www.info.usaid.gov/welcome/`
`bur/asia.html`

The BBC.

WWW Address: `http://`
`a54.cc.umist.ac.uk/~james007/`
`tv.html`

Foreign Affairs in Space

NASA's home page.

WWW Address: `http://`
`www.gsfc.nasa.gov/`
`NASA_homepage.html`

International Space Station Alpha.

WWW Address: `http://issa-www.jsc.nasa.gov/ss/SpaceStation_homepage.html`

The Space Activism home page.

WWW Address: `http://muon.qrc.com/space/start.html`

Guidelines for space activists.

WWW Address: `http://muon.qrc.com/space/guide-lines/start.html`

The European Space Agency.

WWW Address: `http://mesis.esrin.esa.it/html/esis.html`

The Japanese Space Agency.

WWW Address: `http://hdsn.eoc.nasda.go.jp`

The Center for Advanced Space Studies.

Gopher Address: `gopher://cass.jsc.nasa.gov`

Once connected, select the following directory:

`pub`

The UN Office for Outer Space Affairs.

WWW Address: `ftp://ns3.hq.eso.org/pub/un/un-homepage.html`

The NASA Technical Report Server.

WWW Address: `http://techreports.larc.nasa.gov/cgi-bin/NTRS`

PART III

Political Places and Things

Chapter 11

The Branches of Government

You can use the Net to tap the resources of the three branches of government.

In this chapter

- *The Executive Branch—the President and more*
- *The Legislative Branch—the Congress and more*
- *The Judicial Branch—the Courts*

In other chapters

← *The Office of the President is featured in Chapter 3.*

← *The Bill of Rights and the Supreme Court are covered in Chapter 7.*

← *Cabinet departments and Executive Branch agencies are covered in Chapters 8, 9, and 10.*

→ *Repositories for government documents are described in Chapter 13.*

→ *The Senate Gopher is covered in Chapter 14.*

This book deals primarily with domestic politics. Much American political activity (hence much of this book) focuses on parts of the Federal Government. This chapter helps you put everything in context by examining the three branches of the U.S. Government: the Executive Branch, the Legislative Branch, and the Judicial Branch.

As specified in the Constitution, the three branches make up a system of checks and balances. Each branch is limited in what it can do by itself. One example of this is the making of laws. The Congress can write laws, but the Executive Branch is responsible for enforcing them, and the Judicial Branch determines the constitutionality of them.

This chapter looks at each branch of the government. You will find background information on each branch, as well as examples of Net sites. In addition, there are lists of the major elements of each branch, information you can use to fit the government sites in the book into their proper place in the Federal Government.

Newsgroups and Mailing Lists

Various parts of the U.S. Government use newsgroups and mailing lists to make information available to the public. Some of these sources are unmoderated and open to comments from anyone. Others, like the federal courts newsgroup, are moderated, and allow only official material to be posted.

 Congressional Politics

alt.politics.usa.congress

This newsgroup is dedicated to discussions of Congressional politics. Congressional news reports appear here, as do other threads dealing specifically with Congress (see fig. 11.1).

While many of the messages in the congressional politics newsgroup are useful and informative, this is an unmoderated newsgroup. As a result, some threads and individual messages have little or nothing to do with Congress. Clinton bashing is popular in this newsgroup. Take a good look at some of the thread names in figure 11.1—Clinton's Welfare for the Rich is one thread name.

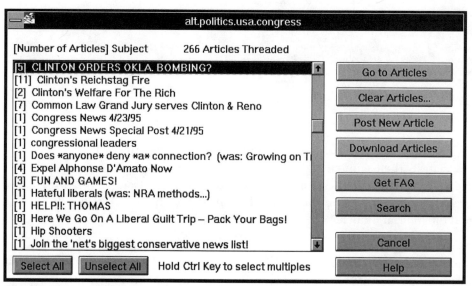

Figure 11.1 alt.politics.usa.congress
A Congressional politics newsgroup.

U.S. Supreme Court Decisions

`courts.usa.federal.supreme`

This moderated newsgroup carries copies of recent Supreme Court decisions. Each case is identified by number and the Court's opinion on each is posted. Concurring and dissenting opinions are also posted if they are available. Because this is a moderated newsgroup, and only authorized people can add messages to it, you can be confident that the material posted here is authentic.

The Department of Health and Human Services Mailing List

`hhsonet@list.nih.gov`

This mailing list carries news and information from the Office of the Secretary of the Department of Health and Human Services. To subscribe, send e-mail to `listserv@list.nih.gov`.

The Executive Branch

The Executive Branch of the government was created from Article II of the Constitution, which established the office of President. The President has many powers and responsibilities. The Executive Branch, which consists of the White House Office, the Executive Office of the President, 14 departments, and any number of independent agencies and commissions, exists to help him do his job. Figure 11.2 shows the Executive Branch page at the White House Web site.

The 14 departments of the Executive Branch are also present on the Net. Many of them are covered in other chapters, and we'll look at one more—the Justice Department—in this chapter. Following is a list of the 14 departments in the Executive Branch.

- Department of Agriculture
- Department of Commerce
- Department of Defense
- Department of Education
- Department of Energy
- Department of Health and Human Services
- Department of Housing and Urban Development
- Department of the Interior
- Department of Justice
- Department of Labor
- Department of State
- Department of Transportation
- Department of the Treasury
- Department of Veterans Affairs

> **NOTE**
>
> The heads of the 14 Executive Branch departments make up the President's Cabinet. The Cabinet members serve as advisors to the President, and direct their departments to achieve his goals.

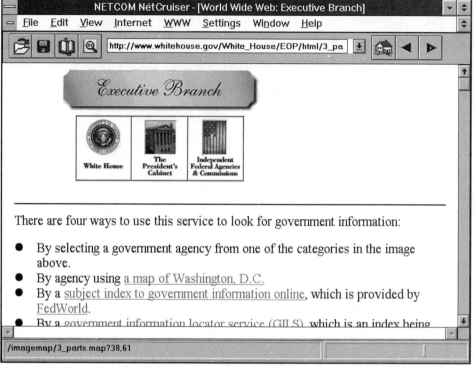

Figure 11.2 `http://www.whitehouse.gov/White_House/EOP/html/3_parts.html`
You can reach the online resources of the Executive Branch through this Web page.

 The U.S. Postal Service

`http://www.usps.gov/`

The United States Postal Service (USPS) is probably the most criticized of all government agencies. When the Postal Service makes the news, it's usually because of piles of undelivered mail and rate increases. Yet if you look behind the headlines, you see a different organization.

The USPS moved about 177 billion pieces of mail in 1994, 40 percent of all the mail moved on earth that year. That's over a half billion pieces of mail a day. To do its job, the USPS owns almost 7000 buildings, over 200,000 vehicles, and employs more than 700,000 people. These facts and more are available on the USPS Web server (see fig. 11.4).

The Postal Rates link gives you a synopsis of current rates or the complete rate tables. The synopsis alone runs to six printed pages.

Another link leads to consumer services. Here you can find a layman's guide to the services of the USPS, mailing tips, and even instructions on attending auctions of unclaimed mail. If you're moving, you can find out about the service's Mover's Guide, a booklet of moving tips and discount coupons.

The White House

The White House is the home of the President, the most powerful person on earth. The place where every President except George Washington lived, the White House is a museum of American artwork and craftsmanship. Walking tours of the White House are conducted frequently —thanks to the Clinton Administration, anyone on the World Wide Web can now take an online tour whenever he or she wishes. The tours consist of photographs of historic areas in and around the White House, photographs like figure 11.3, which shows the Oval Office.

But the White House is much more than the President's house—it is where he and his aides do much of their work. Press briefings, speeches, and many other Executive Branch products emanate from this old building, often finding their way onto the Net. Many of their online storage places are identified in this book.

In political newsgroups and mailing lists you find frequent mention of the White House. In these cases it usually represents the President and the Executive Branch. The building itself has made the news several times in recent years as the result of politically motivated assaults on the building and its occupants. The White House is more than just a building—it is one of the focal points of U.S. and world politics.

Figure 11.3 `http://www.whitehouse.gov/White_House/Tours/Welcome.html`
The Oval Office, part of a White House tour.

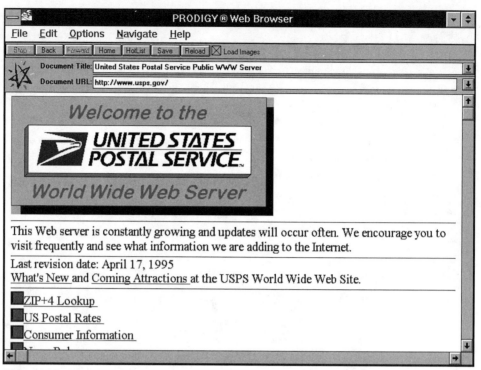

Figure 11.4 http://www.usps.gov/
The U.S. Postal Service home page.

Other links from the USPS home page can lead you to news releases, stamp images, even more postal service information, and an experimental ZIP+4 lookup form. Finally, an About the USPS link leads you to background information on the service, including the facts cited earlier.

 ### The Department of Justice

http://www.usdoj.gov/

The Department of Justice (DOJ) is the law firm of the United States. It prosecutes criminals, from individuals to giant corporations, ensuring that the nation's laws are observed. The depart-ment represents the United States in court, and advises the President and Cabinet on legal matters.

But the Department of Justice is more than just lawyers. It actively enforces the laws through the actions of organizations like the Federal Bureau of Investigation (FBI) and the Drug Enforcement Administration (DEA). The Department of Justice home page lets Net citizens find out more about this powerful organization (see fig. 11.5).

The DOJ home page has links to a variety of resources and information. One set of links provides information on Justice Department organizations like the Civil Rights Division. Each division has differing information, but you may

Figure 11.5 http://www.usdoj.gov/
The Justice Department home page has links to a variety of resources and information.

find an overview of the division, details of important cases it has conducted, and a link to a Gopher site with more information.

Another set of links addresses important DOJ issues like the Violent Crime and Law Enforcement Act of 1994, or Information on the UNABOM Case, a series of unexplained bombings across the country.

Other links from the Department of Justice home page take users to related Web and Gopher sites. There's also an extensive biography of Janet Reno, the first woman Attorney General of the United States.

The Legislative Branch

The Legislative Branch of the government is embodied by the Congress. The Congress is divided into two houses, the Senate and the House of Representatives, which between them have the responsibility to make federal laws. Much of the work done by the Senate and the House is handled by committees and subcommittees. The Senate has 16 standing committees and the House has 20. Each has numerous subcommittees.

The Oklahoma City Bombing

The FBI is quick to enlist the online community when it comes to bombings. Within days of the terrorist attack on the Alfred P. Murrah Federal Building in Oklahoma City, the FBI posted requests for assistance on the Net. The pages contained descriptions of the two suspects, a warning about how dangerous they were, and sketches of them. Figure 11.6 shows one of the pages, with a sketch of Suspect 1.

To make it easy for people to help, an 800 number and an e-mail address were provided for people to report leads. To help motivate people to provide tips, up to a $2,000,000 reward was offered for infor-

mation leading to the arrest and conviction of the suspects. You can see this page in its entirety by browsing to:

> WWW Address: `http://www.usdoj.gov/fbi/reward.html`

Another information page is at:

> WWW Address: `http://naic.nasa.gov/fbi/okbomb.html`

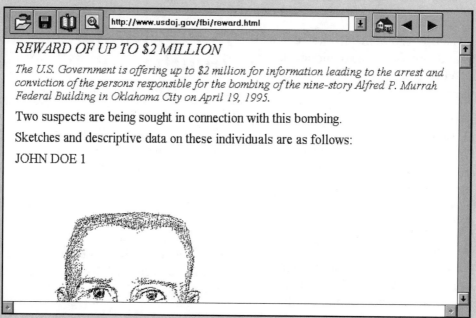

`http://www.usdoj.gov/fbi/reward.html`

REWARD OF UP TO $2 MILLION

The U.S. Government is offering up to $2 million for information leading to the arrest and conviction of the persons responsible for the bombing of the nine-story Alfred P. Murrah Federal Building in Oklahoma City on April 19, 1995.

Two suspects are being sought in connection with this bombing.

Sketches and descriptive data on these individuals are as follows:

JOHN DOE 1

Figure 11.6 `http://www.usdoj.gov/fbi/reward.html`
Wanted: An Online Wanted Poster for the Oklahoma City Bombers.

Besides the Congress, the Legislative Branch includes eight agencies that are responsible to Congress. They are:

- Architect of the Capitol
- United States Botanic Garden
- General Accounting Office (GAO)
- Government Printing Office (GPO)
- Library of Congress
- Office of Technology Assessment
- Congressional Budget Office
- Copyright Royalty Tribunal

The rest of this section looks at the Legislative Branch's presence on the Internet. Sites representing the Senate and the House of Representatives are included. But first, here's a look at Congressional Quarterly (CQ), a company that provides independent observations and commentary on the Congress.

 ### The Congressional Quarterly Gopher

`gopher://gopher.cqalert.com/`

Congressional Quarterly (CQ), founded in 1945 by newspaperman Nelson Poynter, is a company that observes and comments on Congress. It was created to provide the unbiased presentation of government information necessary for democracy to flourish. The company also maintains a Gopher site (see fig. 11.7).

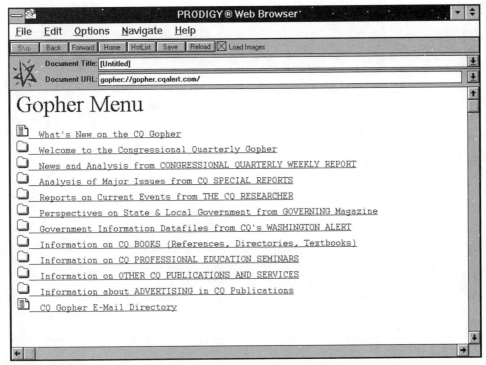

Figure 11.7 `gopher://gopher.cqalert.com/`
The Congressional Quarterly Gopher site.

The CQ Gopher contains documents from five CQ publications: *CQ Weekly Report, CQ Special Reports, the CQ Researcher, CQ's Washington Alert,* and *Governing* magazine. The site provides some free information from each source, as well as instructions on subscribing to the full publication.

The CQ Weekly Report directory contains the cover stories from past and current issues of the magazine. Recent titles include "GOP Tries to Spark Debate on Defense Plans," and "Clinton Wants GOP to Take the Lead on Budget." The Washington Alert directory includes some of the data from CQ's full Washington Alert database. The status of appropriations and major legislation is available, as are voting records, election results, and more.

The directories for the other three publications are similar to the two just described.

 The House of Representatives Home Page

`http://www.house.gov/`

The House of Representatives maintains this Web page as a public source of legislative information (see fig. 11.8). It also serves as a source of information about members, committees, and organizations of the House. Background information, specifics about legislation in progress, and even Washington D.C. visitor information are available here.

Figure 11.8 `http://www.house.gov/`
The House of Representatives home page is a great source for legislative information.

The Legislative Process link takes you to a page with complete information on bills and resolutions under consideration in Congress. The action on the House floor is also covered, as is the voting record of each member of the House. The Legislative Process page itself contains 20 links to different types of information, things like Bill Status, Committee Votes, the Congressional Record, and the Bill Text for the 103rd Congress.

The Legislative Process link takes you to information on bills being considered.

Some parts of the House maintain their own Net resources. The Member, Committee, and House Organizations' Published Information link leads to a collection of these WWW and Gopher resources. Members from 14 states have their own Gopher sites, while two have their own Web sites. Expect more of them to be online by the time you read this.

The Judicial Branch

The Judicial Branch of the government—also known as the third branch—was formed in response to Article III of the Constitution. Article III calls on Congress to create a Supreme Court and any inferior courts it deems necessary. The result, after 200 years of evolution, is the Federal Court system we have today.

11

BRANCHES OF GOVERNMENT

The Supreme Court is the highest court in the land. It rules on the constitutionality of federal and state laws, and decides cases that the lower courts can't. Below the Supreme Court are two layers, the federal appeals courts—also called the circuit courts—and the district courts. There are also six special courts named the:

- Court of Appeals for the Federal Circuit
- Temporary Emergency Court of Appeals
- Claims Court
- Court of International Trade
- Court of Military Appeals
- The Tax Court

This section of the chapter looks at some of the Judicial Branch resources on the Net. It includes two sites related to different aspects of the Supreme Court, and the Federal Court's home page, a clearinghouse for information by and about the Judicial Branch.

 Decisions of the Supreme Court

`http://www.law.cornell.edu/supct/`

Cornell Law School is a prime source of Supreme Court information on the Net. The full text of the Court's opinions from the year 1990 to present is available from this particular page (see fig. 11.9). In many cases, summaries (syllabi) and dissenting or concurring opinions are also available. The material is organized in three different ways to facilitate browsing, and a keyword search tool is available.

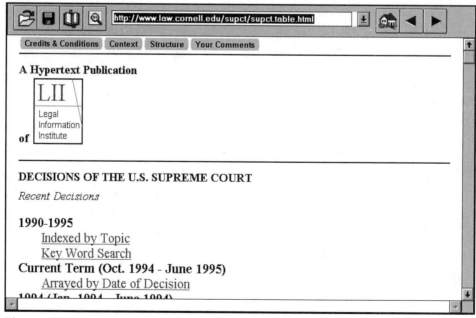

Figure 11.9 `http://www.law.cornell.edu/supct/supct.table.html`
This page provides access to recent Supreme Court decisions.

All the decisions are indexed by topic, ranging from abortion to workers' compensation. Decisions made in the current term are also sorted by decision date, while cases prior to the current term are indexed by the names of the parties involved. The search tool does Boolean searches on words in the titles and bodies of the decisions.

tions, Inc. v. Rural Telephone Service Co., Inc., a decision on copyright infringement, and the *Roe v. Wade* decision, which established a constitutional right to an abortion. These documents are in hypertext form, giving the reader easy access to concurring and dissenting opinions, as well as the full opinion of the court.

NOTE

The same material is available at the Supreme Court Decision Gopher. Its address is included in the list at the end of this chapter.

Besides current decisions, this page contains summaries of two historic Supreme Court decisions, *Feist Publica-*

 Justices of the Supreme Court

`http://www.law.cornell.edu/supct/justices/fullcourt.html`

Another Supreme Court resource maintained by Cornell Law School is the Justices of the Supreme Court page (see fig. 11.10). It's a collection of data about the current justices.

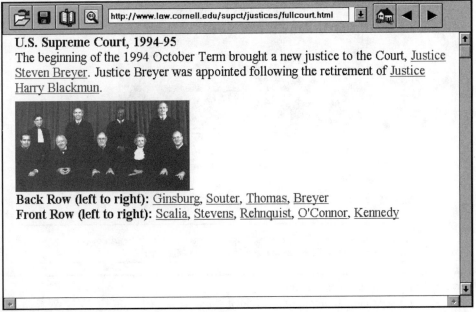

> `http://www.law.cornell.edu/supct/justices/fullcourt.html`
>
> **U.S. Supreme Court, 1994-95**
> The beginning of the 1994 October Term brought a new justice to the Court, Justice Steven Breyer. Justice Breyer was appointed following the retirement of Justice Harry Blackmun.
>
> **Back Row (left to right):** Ginsburg, Souter, Thomas, Breyer
> **Front Row (left to right):** Scalia, Stevens, Rehnquist, O'Connor, Kennedy

Figure 11.10 `http://www.law.cornell.edu/supct/justices/fullcourt.html`
Backgrounds of the Supreme Court Justices.

11

BRANCHES OF GOVERNMENT

For each justice there is a brief biography: birth date, education, and family information. In addition, there is material on government and judicial service, and a link to a page of recent legal opinions by that justice. This page contains the title of the opinion and a link to a summary of it. These summaries are the same as those described earlier in the section on the Supreme Court Decisions page.

The Federal Court's Home Page

http://www.uscourts.gov/

The Federal Court's home page is the place to find information from and about the Judicial Branch (see fig. 11.11). The site is maintained by the Administrative Office of the U.S. Courts. Although still under construction, this page already connects to a number of useful resources. These include:

- Understanding the Federal Courts, a hypertext description of how the federal court system operates

- Articles from the Third Branch, the monthly newsletter of the federal courts

- Recent press releases from the federal court system

- The Directory of Electronic Public Access Services, a guide on getting federal court information online

Figure 11.11 http://www.uscourts.gov/
This site is a great source of information about the Judicial branch.

Few people understand how the Federal court system works. The Understanding the Federal Courts link takes you to a hypertext document that explains the entire system. More than 20 linked documents provide a complete overview of the system, as well as details on each element of it. Features like maps and historical tidbits liven up the material. One such tidbit explains why the Courts of Appeals are called the circuit courts.

Another useful resource at the Federal Court's home page is the directory of Electronic Public Access Services. Following this link takes you to a list of places where you can electronically retrieve information from the federal court system. The list contains phone numbers for hundreds of electronic bulletin boards that contain Circuit Court, District Court, and Bankruptcy Court information. The Judicial Branch hopes to provide access to every federal circuit, district, and bankruptcy court in the nation by the time you read this.

The Branches of Government on the Online Services

Most of the resources on the online services that relate to the branches of government are more appropriately covered in other chapters:

- The White House on AOL and Prodigy—Chapter 2
- Tax information on AOL—Chapter 9
- State Department coverage—Chapter 10
- Tax information on CompuServe—Chapter 13

What are Circuit Courts?

When someone uses the term circuit court, they are referring to one of the Federal Courts of Appeals. The name comes from the early history of the Courts of Appeals. Each Court covers a territory consisting of at least three states.

The early appeals court judges had to travel around their territory on horseback, visiting each courthouse. They would make a complete round trip, or circuit, of their territory, then start around again.

IN RECESS

In the following sections, we'll look at some relevant items in America Online's Capital Connection, as well as the State Department coverage on CompuServe.

 ## AOL's Capital Connection

Keywords: **POLITICS, CAPITAL**

One of the nice features of the AOL's Capital Connection is the way it integrates Internet resources into the service. There are links to the House of Representatives Gopher, White House information, the Legi-Slate Gopher and Supreme Court decisions, and other Net resources. Figure 11.12 shows the information from the House Gopher.

Other resources related to the branches of government reside on AOL itself. One of these is the Federal Employment Service directory, which lists jobs across all branches of the government.

 ## CompuServe's State Department Forum

Go: **CIS:STATE**

The State Department forum on CompuServe carries travel advisories

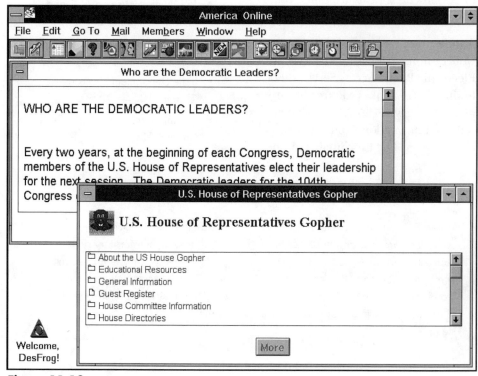

Figure 11.12 Keyword: CAPITAL
The House Gopher on AOL.

and consular information sheets. In addition, it includes the text of recently issued information sheets like the one shown in Figure 11.13.

The State Department forum is similar to the State Department resources on the other services, but it doesn't seem to work quite right—I had problems getting where I wanted to go. The Country Menus and Recently Issued Travel Information options work fine. But when I selected the About the State Department Forum option, I got a travel advisory on Burundi instead. When I selected the Using the Service option, I got an advisory on Ethiopia. By the time you read this, I expect that these problems will be ironed out.

Recommended Sites to See

The remainder of this chapter consists of addresses for government sites on the Net. The addresses are divided into three sections, one for each of the major sections of the chapter.

Each address is identified by its type and a very short description of what you can find there. Many of these addresses are discussed in more detail in the body of the chapter, so if you see one that looks interesting, skim through the appropriate section before logging onto the Net.

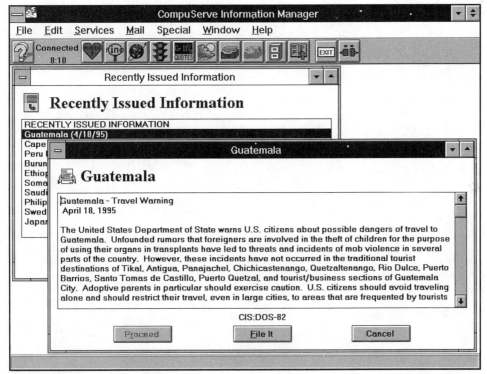

Figure 11.13 Go: CIS:STATE
The State Department on CompuServe.

Newsgroups and Mailing Lists

Discussions of politics in Congress.

UseNet Address:
`alt.politics.usa.congress`

Copies of recent Supreme Court decisions.

UseNet Address:
`courts.usa.federal.supreme`

News from the Department of Health and Human Services.

LISTSERV Address:
`hhsonet@list.nih.gov`

Discussions about the FBI.

UseNet Address:
`alt.politics.org.fbi`

Judicial affairs mailing list.

LISTSERV Address:
`judaff-l@bingvmb.cc.binghamton.edu`

To subscribe, send e-mail to:
`listserv@bingvmb.cc.binghamton.edu`

News from the Supreme Court.

UseNet Address:
`clari.news.usa.law.supreme`

News from the White House.

UseNet Address:
`clari.news.usa.gov.white_house`

The Executive Branch

Tours of the White House.

WWW Address: `http://www.whitehouse.gov/White_House/Tours/Welcome.html`

The President's Cabinet page at the White House.

WWW Address: `http://www.whitehouse.gov/White_House/Cabinet/html/cabinet_links.html`

The US Postal Service.

WWW Address: `http://www.usps.gov/`

Postal Service facts.

WWW Address: `http://www.usps.gov/history/pfact95.html`

Oklahoma City bomber rewards.

WWW Address: `http://www.usdoj.gov/fbi/reward.html`

More on the Oklahoma City bombers.

WWW Address: `http://naic.nasa.gov/fbi/okbomb.html`

White House Information from 1992-1994.

WWW Address: `http://english-server.hss.cmu.edu/WhiteHouse.html`

More White House Information.

WWW Address: `http://sunsite.unc.edu/govdocs.html`

Justice Department Information by Gopher.

Gopher Address: `gopher://marvel.loc.gov`

> Once connected, navigate through the following directories:
> `Government Information`
> `Federal Information`
> `  Resources`
> `Information By Branch of`
> `  Federal Government`
> `Executive Branch`
> `Justice Department (DOJ)`

A list of Executive Branch resources.

WWW Address: `http://www.alw.nih.gov/executive-govt.html`

A FAQ on the White House.

WWW Address: `http://www1.ai.mit.edu/White-House-FAQs.text`

The President's Cabinet with fax numbers.

FTP Address: `ftp://vector.casti.com/pub/QRD/usa/federal/cabinet.with.faxes`

The Legislative Branch

The Congressional Quarterly Gopher.

Gopher Address: `gopher://gopher.cqalert.com/`

The Senate Gopher.

Gopher Address: `gopher://gopher.senate.gov/`

The House of Representatives Web page.

WWW Address: `http://www.house.gov/`

A searchable Congressional directory.

Gopher Address: `gopher:/gopher.ucsc.edu`

> Once connected, navigate through the following directories:
> `The Government`
> `Congressional Directory`
> `104th (Searchable)`

The House of Representatives Gopher.

Gopher Address: `gopher://gopher.house.gov/`

The Senate by FTP.

FTP Address: `ftp://ftp.senate.gov/`

Search for Congressmen's phone and fax numbers.

Gopher Address: `gopher://marvel.loc.gov`

11

BRANCHES OF GOVERNMENT

Once connected, navigate through the following directories:
`U.S. Congress Congressional Directories Search Phone & Fax Numbers...`

The C-SPAN Gopher.

Gopher Address: `gopher:// c-span.org`

Once connected, navigate through the following directories:
`Inside Washington: Government Resource... Congressional Information...`

A list of Legislative Branch resources.

WWW Address: `http:// www.alw.nih.gov/ legislative-govt.html`

The Judicial Branch

The Justices of the U.S. Supreme Court.

WWW Address: `http:// www.law.cornell.edu/supct/ justices/fullcourt.html`

Recent and historic decisions of the U.S. Supreme Court.

WWW Address: `http:// www.law.cornell.edu/supct/`

The Federal Court's home page.

WWW Address: `http:// www.uscourts.gov/`

Supreme Court decisions by Gopher.

Gopher Address: `gopher:// gopher.inforM.umd.edu`

Once connected, navigate through the following directories:
`Educational Resources Academic Resources by Topic United States and... United States of America National Agencies... The Judicial Branch... Supreme Court Decisions`

The Federal Judicial Center home page.

WWW Address: `http:// www.fjc.gov/`

Opinions of the Eleventh Circuit Court.

WWW Address: `http:// www.law.emory.edu/11circuit/`

Chapter 12

State and Local Politics

State and local governments address many interesting issues on the Internet.

In this chapter

- *State-level political sites on the Net*

- *Local political sites on the Net*

- *Directories to state and local political sites*

- *State and local politics on the online services*

In other chapters

← *Rights and responsibilities are as relevant at the state and local level as they are at the national level; see Chapter 7.*

← *Federal policies and programs affect state and local government; see Chapter 8.*

→ *State and local government documents are sometimes found with the federal documents described in Chapter 13.*

I n this chapter, we look at a group of Net sites created by states and localities. By examining these sites, you will get an idea of the information state and local governments are putting on the Net. In addition, I've covered a few sites that will take you to the states and localities you are interested in.

Think about it this way. There are 50 states and thousands of cities and municipalities that could be online, and most of the states, and many of the cities and localities *are* online. Each location does things a little differently, and each, of course, focuses on its own concerns. The result is that there is no way to thoroughly cover all these resources in one chapter.

Newsgroups and Mailing Lists

Several states and cities use the Net as a way to keep their citizens informed. In this section, you find newsgroups and mailing lists associated with several of the cities and states discussed in this chapter. Because so many states and localities can have their own newsgroup, some of those included here are meant to represent broad classes of newsgroups.

 State and Local Politics on ClariNet

`clari.news.usa.gov.state+local`

This newsgroup is the best way to get the news on state and local politics (see fig. 12.1). It's provided by the ClariNet **e.News** service, and is available through most Internet providers. See the "What is ClariNet?" sidebar for more details.

As you can see in figure 12.1, ClariNet newsgroups are orderly. They have no discussions, no flames, no one posting irrelevant messages. This group has nothing but news articles about state and local politics. Because they come from major sources like the Associated Press and Reuters, you can be sure that the articles are factual and balanced.

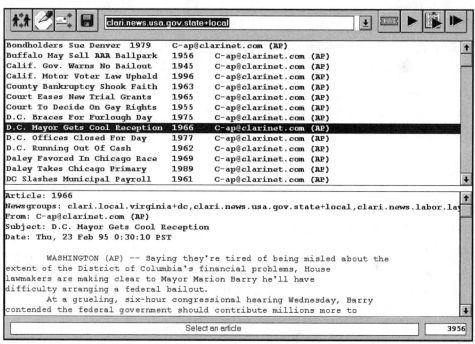

Figure 12.1 `clari.news.usa.gov.state+local`
State and Local Political news on UseNet.

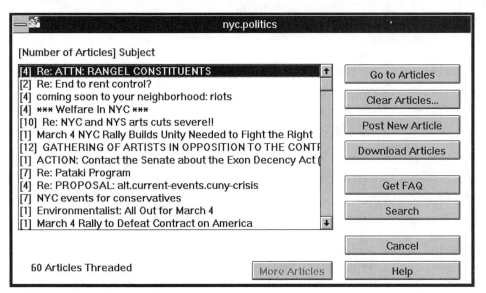

Figure 12.2 `nyc.politics`
The New York City politics newsgroup.

 New York City

`nyc.politics`

New York City, with a population of about seven million, is certainly large enough to support its own newsgroup (see fig. 12.2). In keeping with the city's reputation, the messages here are often rude or even obscene. Some of the thread titles are even obscene!

If you can look past the rough edges of the newsgroup, you can find a lot of local political information. Protests, discussions of current events, and philosophical musings are all there for the reader.

Several cities have their own newsgroups.

What Is ClariNet?

ClariNet **e.News** is an electronic newspaper. Covering a range of topics, from technology to business to politics and news, ClariNet **e.News**, provides immediate delivery of the text of news stories. The articles are taken from professional sources such as Reuters and the Associated Press.

ClariNet is a subscription service; your Internet Service Provider must pay a fee to carry the service. Not all of the providers do that at this time, so you may not have access. If your newsgroup reader doesn't show groups starting with *clari*, your provider doesn't subscribe to the service.

Several other cities have their own newsgroups. The preceding one illustrates the typical naming convention, which starts with the name or initials of the locale, followed by *.politics*. To find citywide information for Seattle, you look under **seattle.politics**.

 Community FreeNet Newsgroups

alt.online-service.freenet

FreeNets are community computer systems. Accessible by phone, and often through the Net, these systems provide an assortment of services to their local community. The services frequently include political and government resources. The **alt.online-service.freenet** newsgroup is for general discussions related to FreeNets, including their locations and availability.

 Arizona and Other State Newgroups

az.politics

Some cities have their own newsgroups; so do some states. Not surprisingly, they cover statewide political issues, as well as local issues. The Arizona politics newsgroup illustrates how they are typically named. The first two characters of the sites are the postal code for that state. The site listed above is the state of Arizona. The Iowa site is called **ia.politics**, and so on.

The state newsgroups are usually unmoderated and often plagued with topic drift, flames, and all the other afflictions of general interest newsgroups. If you can ignore the chaos, rudeness, and obscenity that sometimes appears in these groups, you may find useful political information.

 New Hampshire and Other State ClariNet Newsgroups

clari.loc.new-hampshire

One other way to get news about state and local politics is through ClariNet newsgroups like this one. They provide local news stories on all topics, including politics and government. Look for a group for the states you are interested in.

State Politics on the Net

With 50 states, you could conceivably have 50 completely different state government sites. There are a lot of differences between the state sites, but there are similarities, too. For example, you'll usually see links to state agencies, schools, and state legislative information. Beyond that, the sites tend to focus on their own interests.

The states usually use Web and Gopher sites. You will usually find that the state Web sites are more attractive and easier to use, but have less information than the Gopher sites.

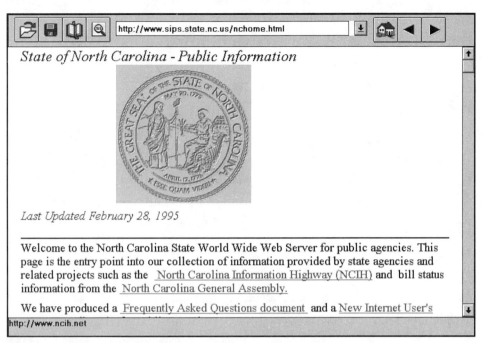

Figure 12.3 `http://www.sips.state.nc.us/nchome.html`
The State of North Carolina Public Information WWW page.

 Public Information from North Carolina

`http://www.sips.state.nc.us/`
`nchome.html`

North Carolina has created a Web page that serves as the central point for information from the state's public agencies (see fig. 12.3). Like most of the pages created by the states, it provides links to a number of state agencies. In this particular case, some of the state agencies include the Department of Insurance, the Employment Security Commission, the Office of State Personnel Job Vacancies, and several others. Another link takes browsers to the North Carolina General Assembly Gopher, where the status of legislation can be checked.

This page has links to all sorts of information. The Department of Agriculture and other state departments are represented, as are the state colleges and universities. One link goes to the state legislature, while another takes you to the North Carolina Information Highway page.

The North Carolina Information Highway

Not content to wait for the eventual appearance of a national information infrastructure (the Information Superhighway everyone is talking about), several states are implementing their own statewide information networks. North Carolina is one of those states.

The North Carolina Information Highway (NCIH) began operation in August 1994. The NCIH continues to expand, with the initial objective being to get the state government online. Other users are expected on the system beginning sometime in 1995.

The system is a high-speed fiber-optic network. Run by the state's telephone companies, it is designed for high speed data transmission, interactive video, and other high-bandwidth applications. Connections to the state's schools and to the Internet are part of the plan. To stay up to date on the development of the NCIH, check out their Web page (see fig. 12.4).

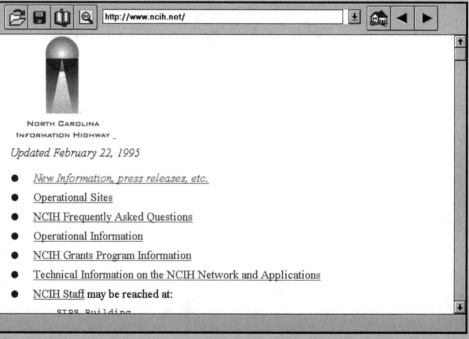

Figure 12.4 `http://www.ncih.net/`
The North Carolina Information Highway page on the WWW.

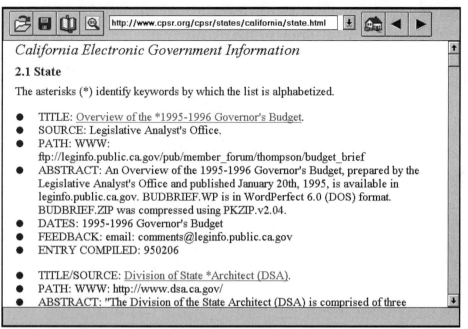

California Electronic Government Information

2.1 State

The asterisks (*) identify keywords by which the list is alphabetized.

- TITLE: <u>Overview of the *1995-1996 Governor's Budget</u>.
- SOURCE: Legislative Analyst's Office.
- PATH: WWW:
  ftp://leginfo.public.ca.gov/pub/member_forum/thompson/budget_brief
- ABSTRACT: An Overview of the 1995-1996 Governor's Budget, prepared by the Legislative Analyst's Office and published January 20th, 1995, is available in leginfo.public.ca.gov. BUDBRIEF.WP is in WordPerfect 6.0 (DOS) format. BUDBRIEF.ZIP was compressed using PKZIP.v2.04.
- DATES: 1995-1996 Governor's Budget
- FEEDBACK: email: comments@leginfo.public.ca.gov
- ENTRY COMPILED: 950206

- TITLE/SOURCE: <u>Division of State *Architect (DSA)</u>.
- PATH: WWW: http://www.dsa.ca.gov/
- ABSTRACT: "The Division of the State Architect (DSA) is comprised of three

Figure 12.5 `http://www.cpsr.org/cpsr/states/california/state.html`
CEGI State Information List on the WWW.

NOTE

The state of Iowa is also building its own information highway. Called the Iowa Communication Network (ICN), it appears to be similar in concept to NCIH. Perhaps these projects and others like them will serve as the prototypes for statewide information systems.

To make it easier for North Carolina state agencies to put their resources online, the site has links to resources for Net neophytes at state agencies. A Frequently Asked Questions (FAQ) file and reading list for new Net users are two of the documents designed to help state employees get up to speed on using the Net.

California State Government Information

`http://www.cpsr.org/cpsr/states/california/cal_gov_info_FAQ.html`

California has one of the most comprehensive state sites on the Net. The California Electronic Government Information (CEGI) Project is a compilation of information about California government resources available electronically. It's divided into eight sections, including State information, California Politicians and Candidates, and Municipal information. The goal is to make the citizens of the state aware of what is available and to stimulate the placement of more resources online.

Figure 12.5 shows the State information section of the list. One thing that makes this list particularly useful is the detailed summary of each site in the list. Features listing the source of the information, the path to it, and an abstract of what is available at the location are included. After you find a site you are interested in, click the hotlink and you are there.

By gathering dozens of links, this list improves your access to state resources. By providing detailed information on each site, it saves you time and effort when you are not sure where to find specific information. The CEGI State Information List is a great resource for users in California.

NOTE

County-, region-, and city-specific information is also available from the main page of this site. It's fairly common for state pages to have at least some local information sources as well.

The New York State Department of State Gopher Site

`gopher://`
`rain.health.state.ny.us`

The New York State Department of State Gopher is designed to pass

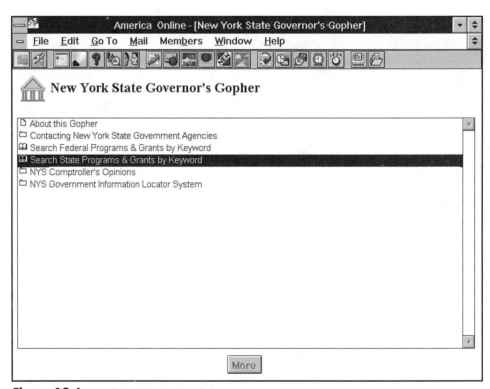

Figure 12.6 `gopher://rain.health.state.ny.us`
The New York State Rural Assistance Information Network.

information from the Governor to the citizens of New York State, as well as the broader Net community. The goal is to make government more accessible. Also known as the Rural Assistance Information Network (R.A.I.N.), this gopher site provides both federal and state resources. Figure 12.6 shows the top level of this Gopher.

Specific resources at this site include three different search systems. One covers state grants and programs. The second one covers federal grants and programs. The third one, a prototype project of the State Library and the State Archives and Records Administration, is known as the Information Locator System.

Local Politics on the Net

Local government sites on the Net exhibit a wide variety of features. Although they are geared to the specific needs of their communities, they usually include some common resources. Local commissions and boards are included, as are links to the next larger political entity—communities to the nearest city, cities to the state. More and more, they also contain links to the nearest FreeNet.

 The City of Boulder, CO

```
http://bcn.boulder.co.us/
government/boulder_city/
center.html
```

Boulder County, Colorado has a major presence on the Net. The Boulder Community Network (BCN) provides an online home for all sorts of information, from the Arts to Weather, for the cities and towns of the county. Local governments are also represented, such as the City of Boulder's Government page.

The City of Boulder Government page has three sections (see fig. 12.7). The first covers the city government, with names and contact information for each city council member. Another link covers every board and commission in the city government, along with meeting and contact notes.

The next section covers information from the City of Boulder Government. It includes city council agendas, news briefs, and more. One unusual item here is the link to emergency preparedness information and a crime fact sheet.

The final section is perhaps the most interesting. The Boulder Neighborhood Handbook is a project to disseminate information about neighborhood interests and goals and aid Boulder neighborhoods in organizing and dealing with the city. This project helps to bring politics to all levels of the community.

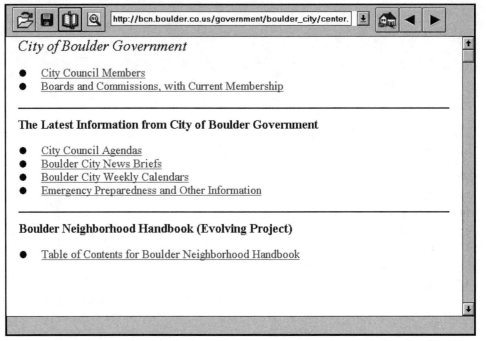

Figure 12.7 `http://bcn.boulder.co.us/government/boulder_city/center.html`
The City of Boulder's Government page.

 The Boulder Community Network

`http://bcn.boulder.co.us/`

The Boulder Community Network, the system that hosts the City of Boulder Government page, is a FreeNet. A FreeNet is a free, community-based computer system that provides information of interest to the local community. FreeNets are normally supported by volunteers and contributions. Access to a FreeNet varies. Some support little more than modem dial-up, and others such as BCN connect to the Net and have their own Web pages (see fig. 12.8).

By giving the community free access to this information and these telecommunication resources, BCN hopes to provide the benefits of these resources to all members of the community. To that end, BCN will include public access kiosks in locations throughout the county, including libraries, government offices, and schools.

A FreeNet is a free, community-based computer system that provides information of interest to the local community.

The BCN is an affiliate of the National Public Telecomputing Network (NPTN), an organization that works to stimulate the growth and interconnection of FreeNets. You can learn more about NPTN and its founder, Tom Grundner, in the sidebar Tom Grundner—The Father of the FreeNet.

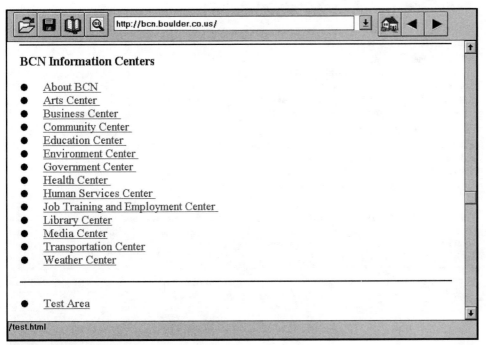

Figure 12.8 `http://bcn.boulder.co.us/`
The Boulder Community Network on the WWW.

Tom Grundner—The Father of the Free-Net

Tom Grundner certainly isn't a household name, yet he is an important person. In 1986, Mr. Grundner developed the Cleveland FreeNet, the first free, open-access, community-based computer system.

The success of the Cleveland FreeNet inspired him to found the National Public Telecomputing Network (NPTN) in 1989. NPTN is a nonprofit organization that helps groups set up FreeNets throughout the United States and other countries. The goal is to foster the

growth of community computer systems in the United States and overseas, linking them together into a network similar to National Public Radio or PBS on television.

Although you won't often see Mr. Grunder's name, his brainchild is providing free public Internet access to people all over the world. If you want more information on Mr. Grundner, check out his home page on the Web (see fig. 12.9).

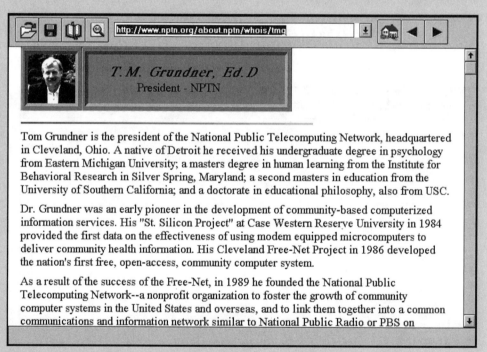

Figure 12.9 http://www.nptn.org/about.nptn/whois/tmg
Tom Grundner's home page.

Searching for Information on Your State and Local Government

This section covers some places where you can start a search for state and local political information. With them, you can quickly find the major resources in your area. Once you reach them, you are likely to find that they point you to even more information.

 The State and Local Governments Page at the Library of Congress

`http://lcweb.loc.gov/global/state/stategov.html`

This site, which is part of the Library of Congress' information services, contains a number of links to state government information (see fig. 12.10). Besides links to most of the 50 states, the page has links to other sites that maintain lists of state and local government information.

 City Net

`http://city.net/countries/united_states/`

City Net is a guide to communities around the world. Currently, 251 countries and 500 cities are represented at this site. All 50 states are represented; as is the District of Columbia. Since City Net covers the world, American cities and states are grouped on the United States page (see fig. 12.11).

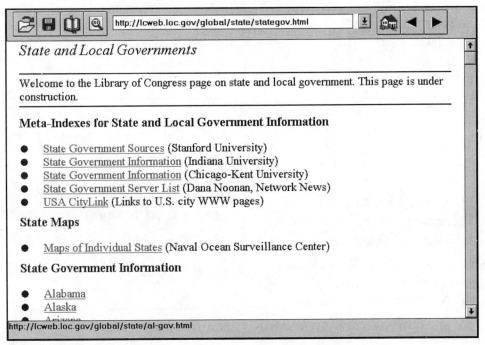

Figure 12.10 `http://lcweb.loc.gov/global/state/stategov.html`
The Library of Congress State and Local Government page on the WWW.

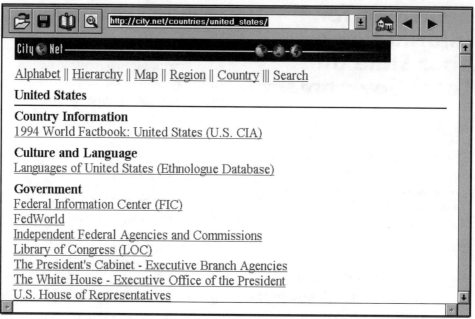

Figure 12.11 `http://city.net/countries/united_states/`
U.S. city and state information is available on City Net.

For each city or state, there is a mix of common and unique information. Common political information for the states include links to state government sites, and to individual cities within the state. For many cities, there are links to government and community organizations. What you'll find for your own city or state is of course dependent on what they have made available. City Net is an easy way to find information.

National Public Telecomputing Network Affiliated FreeNets

As the organizing group for United States and international FreeNets, the NPTN is the ideal place to start a search for a FreeNet near you. The NPTN Affiliates and Organizing Committees page contains links to the contact information for all the active FreeNets (see fig. 12.12).

For each city or state, there is a mix of common and unique information. What you'll find for your own city depends on what it has made available.

State and Local Politics on Online Services

You can find some state and local political information on all three of the online services. AOL and CompuServe have forums specifically for certain states. These forums cover a range of subjects, including politics and government. The Virginia Government forum on AOL and the Florida Today forum on CompuServe are profiled in the following sections.

Prodigy takes a somewhat different approach. Instead of forums for individual states, Prodigy has useful bulletin boards. It contains state and local information combined into a number of topics in a national bulletin board. This means that you can find information from Alaska and Arizona, as well as data from the other 48 states and some locales, all in one bulletin board.

 AOL

Keyword: VIRGINIA

AOL's Virginia forum is a location for just about anything related to the state of Virginia. Figure 12.13 shows some of the material in the Government section of the forum.

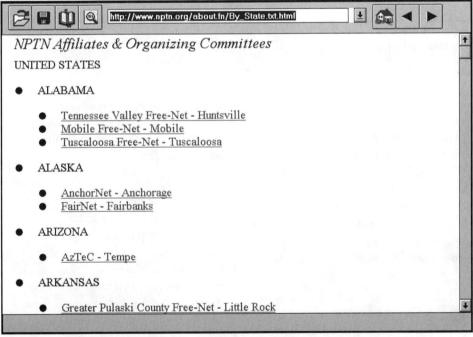

Figure 12.12 `http://www.nptn.org/about.fn/By_State.txt.html`
The NPTN Affiliates and Organizing Committees WWW page.

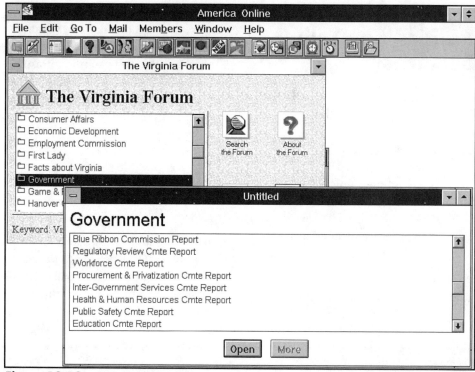

Figure 12.13 Keyword: VIRGINIA
The Government section of the Virginia Forum on AOL.

As you can see in this figure, the resources are primarily reports from the state government. Other sections of the forum include information from sources such as the attorney general's office, the lieutenant governor's office, and various state agencies. Because the forum also contains a message board, visitors can participate in discussions of the issues. Michigan and Utah are two other states that have forums on AOL.

CompuServe

Go: **CIS:CALFOR**

California politics is just one of the many subjects covered here. At this site, there's a message area for political discussion, as well as a library of government documents. Figure 12.14 shows some of the material you can find in this forum.

The messages deal with local, state, and even national events—basically, anything the public cares to talk about. Although the participants may disagree, often violently, there seem to be few flame wars here. The documents in the library deal primarily with state politics—for example, propositions and statements by state politicians.

Prodigy

Jump: AMERICA BB

The America on the Go bulletin board on Prodigy is the place to find state and local political information from around the country. The topics in the forum cover the entire spectrum—two of these topics are sources of political information. The State Laws and Agencies topic includes exactly that: information about state laws and state agencies from around the nation. The other topic, Your Town and Mine, is relatively new, but is becoming a very good source of information as it evolves (see fig. 12.15).

This topic is divided into threads for each state and many localities. The idea is that Prodigy members will add to these threads and provide messages on politics, government, and other subjects that strike their fancy. If the members actively contribute, these threads can become Prodigy's equivalent to message sections or UseNet newsgroups for the states.

You can find state and local political information on Prodigy's America on the Go bulletin board.

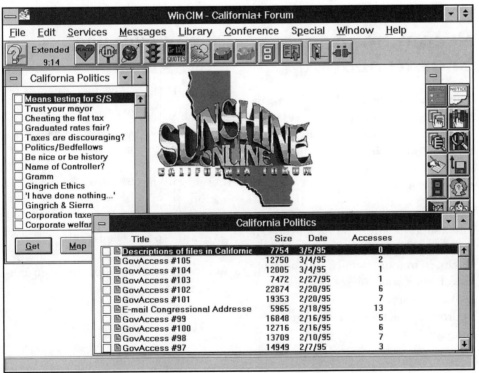

Figure 12.14 Go: CIS:CALFOR
Government information in the California Forum on CompuServe.

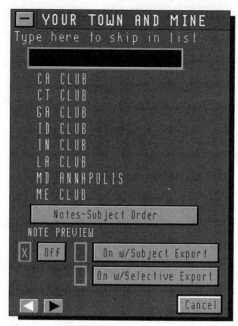

Figure 12.15 Jump: AMERICA BB.
The Your Town and Mine topic in Prodigy's America on the Go Bulletin Board.

Recommended Sites to See

The remainder of this chapter consists of the addresses for Net resources that deal with state and local politics. The addresses are divided into sections that correspond to the major sections of this chapter.

Each address is identified by its type and a short description of what you can find there. Many of these addresses are discussed in more detail in the body of this chapter, so if you see one that looks interesting, skim through the appropriate section before logging onto the Net.

Newsgroups and Mailing Lists

State and local political news from around the country.

UseNetAddress: `clari.news.usa. gov.state+local`

Local headlines from around the nation.

UseNet Address: `clari.local.headlines`

Low-volume newsgroup of state government news.

UseNet Address: `clari.news.gov.state`

New York City political discussions.

UseNet Address: `nyc.politics`

Political topics for the state of Arizona.

UseNet Address:
`az.politics`

Local news from New Hampshire, including political news.

UseNet Address:
`clari.loc.new-hampshire`

News briefs from New Hampshire, including political briefs.

UseNet Address: `clari.loc.new-hampshire.briefs`

State Politics on the Net

Public information from the state of North Carolina.

WWW Address: `http://www.sips.state.nc.us/nchome.html`

The North Carolina Information Highway.

WWW Address: `http://www.ncih.net`

CEGI California state and local government information.

WWW Address: `http://www.cpsr.org/cpsr/states/california/cal_gov_info_FAQ.html`

CEGI California state government information.

WWW Address: `http://www.cpsr.org/cpsr/states/california/state.html`

The New York State Department of State gopher.

Gopher Address: `gopher://rain.health.state.ny.us`

The Texas Secretary of State home page.

WWW Address: `http://register.sos.texas.gov/`

The Institute of Government at UNC.

WWW Address: `http://ncinfo.iog.unc.edu/`

Minnesota state government information.

Gopher Address: `gopher://gopher.revisor.leg.state.mn.us`

Local Politics on the Net

The City of Boulder.

WWW Address: `http://bcn.boulder.co.us/government/boulder_city/center.html`

The Boulder Community Network.

WWW Address: `http://bcn.boulder.co.us/`

Tom Grundner's page at NPTN.

WWW Address: `http://www.nptn.org/about.nptn/whois/tmg`

Washington D.C.'s city page.

WWW Address: `http://teal.nosc.mil/planet_earth/washington.html`

The Association of Bay Area Governments home page.

WWW Address: `http://www.abag.ca.gov/index.html`

The state of Pennsylvania page.

WWW Address: `http://www.NeoSoft.com/citylink/pa.html`

The city of Ann Arbor Michigan.

Gopher Address: `gopher://umcc.umcc.umich.edu`

Once connected, navigate through the following directories:

`Special Interest Gopher Servers and Information City of Ann Arbor Government Information`

California counties and cities.

WWW Address: `http://www.cpsr.org/cpsr/states/california/municipal.html`

Some Indexes of State and Local Political Information

All about FreeNets, including politics.

UseNet Address: `alt.online-service.freenet`

NPTN affiliated FreeNets.

WWW Address: `http://www.nptn.org/about.fn/By_State.txt.html`

The Library of Congress State and Local Government page.

WWW Address: `http://lcweb.loc.gov/global/state/stategov.html`

Collection of political information for most states.

Gopher Address: `gopher://marvel.loc.gov`

Once connected, navigate through the following directories:

`Government Information State and Local Government Information (U.S.)`

Links to FreeNets around the world.

WWW Address: `http://www.uwec.edu/info/freenets.html`

More links to FreeNets around the world.

WWW Address: `http://herald.usask.ca/~scottp/free.html`

An index of state gophers.

Gopher Address: `gopher://link.tsl.texas.gov`

Chapter 13

The End Product: Laws and Other Documents

The Net makes government documents readily available to anyone, and this chapter tells you where to find them.

I f there's one thing that the United States government does well, it is to generate documents. They're the end result of just about all the government's activities. Our government is the largest publisher in the world, generating millions of pages of paper every year. Until recently, these mountains of documents were of little use to the average person or business for two reasons:

- Only physical (paper) documents existed, and they were held at various repositories around the country.
- Writing and printing these documents took time.

Even if you knew which document you wanted, you had to find a physical copy of it. For the most important and famous documents, things like the Declaration of Independence, or the most recent State of the Union address, that wasn't too hard. But, if you wanted something more obscure, finding a copy of it might be almost impossible.

Another problem was timeliness. When a document was created, it had to be printed and distributed. Complete, rapid access to regulations, laws, and other government documents is a competitive edge. Think of the advantages of knowing about new government regulations or Supreme Court decisions before your competitors know about them. If you rely on printed documents, your information can be days, or even weeks, old.

With documents available online, the situation is different. Now:

- Anyone can find and obtain a document.
- Internet users can access this information instantly.

Anyone with access to the Net can get the latest government documents

almost instantly. Documents such as Supreme Court decisions are posted within minutes of being made. Everyone can have almost equal access to these important government products.

This chapter looks at a number of online sources of government documents. Some of these are official government sites, run by agencies, departments, or, in some cases, the Library of Congress. Next, this chapter looks at nongovernment sources for government documents. Although this may seem redundant, you'll see that there are good reasons for them to exist. Finally, you'll find some coverage of sources of government documents on the online services.

Getting the Newsgroups and Mailing Lists

Although tens of thousands of Government Printing Office publications documents are printed every year (or even month!), there aren't many newsgroups or mailing lists dedicated to government documents. The two UseNet newgroups described in the next section are good sources of information.

 UseNet Newsgroups

`bit.listserv.govdoc-l`
`courts.usa.federal.supreme`

The `bit.listserv.govdoc-l` newsgroup is for the discussion of government documents and issues

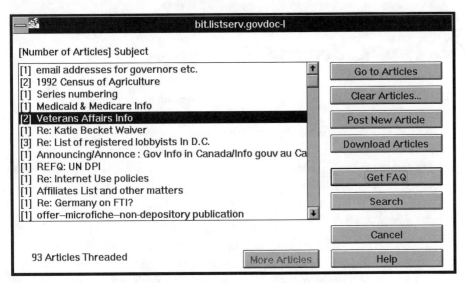

Figure 13.1 `bit.listserv.govdoc-l`
The Government Documents newsgroup is a good source for information.

related to government documents. Figure 13.1 shows some typical articles.

You don't find too much controversy here. What you do find is information about government documents and, perhaps more importantly, answers to questions about them. Officials from government agencies use this newsgroup, and they answer questions about documents.

 Supreme Court Decisions

`courts.usa.federal.supreme`

The `courts.usa.federal.supreme` newsgroup is a moderated newsgroup containing Supreme Court decisions. It carries the text of the decision, a summary, dissenting opinions, and related documents.

Government Archives

The government runs many of its own Net sites. These are obviously the places to go if you want to get the word straight from the horse's mouth. There are dozens of sites, primarily Gopher and Web sites. There isn't one central location where you can find all government documents, so you'll have to use the information in this chapter to guide you.

This section looks at archives representing different branches of the government. The executive and legislative branches are each represented by a Gopher and Web site. Numerous other government sites are listed at the end of the chapter.

What Is a Moderated Newsgroup?

Most UseNet newsgroups are *unmoderated*. That means that anyone can post any article they want to that newsgroup. Random, disruptive, and even obscene messages can be posted to an unmoderated newsgroup. The only control for the content of an unmoderated newsgroup is the self-control of the people who use it.

A *moderated* newsgroup is different. A moderator controls what is posted to the

newsgroup. All materials are filtered (you might also call it censored) by the moderator, and only articles approved by the moderator get into the newsgroup.

The `courts.usa.federal.supreme` newsgroup is a perfect example of a newsgroup that *must* be moderated. Imagine the chaos that would result if someone could post false Supreme Court decisions. The moderator prevents that.

The White House Publications Page

`http://www.whitehouse.gov/ White_House/Publications/html/ Publications.html`

The White House is a major source of government documents. Its primary products are press briefings, speeches, and other output from the President and Vice President. With Mrs. Clinton's involvement in major administrative actions, such as health care, she too generates important documents. The White House Electronic Publications page is one place on the Net to find these documents (see fig. 13.2).

Government documents are available on the Net.

> **NOTE**
>
> The Hillary Clinton profile in Chapter 8, "Policies and Programs," lists some sources of documents related to her national health care plan.

This page is part of the White House Web site set up by the Clinton administration. It includes virtually anything that comes out of the White House—speeches, press releases, executive orders, whatever. The documents are organized in several different ways, to make it easy for visitors to find specific information. Daily releases and summaries cover the latest information. The Topical Releases area gathers all the documents on subjects like health care and the environment. The Major Documents section contains presidential speeches and the text of documents such as the Health Security Act.

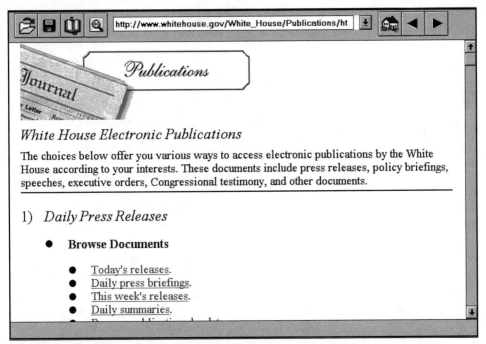

Figure 13.2 `http://www.whitehouse.gov/White_House/Publications/html/`
`Publications.html`
The White House Publications page.

Two other features increase the value of this page. The Document Retrieval section provides a number of different ways to search for documents. You can search for keywords in all available documents or within specific categories. Just follow the directions on the page. The page also provides a link to an e-mail subscription service. By subscribing to this service, anyone can receive the White House's daily publications by e-mail.

 Executive Branch Documents at the LC Marvel Gopher

`gopher://marvel.loc.gov`

Select the following directories:

> `Government Information`
> `Federal Information`
>   `Resources`
> `Information by Branch of`
> `Federal Government`
> `Executive Branch`

The Executive Branch directory on the LC MARVEL Gopher site is a one-stop source for executive branch documents. Although the first thing people think of when they think of the executive branch is the White House, this branch of government contains dozens of agencies, as well. The agencies range from the Department of Agriculture to the Veteran's Administration, to include all groups that report to the president, rather than to Congress or the judiciary.

NOTE

See chapter 11, "The Branches of Government," for more information about the Executive Branch.

The Executive Branch directory contains links to resources from all of these organizations (see fig. 13.3). The Federal Reserve System's directory contains subdirectories for each of the Federal Reserve banks, the Federal Reserve Board of Governors, and an index of Federal Reserve documents in print. Opening one of these directories

leads you to related documents, such as Federal Reserve Bulletins and various studies.

The Thomas Legislative Information Service— Congressional Documents

`http://thomas.loc.gov`

On January 5, 1995, Newt Gingrich introduced the Thomas Legislative Information service, a World Wide Web link to documents and information from Congress (see fig. 13.4). Incorporating the pre-existing House of Representatives Gopher site, Thomas provides an easy-to-use interface to the full text of all House and Senate bills, the Congressional Record, and other resources.

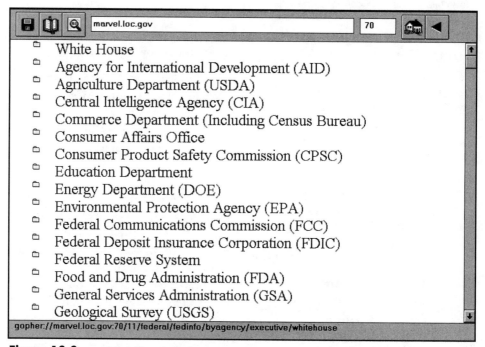

Figure 13.3 `gopher://marvel.loc.gov`
Executive Branch directories on LC Marvel.

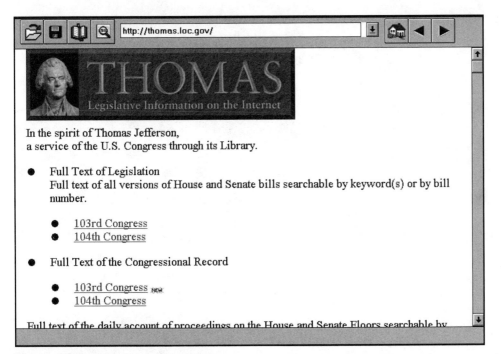

In the spirit of Thomas Jefferson,
a service of the U.S. Congress through its Library.

- **Full Text of Legislation**
  Full text of all versions of House and Senate bills searchable by keyword(s) or by bill number.

  - 103rd Congress
  - 104th Congress

- **Full Text of the Congressional Record**

  - 103rd Congress *NEW*
  - 104th Congress

Full text of the daily account of proceedings on the House and Senate Floors searchable by

Figure 13.4 `http://thomas.loc.gov`
The Thomas Legislative Information Service.

The service was an instant success. In the first four days, over 28,000 people visited the site. Besides searching for bills and browsing the Congressional Record, visitors can send e-mail to members of Congress and learn about the rules and processes by which laws are made. Future plans call for integration of bill digests, summaries, and chronologies of legislation with the full text of bills.

Thomas also provides two links to the Library of Congress. One link goes to the library's Web page, and the other takes users to LC MARVEL, the Library of Congress Gopher site.

 The Senate Gopher

`gopher://gopher.senate.gov`

The U.S. Senate Gopher site is run by the Office of the U.S. Senate Sergeant at Arms and the Senate Committee on

The Library of Congress

The Thomas Legislative Information Service and the Executive Branch documents page at LC MARVEL have something in common (besides being sources of government documents). Both are part of the Library of Congress (LOC). The LOC is the largest library in the world, with vast resources and a seemingly limitless supply of information. The Library of Congress Web home page gives you some idea of the wealth of available online material (see fig.13.5).

As you can see, Thomas and LC MARVEL are just two facets of the library. The LOC maintains numerous exhibits and collections, with some of these online. Some of the exhibits available when this chapter was written are the Gettysburg Address, images from the Russian Church and Native Alaskan Cultures, and the Dead Sea Scrolls.

The LOC is housed in a massive old building that is itself a landmark. To find out more, you can look on the Famous Houses and Buildings list at:

WWW address: `http://www.co.arlington.va.us/houses.htm`

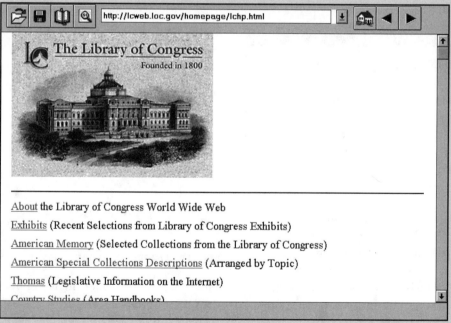

Figure 13.5 `http://lcweb.loc.gov/homepage/lchp.html`
The Library of Congress Web home page.

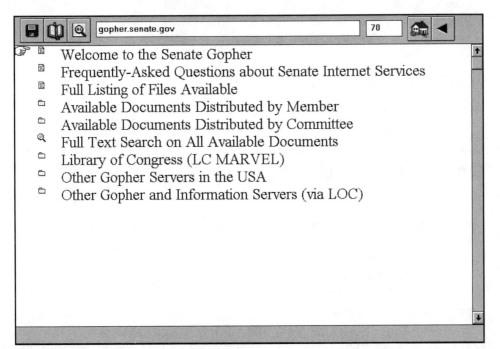

Figure 13.6 `gopher://gopher.senate.gov`
The top menu in the Senate Gopher.

Rules and Administration (see fig. 13.6). The site provides access to documents and other materials from the offices of many, but not all, senators.

The information here is divided into two main directories, Available Documents Distributed by Committees and Available Documents Distributed by Senator. I'll refer to them as the Committees and the Senators directories. Documents generated by a specific committee are found under the Committees directory, and documents from individual Senator's offices are found in the Senators directory.

Available Documents by Senator

The material in the Senators directory is divided into states, and from there into individual senators. When you look at this directory, you notice that not all the states, and therefore not all the senators, are represented. Because the documents are posted by the individual committees and Senator's offices, missing directories indicate that the responsible Senator's offices have not provided documents. For those offices that have provided documents, their documents are typically divided into press releases and general information.

Available Documents by Committee

The Committees directory is structured similarly, with individual committees represented by their own directories. The directories might be empty (like that of the Bipartisan Commission on

Entitlements and Tax Reform), or have press releases and other materials.

A search program lets users look for documents regardless of where they are located in the Gopher.

Nongovernment Document Archives

There are several reasons for the existence of nongovernment sources of government documents. One is to facilitate the use of the material for certain users. A good example of this is the Decisions of the U.S. Supreme Court Web page, maintained by the Legal Information Institute of the Cornell Law School. By gathering these decisions and converting them to hyperlinked documents, the site makes it easier for staff and students at the Institute (and visitors, too) to use the material.

Another reason to maintain separate collections of government documents is to sell the information, which is what Legi-Slate, Inc. does. By gathering and organizing material related to current legislation, Legi-Slate creates a product that people will pay for.

Other sites, such as the Internet Wiretap, maintain seperate collections as a public service. You can see what all three of these sites do with government documents in the following sections.

 Supreme Court Decisions

`http://www.law.cornell.edu/ supct/`

The Legal Information Institute (LII) of Cornell Law School is one of the prime Net locations to find Supreme Court decisions. The decisions are received on the day they are made. The staff at the LII integrates the decisions into an indexed, searchable, hypertext document, and makes them available to the public. Figure 13.7 shows the Decisions of the U.S. Supreme Court page.

The Cornell Law School's Supreme Court Decisions page covers from 1990 to the present. Decisions are indexed by topic. This indexing is extensive, with the decisions divided into almost 150 different topics. These decisions can also be searched by keyword, words in the case name, year, or docket number. A yearly index by Party Name is also provided. The decisions are actually located in an archive at Case Western Reserve University.

This page, and the LII site in general, has a number of other interesting resources. The page has links to two historic decisions: *Feist Publications, Inc. vs. Rural Tel. Serv. Co.* and *Roe vs. Wade.* Other pages at this site contain a hypertext version of the full text of the U.S. Code of Laws, as well as many other legal documents. Some Current interest items here include Lawyers on the Internet and Public Information on the National Information Infrastructure.

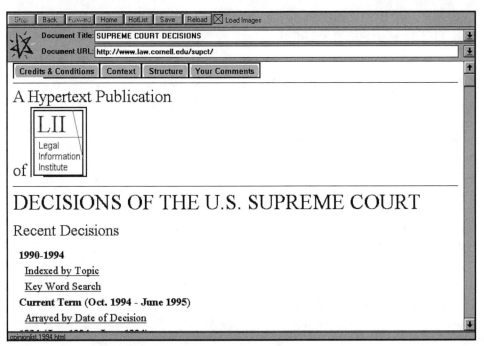

Figure 13.7 `http://www.law.cornell.edu/supct/`
Cornell Law School's Supreme Court Decisions page indexes Supreme Court decisions by topic.

 The Internet Wiretap

`gopher://wiretap.spies.com`

The Internet Wiretap is an unusual site. It is filled with a disparate collection of materials, ranging from government documents, to electronic books, to a "collection of useful and entertaining information, culled from UseNet and elsewhere, and arranged by subject." This section concentrates on the government documents.

The site has two separate directories for government documents. The first is for White House press releases, speeches, and press conferences. Like most other sites that carry this informa-

tion, it is displayed exactly as it comes from the government. The documents in this section are updated daily.

The other directory is entitled Govt. Documents (U.S. & World) and contains exactly that. Figure 13.8 shows some of the documents and subdirectories of additional documents that are found here.

The Internet Wiretap provides a search program that can access all the documents on the site. Users can also reach this site by anonymous FTP at:

> FTP address: `ftp://`
> `ftp.spies.com/Gov`

The Legi-Slate Gopher

`gopher://gopher.legislate.com`

The Legi-Slate Gopher provides strong coverage of federal legislative and regulatory bills, resolutions, and other documents. Run by Legi-Slate, Inc., the service combines free public access resources with subscriber-only resources. Subscribers choose to pay for this service because of the additional value it adds. This value is in the form of additional information related to the documents in question.

For each bill or resolution, the site provides up to 17 supporting documents, ranging from the names of the bills' sponsors to analyses and related articles. The related articles, when available, come from respected sources such as the *Washington Post* or the *Congressional Quarterly Weekly Report.*

The site covers every bill and resolution introduced in Congress since 1993. Its search program allows users to locate documents in several ways (see fig. 13.9). Users can search by date, issuing agency, title, and other methods. The specific search routines available depend on whether the user is a subscriber. As you might expect, in this and every other aspect of the Legi-Slate site, subscribers have more options and can get more information than nonsubscribers.

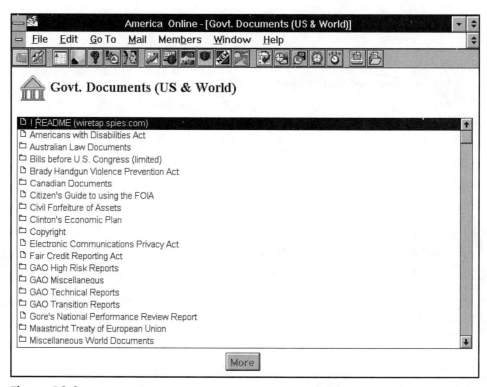

Figure 13.8 `gopher://wiretap.spies.com`
Some of the government documents available at the Internet Wiretap.

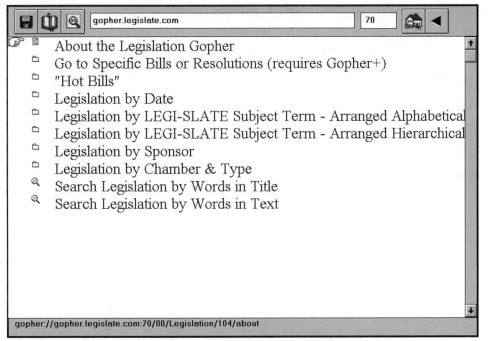

Figure 13.9 `gopher://gopher.legislate.com`
Searching the 104th Congress database on the Legi-Slate Gopher.

In addition to the Congressional documents, the site provides access to all of the regulations published in the Federal Register since January 3, 1994. The full text of the regulations, an official summary, and an abstract are included.

Laws and Government Documents on the Online Services

All three online services give you access to some government documents, but none comes close to the combined range of all the sites on the Net. America Online and Prodigy both carry documents released by the White House. These forums are nearly identical. In addition, the IRS and Compuserve have created a forum that can make tax time less stressful.

The Government Printing Office is a good source for documents that aren't on the Net. It has its own forum on CompuServe at:

> CompuServe address:
> **Go: CIS:GPO-1**

 CompuServe

Go: **CIS:TAXFORMS**

One of the least popular government documents is the tax form, and one of

```
┌──────────────────────────────────────────────────────────────────┐
│ ─ ☜     CompuServe Information Manager - [ IRS Tax Documents+ ]  ▾ ▲│
│ ─  File  Edit  Services  Mail  Special  Window  Help            ▲ │
│ ┌──────────────────────────────────────────────────────────────┐ │
│ │?│ Extended │♥│🔍│🌐│🚦│QUOTES│🐾│🖨│📄│▯│📖│ EXIT │👥│        │
│      7:10                                                         │
│  ☰  IRS Tax Documents+                                            │
│ ┌──────────────────────────────────────────────────────────────┐ │
│ │ Current Selection: 528 document(s)                           │ │
│ │ SEARCH SELECTION CRITERIA                                    │ │
│ │ Document Name/Description      [   ]                          │ │
│ │ Document Number               [   ]                          │ │
│ │ Revision/Publish Date         [   ]                          │ │
│ │ IRS Catalog ID #              [   ]                          │ │
│ │ Display Documents                                            │ │
│ │ Begin New Search                                             │ │
│ │                                                              │ │
│ │                                                              │ │
│ │           ┌────────┐          ┌────────┐                     │ │
│ │           │ Select │          │ Cancel │                     │ │
│ │           └────────┘          └────────┘                     │ │
│ └──────────────────────────────────────────────────────────────┘ │
└──────────────────────────────────────────────────────────────────┘
```

Figure 13.10 Go: CIS:TAXFORMS
Searching for tax forms.

the least popular things about tax forms is that you're always missing one. At the last minute, you end up scurrying around town, going from the post office to the library to the neighborhood accountant, trying to find that one darn form.

CompuServe, together with the IRS, has come up with the solution to this particular problem. They've created the Tax Forms forum. The Tax Forms forum allows you to download copies of every single tax form, as well as most of the instructions for them (see fig. 13.10). The files are in a special format that can be printed in a way that's acceptable to the IRS.

You need special software to do this job. The software is the Adobe Acrobat Reader. Thanks to Adobe Systems, Inc., the publisher, and RR Donnelley & Sons Company, the distributor, you can download the software from this forum, too. When you download and install the reader, you are ready to view and print any of the tax forms on just about any printer.

 AOL

Keyword: WHITE HOUSE

The White House forum on AOL is a good source for presidential press releases, speeches, and other current documents. The material comes from the White House Office of Media Affairs. When received, it is added to a searchable database and made available to forum visitors. Manual searches are also possible. Figure 13.11 shows some of the documents included in the Proclamations library, one of over a dozen categories found here.

The forum contains other document-related features, including the From the White House Library and the White House Library—Archived. These, respectively, contain current and somewhat older White House documents.

The documents here are usually longer than the ones found in the rest of the forum.

The White House Library also contains full copies of the Office of Management and Budget (OMB) reports on upcoming regulations. Each federal workday, the government issues a new report that describes pending and completed regulatory reviews. These reports give the status of each regulation and its Regulation Identification Number (RIN), a unique identifier for each regulation. This number can be used when seeking more information from the agency that issued the regulation.

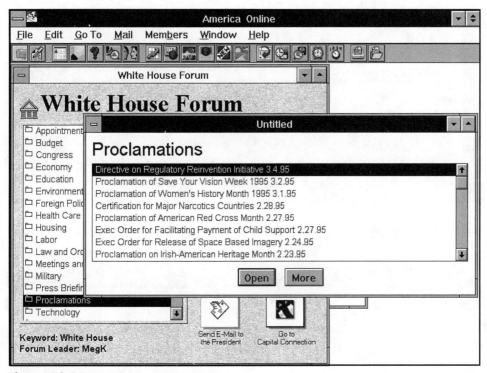

Figure 13.11 Keyword: WHITE HOUSE
Proclamations in AOL's White House forum.

Prodigy

Jump: WHITE HOUSE MEMO

When it comes to government documents, the White House Memo forum on Prodigy is similar to the White House forum on AOL. It, too, is a good source for presidential press releases, speeches, and other current documents. As with the AOL forum, the material here comes from the White House Office of Media Affairs. Prodigy divides the material into a half dozen categories, with an additional index for all of the categories. Automated searches can be run across any of the categories separately or across all the documents. You can do manual searches, too. Figure 13.12 shows some of the documents included in the news section.

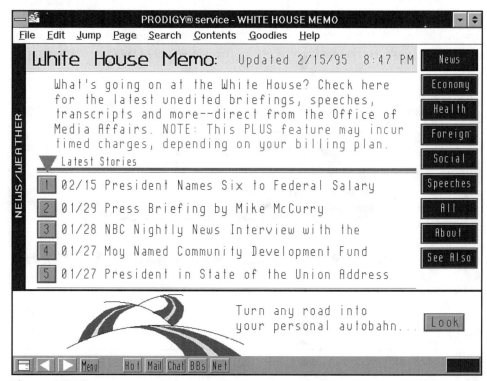

Figure 13.12 Jump: WHITE HOUSE MEMO
The news section of Prodigy's White House Memo forum.

Recommended Sites to See

The following list contains the addresses of locations where you can find laws and other government documents. The addresses are divided into sections, one section for each of the major sections of this chapter.

Each address is identified by its type and a short description of what you can find there. Many of these addresses are discussed in more detail in the body of this chapter; if you see one that looks interesting, skim through the appropriate section before logging on to the Net.

Newsgroups and Mailing Lists

The government documents discussion list.

UseNet address:
`bit.listserv.govdoc-l`

Supreme Court decisions.

UseNet address:
`courts.usa.federal.supreme`

Government Archives

The White House Publications page.

WWW address: `http://`
`www.whitehouse.gov/`
`White_House/Publications/`
`html/Publications.html`

The Library of Congress Marvel Gopher site.

Gopher address: `gopher://`
`lcmarvel.loc.gov`

Select the following directories:
`Government Information`
`Federal Information`
`   Resources`
`Federal Information at the`
`   Library of Congress`

The Thomas Legislative Information Service.

WWW address: `http://`
`thomas.loc.gov`

13

LAWS & OTHER DOCUMENTS

The Library of Congress home page.

WWW address: `http://lcweb.loc.gov/homepage/lchp.html`

The U.S. Senate Gopher.

Gopher address: `gopher://gopher.senate.gov`

The National Archives and Records Administration.

WWW address: `http://www.nara.gov/`

The Bureau of the Census.

WWW address: `http://www.census.gov/`

The Environmental Protection Agency.

WWW address: `http://www.epa.gov/`

The United States Postal Service.

WWW address: `http://www.usps.gov/`

The FedWorld home page.

WWW address: `http://www.fedworld.gov/#usgovt`

The White House home page.

WWW address: `http://www.whitehouse.gov/`

The U.S. budget.

Gopher address: `gopher://gopher.stat-usa.gov`

Select the following directory:
`Budget of the United States Government, Fiscal Year 1996`

The Department of Defense's Advanced Research Projects Agency.

WWW address: `http://www.arpa.mil/`

Famous houses and buildings, including the Library of Congress.

WWW address: `http://www.co.arlington.va.us/houses.htm`

Nongovernment Document Archives

Supreme Court decisions.

WWW address: `http://www.law.cornell.edu/supct/supct.table.html`

The Internet Wiretap.

Gopher address: `gopher://wiretap.spies.com`

Legi-Slate Gopher.

Gopher address: `gopher://gopher.legislate.com`

Searching the 104th Congress database.

Gopher address: `gopher://gopher.legislate.com`

Select the following directories:
`Legislation
(Bills & Resolutions)
104th Congress (1995-1996)`

Presidential and vice presidential press releases, statements, and addresses.

WWW address: `http://sunsite.unc.edu/govdocs.html`

The Government Page on Yahoo.

WWW address: `http:// www.yahoo.com/Government/`

The U.S. Code of Federal Regulations.

Gopher address: `gopher:// gopher.counterpoint.com 2001`

The U.S. Federal Register.

Gopher address: `gopher:// gopher.counterpoint.com 2002`

Government information resources index at the InfoMine.

WWW address: `http://lib- www.ucr.edu/govpub/`

The Government Printing Office.

CompuServe address: `Go: CIS:GPO-1`

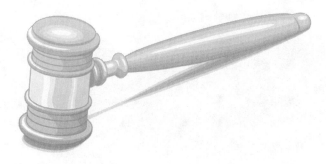

13

LAWS & OTHER DOCUMENTS

PART IV

The International Scene

Chapter 14
Political Hot Spots

Learn about political hot spots around the world, from Bosnia to Mexico's Zapatista rebellion.

In this chapter

- *Newsgroups and mailing lists about political hot spots*
- *Hot spots where the U.N. has troops*
- *Other political hot spots*

In other chapters

← *The United Nations in general is covered in Chapter 10.*

← *U.S. agencies and organizations that provide relief to political hot spots are covered in Chapter 10.*

The Net is a powerful way to make information about a situation available to the rest of the world. As we have seen in recent years, the eyes of the world can moderate the actions of governments and rebel forces. The sites examined in this chapter are using the Net to gain publicity for their cause and influence the behavior of the groups involved in the conflicts. Whether by newsgroup or colorful Web page, each of these sites is having some influence on the events it covers.

Newsgroups and Mailing Lists

While a colorful Web site is the flashiest way to provide information about a political hot spot, newsgroups and mailing lists can be a more efficient way to spread the word. They require fewer computer resources and are more quickly and easily updated than Web pages. Another advantage of newsgroups and mailing lists is that they allow others to comment and discuss the situation.

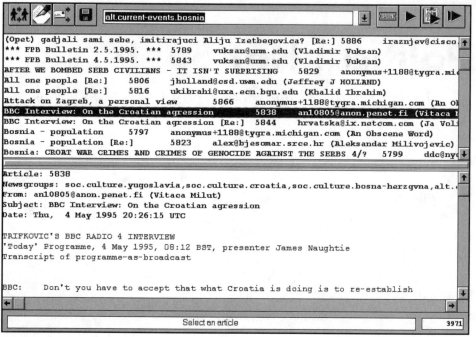

Figure 14.1 `alt.current-events.bosnia`
This current events newsgroup discusses Bosnia.

 **The Bosnian Current Events Newsgroup**

`alt.current-events.bosnia`

This newsgroup is for discussion of the war in Bosnia (see fig. 14.1). The threads in this newsgroup cover all elements of the war. There are personal accounts of the fighting, as well as reports from news agencies like the BBC. There are also more intense messages, accusing one side or the other of war crimes, even genocide. Most, but not all, of the messages are in English.

 Terrorism News Stories

`clari.news.terrorism`

The terrorism newsgroup consists solely of terrorism news stories from sources like the Associated Press. Since the recent bombing of the Edward P. Murrah Office Building in Oklahoma City, most of the stories deal with that. At other times, the stories deal with terrorism around the world. Recent stories have addressed issues like raids on busses in Burundi and the poison gas attacks in Japan. Some of the groups involved in the political hot spots in this chapter use terrorist tactics, so you might find stories about them here.

Hot Spots Involving the U.N.

The countries or regions covered in this section have one thing in common—they all have United Nations (U.N.) forces involved. The U.N. is involved in over two dozen peace-keeping actions around the world, and the presence of U.N. forces tends to focus world attention on the hot spots in which they are involved.

 The U.N. Peace-Keeping Operations Page

`http://ralph.gmu.edu/cfpa/`
`peace/toc.html`

This site contains information about past and present United Nations peace-keeping operations around the world (see fig. 14.2). It begins with a summary of all such U.N. operations from 1948 to 1994, detailing the human and financial costs of the U.N.'s role as a peace keeper.

After the general summary, the site provides a short summary of each of the operations in progress in December, 1994. These summaries list the name of the operation, its start date, cost, troop levels, and fatalities. The name of each operation is also a link to a more detailed report on that operation.

The amount of material in these reports varies, but they all have some common elements. Each report lists details such as the Security Council resolution that authorizes the mission,

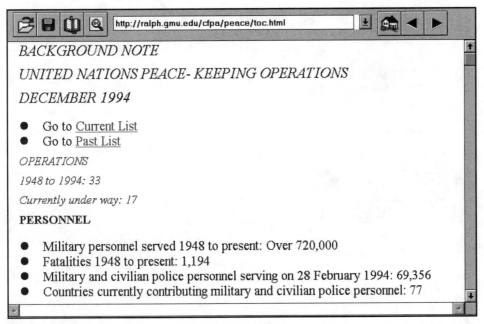

Figure 14.2 `http://ralph.gmu.edu/cfpa/peace/toc.html`
A list of U.N. Peace-Keeping operations.

the mandate for the mission, and which countries provide the forces for the mission. In addition, each report is linked to a map that shows the region for which the mission is responsible.

The amount of additional material varies from mission to mission. The report on UNMOT, the United Nations Mission of Observers in Tajikistan, is one page. The report on UNAMIR, the United Nations Assistance Mission for Rwanda, is 40 printed pages—and it's not even the largest report available at this site.

 Rwanda Crisis Web

`http://www.intac.com/`
`PubService/rwanda/index.html`

The Rwanda Crisis Web site is a public service of the INTAC Access Company, an Internet access provider (see fig. 14.3). The site draws on a wide variety of sources to provide as detailed a picture as possible of the events in Rwanda. Some of these sources include U.N. agencies, the Voice of America, and the Canadian Broadcasting Company.

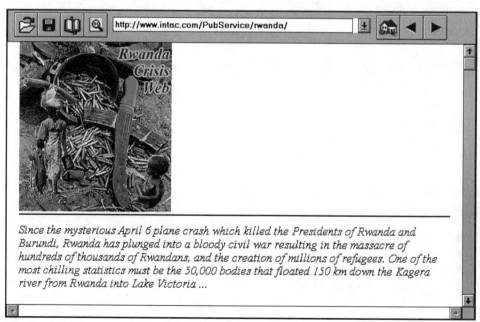

Since the mysterious April 6 plane crash which killed the Presidents of Rwanda and Burundi, Rwanda has plunged into a bloody civil war resulting in the massacre of hundreds of thousands of Rwandans, and the creation of millions of refugees. One of the most chilling statistics must be the 50,000 bodies that floated 150 km down the Kagera river from Rwanda into Lake Victoria...

Figure 14.3 `http://www.intac.com/PubService/rwanda/`
The Rwanda Crisis Web page provides a picture of what is happening in Rwanda.

Rwandan Relief Efforts

The Rwanda Crisis Web provides a link that helps interested people get involved in Rwanda relief efforts. The link takes you to a page that has links to over 30 U.S. based organizations involved in Rwanda. Figure 14.4 shows the start of the page.

For each organization listed, there is a description of the organization's activities in Rwanda, and instructions for contributing money. If you are interested in helping, you can follow the links from the Rwanda Crisis Web page, or browse directly to:

WWW address: `http://` `www.intac.com/PubService/` `rwanda/fund/index.html`

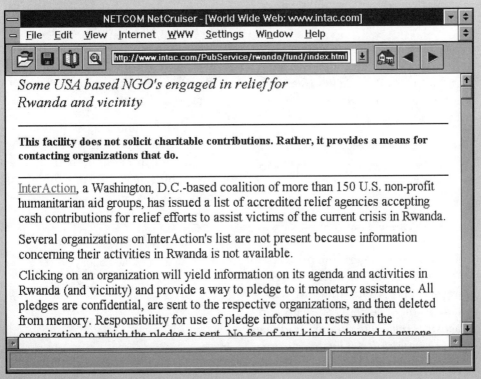

Figure 14.4 `http://www.intac.com/PubService/rwanda/fund/index.html`
Some Rwanda relief organizations accept donations.

The New Information section of the Rwanda Crisis Web page contains recent news and background reports from many sources, with the greatest single source being UNREO, the United Nations Rwanda Emergency Office. Each UNREO report runs several pages. The reports are compilations of information from sources like the Government of Rwanda and UNAMIR.

The April 27, 1995 UNREO report was the most recent when I visited this site. It deals with the needs of refugees, the status of relief centers, and medical information.

In addition to the New section, the Rwanda Crisis Web contains around 60 megabytes of Rwanda information. The information comes from dozens of sources including:

- The Voice of America (VOA)
- The Candian Broadcasting Corporation (CBC)
- Various United Nations Agencies
- Various relief agencies

The material ranges from press releases to emergency information and relief agency reports. Other resources include announcements of events and activities related to Rwanda, and maps of the country and neighboring areas. Much of the information is updated daily.

 The War in Bosnia—The Electronic Archive

http://www.essex.ac.uk/law/
human-rights/balkans/

The War in Bosnia—the Electronic Archives is designed to collect information on Bosnia and make it available in one location (see fig. 14.5). The material here comes from U.S. Government sources, international agencies, and regional sources. The page consists of numerous links to resources like the Bosnia home page, Activities of the Red Cross and Red Crescent Societies in former Yugoslavia, and the Zagreb Daily Bulletin. The age of the material here varies—some information is updated weekly, while other material is years out of date.

The Bosnia home page is an up-to-date source of information on the conflict in Bosnia—from the Bosnian perspective. It provides background information as well as current news. Some of the links here include:

- A brief history of the war
- Images of the tragedy
- Major war criminals/suspects
- Ljiljan, a weekly newspaper from Bosnia.

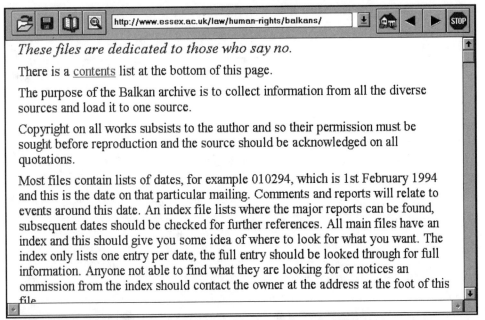

These files are dedicated to those who say no.

There is a contents list at the bottom of this page.

The purpose of the Balkan archive is to collect information from all the diverse sources and load it to one source.

Copyright on all works subsists to the author and so their permission must be sought before reproduction and the source should be acknowledged on all quotations.

Most files contain lists of dates, for example 010294, which is 1st February 1994 and this is the date on that particular mailing. Comments and reports will relate to events around this date. An index file lists where the major reports can be found, subsequent dates should be checked for further references. All main files have an index and this should give you some idea of where to look for what you want. The index only lists one entry per date, the full entry should be looked through for full information. Anyone not able to find what they are looking for or notices an ommission from the index should contact the owner at the address at the foot of this file.

Figure 14.5 `http://www.essex.ac.uk/law/human-rights/balkans/`
The War in Bosnia—the Electronic Archive, has all sorts of information about Bosnia.

NOTE

The War in Bosnia page provides a link that helps interested people get involved in Bosnia relief efforts. The link takes you to a page with links to numerous organizations involved in Bosnia. The page also contains instructions for sending food, money, and medical supplies to the country. If you are interested in helping, you can follow the links from the War in Bosnia page, or browse directly to:

WWW address: `http://www.essex.ac.uk/law/human-rights/balkans/comment/foodaid.html`

The Yellow Ribbon Home Page

`http://www.swaninc.com:80/yellowribbon/`

Although U.S. led forces defeated Iraq in the 1991 Gulf War, Saddam Hussein remained in power. Whether he is harassing U.N. inspectors or making threatening moves toward his neighbors, he remains a thorn in the side of the world. This site, the Yellow Ribbon home page, illustrates one of the many ways that Saddam and Iraq cause trouble (see fig. 14.6).

14

POLITICAL HOT SPOTS

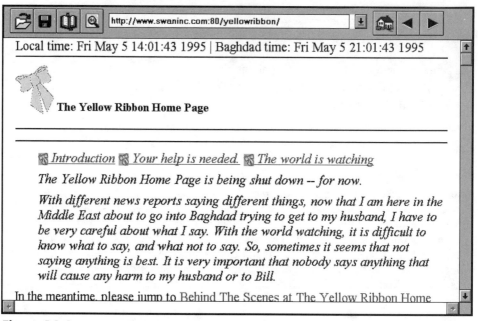

Local time: Fri May 5 14:01:43 1995 | Baghdad time: Fri May 5 21:01:43 1995

The Yellow Ribbon Home Page

Introduction *Your help is needed.* *The world is watching*

The Yellow Ribbon Home Page is being shut down -- for now.

With different news reports saying different things, now that I am here in the Middle East about to go into Baghdad trying to get to my husband, I have to be very careful about what I say. With the world watching, it is difficult to know what to say, and what not to say. So, sometimes it seems that not saying anything is best. It is very important that nobody says anything that will cause any harm to my husband or to Bill.

In the meantime, please jump to Behind The Scenes at The Yellow Ribbon Home

Figure 14.6 `http://www.swaninc.com:80/yellowribbon/`
The Yellow Ribbon home page provides support for two Americans held captive in Iraq.

The Yellow Ribbon page was created for two reasons: to remind the world of the fate of two Americans, David Daliberti and Bill Barloon, who took a wrong turn and ended up in Iraq; and to allow Kathy, the wife of David, to attempt to speak directly to Iraqi officials via the Net.

On May 5, 1995, the page was being temporarily shut down. At that time, Kathy Daliberti was in the Middle East preparing to go to Baghdad, and wanted to ensure that nothing appeared on the Yellow Ribbon page that might irritate the Iraqis. Perhaps by the time you read this, the page will be back up with word that the men have returned home safely.

> **NOTE**
>
> Kathy Daliberti asks that you contact your Senators, Representatives, and the President on behalf of her husband. To make that easier, the Yellow Ribbon page has special links at the end of every page. These links take you to tools that search for the e-mail addresses of Congressmen. Another tool provides a form for sending e-mail to President Clinton.

Other Political Hot Spots

This section of the chapter looks at political hot spots where the United Nations is not involved. One of the sites, the EZLN page, was created by one person to support the Zapatistas cause. It shows how the Net empowers individuals to have an effect on events around the world.

YA BASTA!—The EZLN Page

`http://www.sccs.swarthmore.edu/`
`~justin/Docs/ezln/ezln.html`

EZLN is an acronym for the Zapatista National Liberation Army, the revolutionary forces battling the government of Mexico. The EZLN page is designed to provide information about, and support for, the EZLN (see fig. 14.7).

The EZLN page provides background information on the people and philosophy of the Zapatistas, as EZLN members are called. Links can take you to reports on Comandante Ramona and Subcomandante Marcos, leaders of the EZLN. Another provides a biography of Emiliano Zapata, the dead revolutionary who provided the inspiration for the EZLN. The EZLN Communiqués link leads to dozens of messages issued by the leadership of

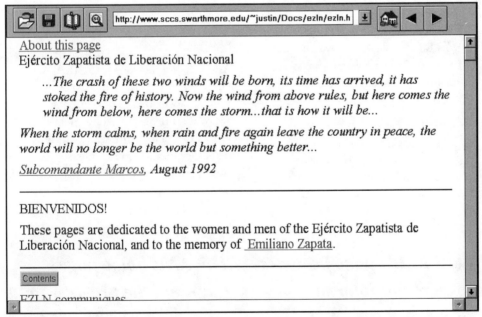

Figure 14.7 `http://www.sccs.swarthmore.edu/~justin/Docs/ezln/ezln.html`
YA BASTA!—The EZLN page, is dedicated to the Zapatista revolution in Mexico.

the Army, addressing their objectives and demands.

The EZLN frequently asked question (FAQ) file can also be reached from the home page. This file contains the answers to several common questions about the EZLN, including the Army's demands and its makeup. The FAQ describes the ideology of the EZLN as postmodern—a mix of Marx and other writers.

NOTE

If you believe that, contrary to what the world's media are reporting, the Mexican government is oppressing and exterminating the people of Chiapas, the Mexican Exiles for Democracy would like to hear from you. They are soliciting money for the State Democratic Assembly of the People of Chiapas. If you want to contribute, you can get more information at:

WWW address: `http://www.sccs.swarthmore.edu/~justin/Docs/ezln/mepd-donations.html`

THE EZLN page provides background information on the people and philosophy of the Zapatistas.

The ANC Information Page

`http://www.anc.org.za`

Apartheid has been abolished in South Africa, and the African National Congress is now the majority party in a Government of National Unity, but peace still eludes South Africa. The ANC home page provides a glimpse into the majority party and news of the progress and problems of the country (see fig. 14.8).

At this time, the most useful resource on the page is the News From South Africa link. Every day, news stories are gathered from the wires of the South African Press Association and linked to the ANC page. A short summary appears for each story, with a link to the entire article.

Another link takes you to the ANC Gopher, which contains ANC documents, Government documents, and reports on programs. The specific contents of the Government document directory include press releases, speeches, copies of legislation, and more.

The ANC home page examines the problems and progress of South Africa.

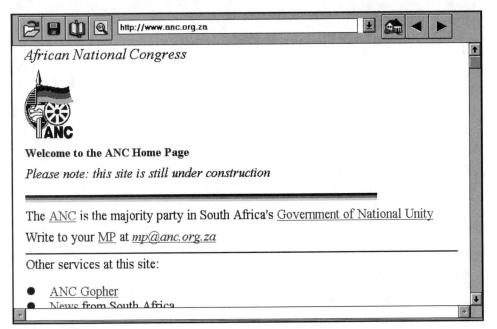

Figure 14.8 `http://www.anc.org.za`
The ANC Information Page covers progress and problems in South Africa.

 The Free Burma Home Page

`http://www.interactivist.`
`virtualvegas.com/`
`freebrma/freebrma.html`

According to the Free Burma home page, Burma has been under martial law since 1962 (see fig. 14.9). The page exists to disseminate information about the plight of the Burmese people, in hopes of eliminating the military government.

The primary resources at this site are news reports from the BurmaNet electronic newspaper and other sources. Since the page changes as the news changes, you won't find the same reports described here, but the reports

can give you an idea of the kinds of things you will find when you visit the page.

> **NOTE**
>
> The author of the Free Burma page is soliciting virtually any kind of support. If you would like to help out, you can send e-mail requesting more information to:
>
> **freeburma@pobox.com**

The most recent report describes Burmese forces crossing into Thailand to destroy Burmese refugee camps. A link to the April 30, 1995 edition of the BurmaNet News provides more details.

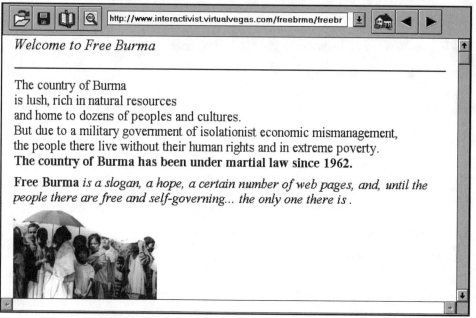

Welcome to Free Burma

The country of Burma
is lush, rich in natural resources
and home to dozens of peoples and cultures.
But due to a military government of isolationist economic mismanagement,
the people there live without their human rights and in extreme poverty.
The country of Burma has been under martial law since 1962.

Free Burma *is a slogan, a hope, a certain number of web pages, and, until the people there are free and self-governing... the only one there is .*

Figure 14.9 `http://www.interactivist.virtualvegas.com/freebrma/freebrma.html`
The Free Burma home page disseminates information about the plight of the Burmese people.

Besides the news reports, the page maintains links to Interviews with Burmese civilians, lists of companies that do business with Burma, and links to other information sources.

Political Hot Spots on the Online Services

The level of coverage for international hot spots varies greatly from service to service. CompuServe has the most extensive coverage, followed by America Online. I was unable to find any significant coverage of hot spots on Prodigy.

 The International Issues Message Board on AOL

Keyword: CAPITAL

The International Issues discussion area in the Capital Connection contains threads covering many political hot spots (see fig. 14.10).

In general, the messages here are controlled, with little of the ranting and flaming that you might expect to find associated with controversial issues.

The Global Crisis Forum on CompuServe

Go: `CIS:CRISIS`

The Global Crisis forum is the place to go when you want information on political hot spots. The forum provides discussion areas and libraries for each major topic covered. Two of the hot spots you looked at earlier in the chapter, Bosnia and Iraq, have their own topics, hence their own discussion areas and file libraries. Figure 14.11 shows some of the files in the Bosnia library.

As you can see in the figure, the libraries contain a range of information—everything from photos of people in Zagreb to a copy of the UNPROFOR's mandate.

Hot spots that don't have their own topics will fit into other sections. There are topics for the major geographic regions of the earth, as well as a general questions area. Other features of the forum include a natural disasters section, coverage of global business and communications, an area to discuss the impact of the media on crises, and more.

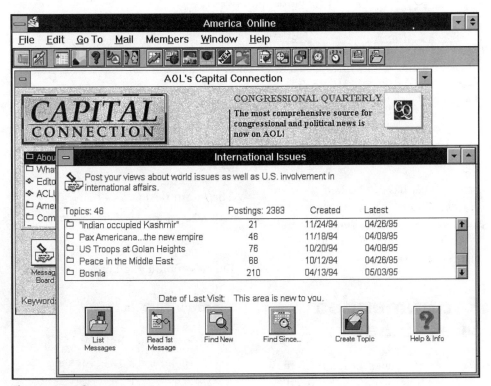

Figure 14.10 Keyword: CAPITAL
The International Issues message board.

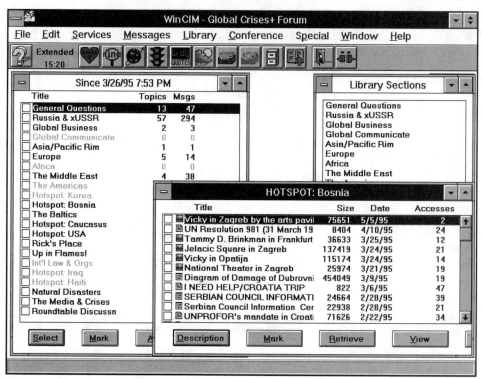

Figure 14.11 Go: CIS:CRISIS
The Global Crisis forum on CompuServe

 Prodigy

Prodigy only has the limited coverage
of international hot spots you get in
news services (**Jump: News**) and the
White House Memo area (**Jump:
White House**).

Recommended Sites to See

The rest of this chapter is a list. This list
contains the information you need to
reach the sites listed in this chapter, as
well as related sites.

Newsgroups and Mailing Lists

The war in Bosnia.

UseNet address: `alt.current-events.bosnia`

Burmese politics and more.

UseNet address:
`soc.culture.burma`

Discussions of the Gulf War.

UseNet address: `alt.desert-storm`

News stories on terrorism.

> UseNet address: `clari.news.terrorism`

Kuwaiti politics and culture.

> UseNet address: `alt.culture.kuwait`

News stories about Iraq.

> UseNet address: `clari.world.mideast.iraq`

Hot Spots Involving the U.N.

A list of U.N. peace-keeping missions.

> WWW address: `http://ralph.gmu.edu/cfpa/peace/toc.html`

The Rwanda Crisis Web.

> WWW address: `http://www.intac.com/PubService/rwanda/`

The War in Bosnia —The Electronic Archive.

> WWW address: `http://www.essex.ac.uk/law/human-rights/balkans/`

The Yellow Ribbon home page.

> WWW address: `http://www.swaninc.com:80/yellowribbon/`

Under the Volcanoes, a Rwanda report.

> WWW address: `http://www.ifrc.org/rwanda/contents.html`

The U.N. peace-keeping Gopher.

> Gopher address: `gopher://gopher.undp.org`
>
>> Select the following directories:
>> `The United Nations, What it is,...`
>> `United Nations Peace-Keeping Operations`

Women for Women in Bosnia.

> WWW address: `http://www.embassy.org/wwbosnia/wwbosnia.html`

Hot Spots That Don't Involve the U.N.

YA BASTA!—The EZLN page.

> WWW address: `http://www.sccs.swarthmore.edu/~justin/docs/ezln/ezln.html`

The ANC home page.

> WWW address: `http://www.anc.org.za/`

The Free Burma home page.

> WWW address: `http://www.interactivist.virtualvegas.com/freebrma/freebrma.html`

An interview with Subcomandante Marcos.

> WWW address: `http://www.igc.apc.org/nacla/zaps/ezln.html`

The ANC Gopher.

> Gopher address: `gopher://gopher.anc.org.za`

14

POLITICAL HOT SPOTS

Chapter 15

Other Interesting International Locations

A grab bag of interesting international locations

In this chapter

- *Getting the news on interesting international sites*
- *Interesting international sites on the Net*
- *International sites on the online services*

In other chapters

← *If you're interested in Japan and its Industry of Trade, you may be interested in the Treaties section of Chapter 9.*

← *The U.S. environmental coverage in Chapter 7 might interest readers of the Australian Wildlife Protection Agency section.*

This chapter is the last political one in the book. Politics can be serious, and, as we saw in the previous chapter, brutal. This chapter isn't like that. It's actually a grab bag of interesting or fun political sites. Hopefully, reading this chapter will get you out of the depression the previous chapter put you into.

The chapter has the same general shape as earlier ones, except that many of the sites here are hard to categorize politically. In general, the more serious sites are in the beginning of the chapter, and the fun ones are toward the end.

Newsgroups and Mailing Lists

This section covers newsgroups and mailing lists that discuss the politics of specific countries or international politics on a global scale.

 Russian Current Events

`alt.current-events.russia`

This newsgroup's name says it all: it's a place to discuss current events in Russia. Figure 15.1 shows some typical threads and part of a message from this newsgroup.

 **Conspiracies**

`alt.conspiracy`

This is the place to go for discussions of conspiracies of every sort. Mind control, alien abductions, cattle mutilation, and various political conspiracy theories show up here. You need an open mind for this discussion group.

Interesting International Sites on the Net

I've selected six Net sites for this section. Each one sparked my interest in

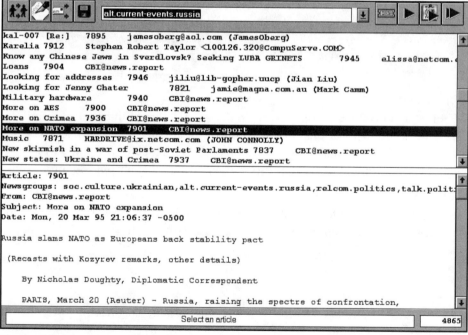

Figure 15.1 `alt.current-events.russia`
The threads cover all sorts of topics, from surplus military hardware, to NATO activities, to looking for a friend.

its own way. The Japanese Executive Branch is here because of Japan's status as our top economic competitor. The Center for World Indigenous Studies is included to show the high-tech nations are not the only ones taking advantage of the Net.

Friends & Partners, a joint effort by American and Russian citizens, illustrates the ways that the Net allows people to work together directly, without waiting for their governments. The World Constitutions Gopher site lets visitors compare the fundamental written laws that are supposed to govern the behavior of nations. The Australian Wildlife Protection Authority is here because I was curious how the Australians preserve their unique plant and animal species.

The Japanese Executive Branch

`http://jw.stanford.edu/GOV/`
`CABINET/cabinet.html`

The Japanese are our greatest economic competitors and allies. The Japanese government, like our own, has begun moving resources onto the Net, allowing you to see how their government compares to our own.

The Japanese Cabinet is part of their Executive Branch (see fig. 15.2). It's divided into 12 ministries, the most famous of which is the Ministry of International Trade & Industry (MITI). MITI is frequently cited as a successful example of industrial planning, and held up as a model for the rest of the world to emulate. Other ministries include Justice, Foreign Affairs, and Health and Welfare. There's also a link to the Prime Minister's office.

The Prime Minister's Web page covers the organization and mission of the office. It describes the 14 Commissions and Agencies reporting to the office, and features a structure map (an organization chart) that shows how everything interrelates. In the future, this page will include more information—things like the office's budget, staff, and activities.

The Center for World Indigenous Studies

`http://www.halcyon.com/FWDP/`

The principle that guides the activities of the Center for World Indigenous Studies (CWIS), a nonprofit research and education organization, is summed up in their introduction:

> Access to knowledge and peoples' ideas reduces the possibility of conflict, and increases the possibility of cooperation between peoples on the

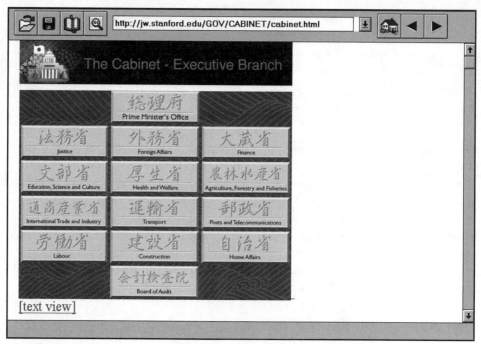

Figure 15.2 `http://jw.stanford.edu/GOV/CABINET/cabinet.html`
The Japanese Cabinet on the Web.

basis of mutual consent. By democratizing relations between peoples, between nations and states, the diversity of nations and their cultures will continue to enrich the world.

> **NOTE**
>
> You can find a copy of the Japanese Constitution, imposed by the U.S. after World War II, at the World Constitutions Gopher site described later in the chapter.

Founded in 1984 by Rudolph C. Ryser of the Cowlitz Tribe, and Chief George Manuel of the Shuswap Nation, the Center seeks to foster "wider understanding and appreciation of the ideas and knowledge of indigenous peoples."

To achieve its goals, the Center gathers, stores, and distributes the written and spoken words of leading contributors from indigenous peoples. The CWIS home page on the Web is one of the distribution points (see fig. 15.3). The page links to the Fourth World Documentation Project (FWDP), which is the actual distribution point for documents. The FWDP page maintains six archives of documents; you can search them by keyword.

The page also has information on other CWIS projects. One project involved the CWIS in relations between the Russian Federation and the more than 65 nations within that federation.

This project resulted in CWIS participation in the Moscow Conference on Indigenous Peoples in 1993. Other projects have taken place in the United States, Canada, Nicaragua, and at the United Nations.

 Friends and Partners

`http://april.ibpm.serpukhov.su/`
`friends/`

From the end of World War II, the United States and the Union of Soviet Socialist Republics—Russia and a number of smaller states—were enemies. With thousands of nuclear missiles aimed at each other, and proxy wars raging around the world, there seemed little chance that the people of the U.S. and Russia could ever become friends. But the USSR is gone, and Russia is an independent nation. Although the leaders of both nations are still squabbling over policy and aid issues, the people have taken things into their own hands. One result is the Friends and Partners Internet Information Service.

To fulfill the goals of better understanding between the people of the U.S. and Russia, the Friends and Partners page provides information—geography, history, literature, and much more from each country (see fig. 15.4).

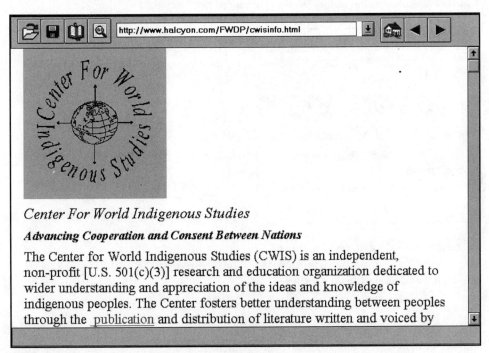

Figure 15.3 `http://www.halcyon.com/FWDP/cwisinfo.html`
The Center for World Indigenous Studies Web site.

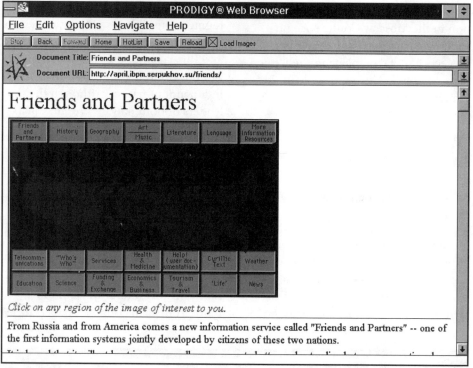

Figure 15.4 `http://april.ibpm.serpukhov.su/friends/`
The Friends and Partners Web page.

The Friends and Partners server provides access to a wide range of information. There is academic and statistical data like Russian and American demographics. There's also art, poetry, literature, and much more. Links to works by Dostoyevsky and Tolstoy are there alongside Twain and literature from around the world.

Other links connect to other resources. Visitors can read the *St. Petersburg Press,* a weekly newspaper. A side trip to a server dedicated to the Ukraine provides information on one of Russia's most important neighbors. For those interested in one of the world's worst nuclear disasters, the Chernobyl accident database is just a click away. Many other resources await the visitor as well.

The World Constitutions Gopher Site

`gopher://wiretap.spies.com`

Once connected, navigate through the following directories:

```
Government Docs (US & World)
World Constitutions
```

Have you ever wondered how the U.S. Constitution compares to those of other countries? If so, this Gopher site is for you. The World Constitutions directory on the Internet Wiretap Gopher contains over two dozen constitutions from various nations and eras (see fig. 15.5). The Constitution of the United States is there, of course. So are the equivalent documents for Australia, Canada, Japan, and other democracies.

A number of more unusual constitutions are also included. Recent documents include the Constitutions of the People's Republic of China and the USSR. Historic texts such as the Magna Carta, the 300-year-old English Bill of Rights, and the Constitution of the Iroquois Nations give the collection additional depth.

The World Constitutions directory contains over two dozen constitutions.

Figure 15.5 `gopher://wiretap.spies.com`
The World Constitutions directory.

Vladimir I. Lenin

Lenin, who lived from 1870 to 1924, was the leader of the Russian revolution, and the first leader of the USSR.

Now that the Soviet Union has collapsed, Lenin seems to be a *persona non grata*. Even the city of Leningrad has reverted to its original name, St. Petersburg.

Lenin's name does still appear on the Net. I found him mentioned in a critique of a book about the fall of the Soviet Empire, as well as in the writings of organizations like the Workers World Party. But the most unusual place that I found Lenin's name on the Net is at the Czar Bazaar (see fig. 15.6).

As you can see from figure 15.6, the political Matryoshka dolls are designed to honor Soviet and Russian leaders. Lenin, being the first Soviet leader, is the smallest doll and nests inside all the others.

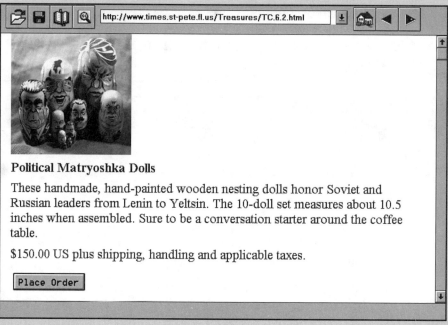

http://www.times.st-pete.fl.us/Treasures/TC.6.2.html

Political Matryoshka Dolls

These handmade, hand-painted wooden nesting dolls honor Soviet and Russian leaders from Lenin to Yeltsin. The 10-doll set measures about 10.5 inches when assembled. Sure to be a conversation starter around the coffee table.

$150.00 US plus shipping, handling and applicable taxes.

Place Order

Figure 15.6 `http://www.times.st-pete.fl.us/Treasures/TC.6.2.html`
Political Matryoshka Dolls at the Czar Bazaar site.

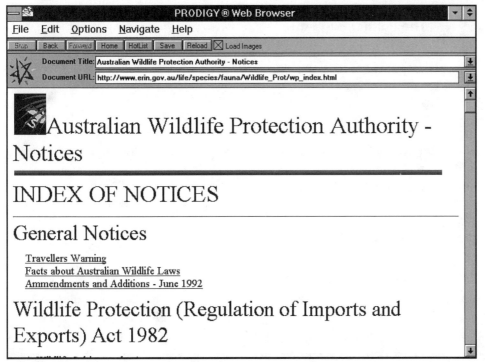

PRODIGY® Web Browser

File   Edit   Options   Navigate   Help

Stop | Back | Forward | Home | HotList | Save | Reload | ☒ Load Images

Document Title: Australian Wildlife Protection Authority - Notices

Document URL: http://www.erin.gov.au/life/species/fauna/Wildlife_Prot/wp_index.html

Australian Wildlife Protection Authority - Notices

INDEX OF NOTICES

General Notices

Travellers Warning
Facts about Australian Wildlife Laws
Ammendments and Additions - June 1992

Wildlife Protection (Regulation of Imports and Exports) Act 1982

Figure 15.7 http://www.erin.gov.au/life/species/fauna/Wildlife_Prot/
wp_index.html
The Australian Wildlife Protection Authority Web site.

**Australian Wildlife
Protection Authority**

`http://www.erin.gov.au/life/`
`species/fauna/Wildlife_Prot/`
`wp_index.html`

Australia is the home of some of the world's most unusual creatures. Kangaroos, emus, and koalas are exotic critters that could be valuable to smugglers. The Australian Wildlife Protection Authority is the guardian of the country's plants and animals, and is featured here.

Although the Authority might seem like a strange choice for a chapter on international politics, it isn't. Aside from being a political organization itself, much of the Authority's work deals with imports and exports of plants and animals. The rules and regulations that govern these activities are determined politically.

The Australian Wildlife Protection Authority Web page is an index of notices, laws, and trade rules (see fig. 15.7). The rules define what can and can't be hunted, imported, or exported. The emu is just one of over a thousand species of plants and animals that are protected. This is also the place to find out about permits for products made from Australian plants and animals.

The Politics Page on Sumeria

http://werple.mira.net.au/
sumeria/politics.html

The parties and organizations examined throughout this book are all legitimate. You can prove they exist, and they make their goals known. You may not agree with them, and some of them may have hidden agendas in addition to their stated goals, but in general, they are what they appear to be.

Some people believe in another kind of political organization. They believe that secret organizations composed of the rich and powerful plan world domination, and in fact already control much of what happens in the world. These people speak of groups like the Bilderbergers, so powerful that the media doesn't even acknowledge their existence. Another favorite is the Trilateral Commission, a real organization, accused of secretly working to subvert U.S. independence and curtail democracy in the name of profits. These people are conspiracy theorists.

The Politics page at the Sumeria Web site is a collection point for conspiracy theories (see fig. 15.8). Here you learn about the Trilateral Commission's plans, find out who the Bilderbergers are, and explore alleged links between

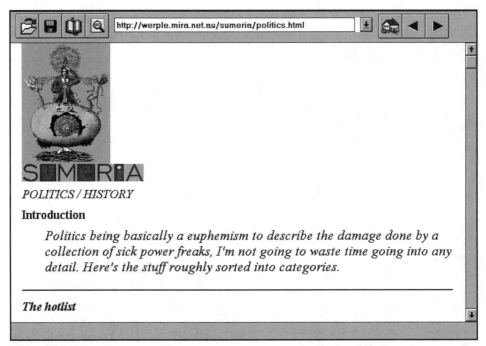

Figure 15.8 http://werple.mira.net.au/sumeria/politics.html
The Sumeria Politics Page on the WWW.

ex-Nazis, the Rockefellers and the UN. Did you think that the Federal Emergency Management Agency was just a harmless government bureaucracy? This site tells you the alleged "truth" about FEMA.

Many other conspiracies and secrets can be explored here, too. The International Monetary Fund, George Bush's CIA involvement, and the bankers are all exposed. So are the occult practices of the Nazis, and the real reason for the A-bombing of Japan. Even the Kennedy assassination is solved here—according to conspiracy theorists.

Other Interesting International Locations on the Online Services

The online services all have some international coverage. Some of their international resources were covered in earlier chapters, and others can be found by searching for particular countries or regions. For this chapter I've included two locations, the World Community Forum on CompuServe, and the Canada Bulletin Board on Prodigy.

The politics page at the Sumeria Web site is a collection point for conspiracy theories.

 World Community Forum

Go: `CIS:WCOMMUNITY`

Even though it isn't strictly a political site, I'm really excited about CompuServe's World Community Forum (see fig. 15.9). The forum is designed as a meeting place where people from different nations can discuss all sorts of issues, including politics. What makes this forum exciting is how it helps people communicate.

The forum has German, French, Spanish, and English forums within it. When a member enters a message in the English forum, it is automatically translated into German, French, and Spanish, and posted in the appropriate forums. The translation is done by machine, and occurs almost instantly. It's sort of like the universal translators that let the people in Star Trek communicate with anyone they meet.

A Collection of "International Conspirators"

When you look into international political conspiracy literature, certain individuals and organizations appear again and again. Here is what I could find out about them.

The Bilderbergers. This group of powerful politicians, industrialists, and financiers is believed to have a secret agenda of world domination. Their plans supposedly call for the United States to subordinate itself to the United Nations, as one step toward a Bilderberger-directed world government. In reality, I can't find any evidence that this group exists.

The Council on Foreign Relations. The CFR was founded in 1921. Conspiracy theorists believe that its goal is to make the United States part of a Socialist world government. Most Presidents and Presidential Candidates in recent years are said to be CFR members, as are the leaders of every major media outlet, schools and universities, labor unions, the military, and so on. In short, if you believe the theories, almost every powerful person in America is secretly trying to subvert it.

The Trilateral Commission. The Trilateral Commission was formed in 1973. Its headquarters are in New York, and has just over 300 members. According to the Sumeria Political Page, the commission's goal is to divide the world into three sections for greater economic efficiency.

David Rockefeller. Billionaire founder of the Trilateral Commission. Often referred to in the literature as David Trismegistus. This apparently means David the thrice-greatest Rockefeller: scion of the House of Exxon, chair of Chase Manhattan Bank, controller of billions of trust fund dollars.

Aside from the parallel forums, the World Community Forum is structured like any other CompuServe forum. If you would like to talk about politics, travel, culture, or just about any other subject you can think of, with CompuServe members from around the world, this is the place to start.

Canada Bulletin Board

Jump: CANADA

The Canada Bulletin Board on Prodigy covers the full range of subjects, including politics. The Politics/Separation Subject deals with many topics, but the dominant one is Quebec and its

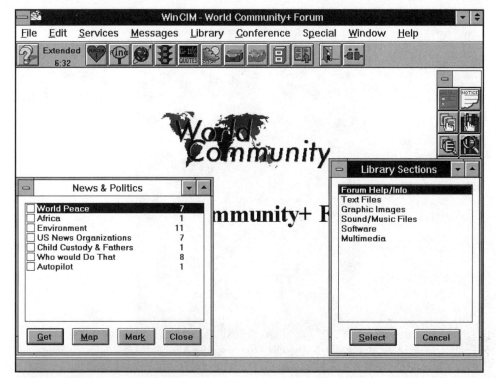

Figure 15.9 Go: CIS:WCOMMUNITY
The World Community Forum on CompuServe.

possible separation from the rest of Canada (see fig. 15.10).

The discussions that I saw on the Canada Bulletin Board were polite, with well-reasoned positions and statistics to back them up. One large thread applied the writings of Alvin and Heidi Toffler, in their book Global Paradox, to the Quebec situation. The writers seem very optimistic about the potential of their country, if only the Quebec problem can be resolved.

The Canada Bulletin Board has other subjects related to politics as well. One discusses the 1995 Canadian Budget, while another deals with the Royal Canadian Air Force.

Recommended Sites to See

The remainder of this chapter consists of the addresses of other interesting international political sites on the Net. The addresses are divided into sections that correspond to the major sections of this chapter.

Each address is identified by its type and a very short description of what you can find there. Many of these addresses are discussed in more detail in the body of the chapter; if you see one that looks interesting, skim through the appropriate section before logging onto the Net.

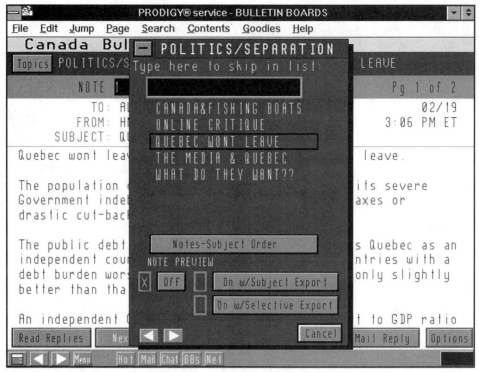

Figure 15.10 Jump: CANADA
The Politics/Separation Subject in the Canada Bulletin Board on Prodigy.

Getting the News

Current events in Russia.

> UseNet address: `alt.current-events.russia`

Conspiracy theories of every sort.

> UseNet address: `alt.conspiracy`

News of, and about, Japan.

> UseNet address: `clari.world.asia.japan`

JFK assassination theories.

> UseNet address: `alt.conspiracy.jfk`

Discussions of aboriginal people around the world.

> UseNet address: `soc.culture.native`

Russian cultural discussions.

> UseNet address: `soc.culture.soviet`

What's happening in the Ukraine.

> UseNet address: `alt.current-events.ukraine`

The Sumeria announcement mailing list.

> LISTSERV address: `sumeria-announce-request@werple.mira.net.au`

Interesting Political Sites

Japanese government organizations.

WWW address: `http://kiku.stanford.edu/GOV/gov.html`

The Japanese Executive branch.

WWW address: `http://jw.stanford.edu/GOV/CABINET.cabinet.html`

The Ministry of International Trade and Industry (MITI).

WWW address: `http://jw.stanford.edu/GOV/CABINET/MITI/home.html`

The Center for World Indigenous Studies (CWIS) home page.

WWW address: `http://www.halcyon.com/FWDP/cwisinfo.html`

The CWIS Fourth World Documentation Project home page.

WWW address: `http://www.halcyon.com/FWDP/fwdp.html`

The EnviroLink Indigenous Rights gopher.

Gopher address: `gopher://envirolink.org`

> Once connected, navigate through the following directories:
> `EnviroIssues...`
> `Indigenous Rights`

The World Constitutions gopher site.

Gopher address: `gopher://wiretap.spies.com`

> Once connected, navigate through the following directories:
> `Government Docs (US & World)`
> `World Constitutions`

A U.S. constitution reference library.

WWW address: `http://tomahawk.welch.jhu.edu:1080/constitution.html`

The Friends and Partners Internet Information Service.

WWW address: `http://solar.rtd.utk.edu/friends/home.html`

An online tour of the Kremlin.

WWW address: `http://www.kiae.su/www/wtr/kremlin/begin.html`

The St. Petersburg, Russia server.

WWW address: `http://www.spb.su/`

The Center for Civil Society International.

WWW address: `http://solar.rtd.utk.edu/friends/ccsi/ccsihome.html`

The Australian Wildlife Protection Authority.

WWW address: `http://www.erin.gov.au/life/species/fauna/Wildlife_Prot/wp_index.html`

The Sumeria Political page.

WWW address: `http://werple.mira.net.au/sumeria/politics.html`

An essay on the Trilateral Commission.

WWW address: `http://werple.mira.net.au/sumeria/politics/trilat.html`

The home page for Sumeria.

WWW address: `http://werple.mira.net.au/sumeria/`

An online bookstore for the conspiracy minded.

WWW address: `http://www.illuminet.com/~ron/inet.html`

PART V

Getting Going and Keeping Up

Chapter 16

Getting Going and Keeping Up on the Net

This chapter gives you a basic understanding of how to get started and keep up on the Internet.

In this chapter

- *What you need to get connected to the Internet*
- *Who provides access to the Internet*
- *What Internet software you need*
- *How to use addresses in this book*
- *How to find other political information on the Net*

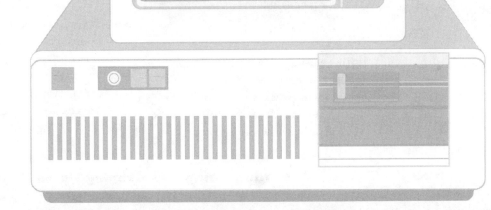

This chapter shows you how to use the software you'll need to find political information on the Net. Keep in mind that this chapter isn't designed as an exhaustive "How To." Instead, it's intended to get you off and running—from choosing a software package to actually dialing up and connecting with many different types of servers on the Internet. At the end of the chapter, several books are discussed that can take you further in the use of Internet software and methods.

Hardware for Connecting to the Net

The Internet began as a text-based medium, which required basic hardware. Today's Net, however, includes graphics, video, audio, and other multimedia components. To get connected and to use the Internet to its fullest, you need a system similar to the type listed here:

- A 486 computer
- 50 MHz or higher
- At least 25-50 MB of free disk space
- 8 MB of RAM
- At least a 14.4 V.32bis/V.42 modem (although 28.8 V.34 modems are already very affordable)
- A sound card
- A video card that will handle at least 256 colors
- Speakers
- A CD-ROM drive
- A mouse

If you're using a Macintosh, the preceding memory, hard-disk, CD-ROM, and modem requirements apply. Although you can do many things on the Net with a Mac Classic, it's recom-

mended that you use a higher-end machine such as the Quadra or PowerMac. Many of the audio and video capabilities you need are built in to the Macintosh.

Software for Connecting to the Net

Much of the information available on the Net is not accessible through a standard connection. In other words, you cannot dial up the Internet with the same modem software you use to call BBSs. For many of these tasks you need to establish a special connection that speaks TCP/IP (the language of the Internet). To do this, you need special software and a service provider that gives you a more direct link to the Internet.

Many commercial services offer their own software to help you establish a TCP/IP connection; they are discussed in the next section. If you already belong to a service provider and do not have access to TCP/IP software, more and more companies are offering dial-in Internet connections through software programs you can purchase at your local retailer. Still other Internet services offer prepackaged software that is already configured for you to use.

Service Providers

Once you have the right hardware and software, you still need a service provider. There are hundreds of service providers—both local and national—and more spring up every day. If you haven't signed up with a service provider, this section offers help.

What to Look for in a Service Provider

A service provider is nothing more than a company or organization that provides (usually for a fee) access to the Internet. Not all service providers are alike. Although they all provide the same service—a connection to the Internet—a number of variables come into play regarding what they allow you to access, how they charge for connecting, what extra services they provide, and many others factors. To find the best value and most capabilities, consider the following criteria:

- *Cost.* What is the bottom line cost for the service? A flat rate service is often a better deal than a per/hour service. Many providers offer an attractive fee but charge extra for connect time, amount of information downloaded, higher connection speeds, and direct PPP/SLIP access. It's very important to

find out all of the obvious and hidden costs when considering a provider.

- *Company Maturity.* It's important to know how much you can rely on a company. Find out how long it has been in business, the number of subscribers, and the number of connections. A mature company with a stable base of customers is probably a good choice.

- *Customer Support and Usability.* Once you sign on the dotted line, are you on your own? Do they have online help? Do they have a toll-free service? Can you instantaneously find out how much you've used the service at any given time? Most good providers have customer support. Also, many providers offer free trial subscriptions to see if you're happy with their services. In addition, you'll want to know how easy a system is to use. Do they provide an integrated menu that lets you access multiple functions from a central application? This can be determined when trying out their "free trial."

- *Connectivity.* It's very important to find out how a provider gives you access. Will you be able to dial a local number or a toll-free number? Make sure the provider has enough lines to support the necessary users, otherwise you may end up getting a busy signal. When talking to providers, ask them what percentage of the time their users get busy signals. If it's a high percentage, ask them if they plan on adding more lines in the future. Also ask what you can do once you're connected. Can you perform all the major functions of the

Net like Web-browsing, FTP, Gopher, and e-mail? And what type of interface does the company offer to complete these functions?

National Providers

Several national providers are listed in Table 16.1.

Providers with Custom Software

In an attempt to keep pace with commercial services such as America Online and CompuServe, some providers have developed their own interfaces to make using them easier. This section briefly looks at two such providers—Netcom, a national provider based in San Jose, and The Pipeline, out of New York City.

Netcom

Netcom offers a comprehensive package to connect to the Net called NetCruiser. NetCruiser is a Windows program and comes on one floppy disk that's easy to install. The software is free, but the service is $19.95 a month, with a $25.00 start up fee.

Table 16.1 Information on National Providers		
Provider	**Address & Phone Number**	**Services**
CERFNET	P.O. Box 85608 San Diego, CA 92186 800-876-2373	14.4 Dial-up SLIP/PPP Toll-free number
JvNCnet	3 Independence Way Berkeley, CA 94704 609-897-7300	14.4 Dial-up SLIP/PPP
PINET	500 Sunnyside Blvd. Woodbury, NY 11797 800-539-3505 or 206-455-3505	14.4 Dial-up SLIP/PPP Menu
Rocky Mountain Internet	2860 S. Circle Suite 2202 Colorado Springs, CO 80906 719-576-6845	14.4 Dial-up SLIP/PPP Toll-free number Menu

One attractive feature of NetCruiser is its connect time policy. The first 40 hours of prime time usage are included in the fee, and all off-peak hours are free (midnight to 9:00 a.m., and all day Saturday and Sunday). This policy is handy for someone who uses the Internet during off hours.

NetCruiser offers WWW, Gopher, FTP, UseNet, including the ClariNet **e.News** service, Telnet, and e-mail. Whereas you might have to go out and find a separate application to perform all of these tasks with other systems or providers—NetCruiser does it all from one application. This makes cruising the Net much easier.

To get more information about Netcom services, contact Netcom at:

> 3031 Tisch Way, Second Floor
> San Jose, CA 95128
> 408-983-5950, 800-353-6600
> Fax: 408-241-9145
>
> WWW address: **http://www.netcom.com/**

The Pipeline

All the software needed to use The Pipeline comes on a single disk that's simple to install. With The Pipeline, there are no hassles with trying to establish a special PPP or SLIP connection—they provide their own connection for you.

The Pipeline offers a free demo account for you to try before you decide to buy. If you decide to use it, accounts begin at about $15 a month. The Pipeline offers e-mail, FTP, online chatting, and Gopher service. Much of its interface is point-and-click and easy to use. As with Netcom, its single software interface successfully replaces separate applications so that you can cruise most places from within one application.

To find out more, contact The Pipeline at:

> 150 Broadway
> New York, NY 10038
> 212-267-3636
> 212-267-6432 (dial-up modem)
>
> WWW address: **http://www.pipeline.com**
> E-mail address: **info@pipeline.com**

How to Access Different Parts of the Internet

If you don't go with a commercial or national provider that supplies its own interface, you will need to get different software to access information in this book. This section tells you what you need, where to get it, and how to use the addresses in this book. In addition to the locations given for specific software, much of the software can be retrieved from Que's FTP site at **que.mcp.com** and at several other sites such as **wuarchive.wustl.edu** and **mac.archive.umich.edu**.

World Wide Web

The World Wide Web (also referred to as Web, WWW, or W3) is a hypertext system that makes jumping from link to link as easy as pointing and clicking. It's also the home for much of the political information on the Internet.

The hypertext format allows you to move to more specific information on your chosen topic, or you can move to another topic altogether by clicking a line of highlighted text.

To cruise the Web, you need a Web browser. Some browsers are better than others, but it should be obvious that a good Web browser is the most important tool for getting political information off the Net.

Web Browsers and Where to Get Them

There are many browsers available via the Internet. The two most popular are listed below.

- *NCSA Mosaic.* Mosaic, the original Web browser, is an excellent choice that offers many attractive features for Windows and Macintosh users. The Windows version is available at `ftp.cyberspace.com` in the directory `/pub/ppp/Windows/mosaic`. The Macintosh version is available at `scss3.cl.msu.edu` in the directory `/pub/mac`.

- *Netscape.* Netscape is a Windows and Macintosh browser that has a lot of people singing its praises. The Windows version is available at `ftp.halcyon.com` in the directory `/pub/slip/www/netscape`. The Macintosh version is available at `ftp.3com.com` in the directory `/netscape`. Netscape also offers many sites for both versions, including `ftp.netscape.com` in the directory `/netscape1.1`.

Using a Web Browser to Find URL Addresses

Every site on the Web can be identified by its URL (Uniform Resource Locator). Basically, a URL tells your Web browser where to find a particular Web site (in this book, a Web address is identified either by the World Wide Web icon or is preceded by "WWW address:").

Both browsers previously listed enable you to enter any URL to get to any page on the Web. Simply type the URL address you'd like and the browser takes you right to it. Another thing to remember is that URL addresses are case-sensitive. That means that if an address has capital letters, you need to use capital letters when typing it. For example, if you wanted to get to the Right Side of the Web page, you would type `http://www.clark.net/pub/jeffd/index.html` (see fig. 16.1).

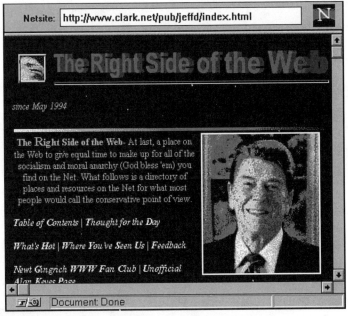

Figure 16.1 `http://clark.net/pub/jeffd/index.html`
Entering the Right Side of the Web's URL in NetCruiser instantly takes you to this web page.

 FTP

File Transfer Protocol (FTP) software enables you to receive (download) files from another computer and send (upload) files to another computer. These files can be anything from documents to complex audio/video files to software programs.

FTP Clients and Where to Get Them

Although Netscape can do FTP, it does have some limitations. For instance, you cannot upload files using Netscape. Most FTP clients offer many additional options that you might find useful if you use FTP a lot. Some good FTP clients for both Windows and Macintosh users are as follows:

- *WS_FTP.* This is probably the best Windows FTP program available. For a complete user's guide for WS_FTP, see Que's *Using FTP.* Among many sites, WS_FTP is currently available at **ftp.halcyon.com** in the directory **/pub/slip/ftp.**

- *Fetch.* The original Macintosh FTP client, Fetch offers a good user interface along with automatic decompression and execution of downloaded files. It can be found at **bitsy.mit.edu** in the directory **/pub/mac/fetch.**

- *Anarchie.* This is an excellent program that allows you to first locate programs (using an FTP search client called Archie) and then instantly access the FTP site once it has been found. This is an excellent program to use if you don't know exactly where a file is located—or even if you do. It can be found at **nic.switch.ch** in the directory **/software/mac /archive.**

Using an FTP Client to Find FTP Addresses

Using FTP with the new graphical-interface clients that are available has become very easy. When getting a file from an FTP site, there are several things to consider.

- You should first be aware of the FTP site, or *host name,* itself. This is the place you actually find the file.

- Know the *path,* or set of directories, that lead you to the file. For instance,

assume you would like to download some Libertarian Party press releases that are available at **ftp.digex.net/pub/access/ lphq/.** You would first tell your FTP client to find the host **ftp.digex.net.** You would then proceed through the **/pub, /access,** and **/lphq** directories.

- The last thing to be aware of is the *file type.* A plain text file (which often ends with **.txt** or **.doc**) can be downloaded as plain text. Most other files should be downloaded as binary data. For instance, if you see a directory with a file in it like **pub/music/ lyrics/text/highway66.txt,** the file can be downloaded as text. However, if a file has a different extension, such as the file found in the directory **/pub/music/ soundfiles/highway66.wav,** you should download the file as a binary. If you're unsure, download as a binary, since a binary download also can handle text data. All of the FTP clients listed in the previous sections enable you to define file type automatically or manually.

NOTE

When using FTP, you're a nobody—literally. All of the FTP sites in this book are referred to as *Anonymous FTP Sites.* This means that when you log on to the host, you enter **anonymous** as your user name. Also—although it isn't required—good etiquette dictates that you use your e-mail address as your password.

UseNet Newsgroups

Newsgroups probably contain more discussion and information than a thousand talk shows and magazines combined. They change almost constantly, with thousands of discussions occurring on hundreds of topics every day.

There are newsgroups covering every aspect of politics all over the Internet. Not only can you get current information from newsgroups, but you can let your opinions be known as well.

Newsreaders and Where to Get Them

Newsreaders help you sort through all of the daily messages that are posted. More than that, though, they help organize newsgroups so that you can easily pick out the topics that interest you. For complete coverage of newsgroups, see Que's *Using UseNet Newsgroups*. Although most web browsers, including Netscape, will read news, some of the more common newsreaders with expanded capabilities, such as on-the-fly decoding, follow:

- *WinVN*. This is one of the best Windows newsreaders available, enabling you to do just about everything with a click of your mouse. The most-recent version is available at **ftp.ksc.nasa.gov** in the directory **/pub/winvn/win3** (the most current version is **wv16_99_03.zip**).

- *NewsXpress*. NewsXpress is a new Windows entry into the newsreader business. Even though it's new, it already enjoys widespread popularity. You can currently find it at **ftp.cyberspace.com** in the directory **/pub/ppp/windows/newsreaders**.

- *Newswatcher*. This is the easiest-to-use and most-complete Macintosh Newsreader. The multi-window design helps you read news quickly and easily. It can be located at **ftp.switch.ch** in the **/software/mac/news** directory.

- *Nuntius*. This is another Macintosh Newsreader. It's probably not as widely used as Newswatcher, but it contains some attractive features. Nuntius is located at the same FTP site as Newswatcher (**ftp.switch.ch** in the **/software/mac/news** directory).

Using Newsreaders to Find UseNet Addresses

Once your newsreader is operational, newsgroups are very easy to locate and to read. Most of the political newsgroups reside in the **alt.** *hierarchy* of UseNet. A hierarchy is simply a way of organizing newsgroups in UseNet. Newsgroups about recreation are in the **rec.*** hierarchy; groups about computers are in the **comp.*** hierarchy, and so on.

If, for example, you wanted to read **alt.politics.usa.gov.foreign-affairs**, you would tell your newsreader to go to that group. Many newsreaders have a Find option that lets you look for a group by name. You may also run into a newsgroup while scrolling through all the possibilities.

Once you have found a newsgroup, subscribe to it (usually by selecting the group and choosing the Subscribe option in most newsreaders. After you've subscribed, you're off and reading.

There are a couple of things to keep in mind when finding, subscribing, and reading newsgroups.

- A lot of news servers don't carry many of the **alt.*** hierarchies due to the high traffic. If your news server doesn't carry a group mentioned in this book, contact your provider and request that they carry the group.

- You may want to *lurk* on newsgroups for a while before subscribing (that is, read some of the messages and get a feel for the group before you plunge in and start contributing articles).

- Remember that politics can be a very emotional topic—try to keep your cool.

 Gopher

Gopher is a means of finding your way around the Internet. It's called Gopher because it was set up at the University of Minnesota—the Golden Gophers—and because it's a way to *go for* files on the Internet.

Gopher was also probably the first non-command-line interface available on the Internet. Instead of using command lines to get you where you want to go, Gopher uses a menu-driven system. Getting from place to place is merely a matter of choosing a menu item.

Gopher Clients and Where to Get Them

Despite Gopher's relative ease of use, there are Gopher clients available that make Gophering even easier. They do so primarily through the use of a point-and-click GUI (Graphical User Interface) that is usually very similar to Netscape's. The two most popular Gopher clients follow:

- *Hgopher.* This is the most popular Gopher client for Windows. You can save electronic bookmarks and use Gopher by using your mouse. Hgopher is located at **ucselx.sdsu.edu** in the **/pub/ibm** directory.

- *TurboGopher.* TurboGopher is a simple Macintosh Gopher client that creates separate windows for each menu. Turbo Gopher can be found at **bitsy.mit.edu** in the **/pub/mac/ gopher** directory.

Using Gopher Clients to Find Gopher Addresses

Gopher addresses work much like FTP addresses. You need to find a Gopher address you would like to use as your home Gopher. In other words, you want to tell your client which Gopher menu you would like to have appear when you first start. Most Gopher clients usually have a preset home Gopher that the user can easily change.

Obviously, you'll want to access more than one Gopher site. There are two basic ways you want to do this:

- Gopher clients generally enable you to go to a Gopher site other than your home Gopher. Choose the menu option that enables you to put in the address of the Gopher site to which you'd like to go. This is the best method to use when first looking at a Gopher site.

For instance, if you wanted to view the World Constitutions Gopher site, you would tell your Gopher client to go to `wiretap.spies.com`. Once there, you would follow the **Government Docs (US & World)** link, which would take you to the World Constitutions.

- The second way to use Gopher sites is to make bookmarks in your Gopher client. Suppose you browse a Gopher site and decide you like it and will probably look at it again. Instead of writing down or remembering the address for future use, set a bookmark using the Gopher client. Once a bookmark has been set, you can instantly access that Gopher site again.

 ## Mailing Lists

E-mail is probably used more than any other function on the Internet. People use e-mail to communicate, transfer files, get information, and so on. While most e-mail is transferred between two individual users privately, there are also instances in which groups use e-mail in a more public way. One of those uses is the LISTS.

LISTSERVs (sometimes referred to as mailing lists) are very similar to newsgroups, with the exception that all LISTSERV discussion is delivered di-rectly to your mailbox. When you find the e-mail address of a LISTSERV, write a message to that address to subscribe to the list. From that point on, all e-mail discussion that is sent to that LISTSERV e-mail address will appear in your mailbox. To use a LISTSERV, you should have a good e-mail client.

E-Mail Clients and Where to Get Them

Surprisingly, there aren't many good e-mail clients out there for public use. One very good one does exist, though.

- *Eudora.* This is the most widely used Windows and Macintosh e-mail client. Although Eudora is now available commercially, a functional shareware version is still available. Eudora, both the commercial and shareware versions, is available for both Windows and Macintosh platforms.

> ### NOTE
> Shareware is software that enables you to use it free on a trial basis, after which you can pay a fee for its continued use and technical support.

The best place to get Eudora is from `ftp.qualcomm.com`. This FTP site is run by Qualcomm, the makers of Eudora. The Windows version can be found at **/quest/windows/eudora/ 1.4**. Version 1.4 is the latest shareware version. For the Macintosh version, go to **/quest/mac/eudora/1.5**.

Using E-mail Clients to Find Mailing List Addresses

As previously mentioned, when you use e-mail to get political information on the Net, you will probably be accessing LISTSERVs (or mailing lists). Using a LISTSERV is really quite easy. There are several important things to keep in mind, however.

- LISTSERVs usually have two addresses. One address is used to subscribe, obtain archives and help files, and so on. The other address is used to post messages to the rest of the subscribers.

- Always read the introductory message (and keep a copy) that you receive when you first subscribe to a LISTSERV. It could save you a lot of hassles.

- When you join a LISTSERV for the first time, check your e-mail every day for a few days after subscribing. This way, you'll know if you've subscribed to a list that either has too much traffic, isn't interesting, or gives you any other reason for wanting to unsubscribe right away.

As an example, suppose you want to subscribe to the Socialist Party's mailing list. Simply follow these steps:

1. The address for the Socialist Party is

   LISTSERV Address:
   `majordomo@world.std.com`
   subscribe `SocNet`

2. To subscribe, open your e-mail program and add the LISTSERV's address, `majordomo@world.std.com` to the TO line. Leave the subject line blank.

3. In the body of the message, type **SUBSCRIBE SocNet *Firstname Lastname***.

4. Now send your e-mail message. You usually receive a message that welcomes you and provides instructions on how to send mail to the list.

How to Find Other Political Information on the Internet

Although this book is full of information, it touches on only a fraction of the political information available on the Net. To make matters worse (or better), the available information is likely to double in six months. Given this fact, it's helpful to be able to find both new and additional sources of information on the Internet. Fortunately, there are ways to do this on the Web.

Using WWW Directory Pages to Find Other Sites

There are lots of directory offerings on the Web to help you find what you're looking for. In fact, many Web browsers—like Netscape—have collected a number of directory pages that are available at your fingertips.

The Whole Internet Catalog

One of the best subject directory pages is *The Whole Internet Catalog* by O'Reilly and Associates. This site offers information on what's new, what's hot, and a

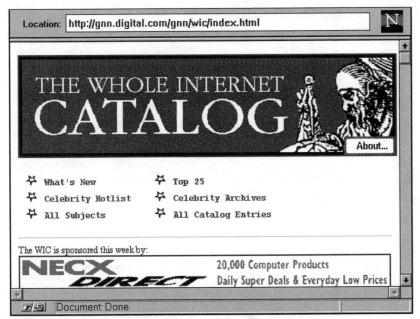

Figure 16.2 `http://gnn.digital.com/gnn/wic/index.html`
The Whole Internet Catalog offers directories on many subjects, including politics.

host of other subjects, including politics (see fig. 16.2). The Whole Internet Catalog is at:

> `http://gnn.digital.com/gnn/`
> `wic/index.html`

The Yahoo Web Site

The Yahoo Web site is another popular subject directory. If you like, Yahoo will even send you to a random Web site. It also offers a wide range of subjects to which you can get directories. You can get the Yahoo directory at the following address:

> `http://www.yahoo.com/`

The CERN Full Server List

Probably the most complete directory page is the full server list available at CERN. It lists the servers by geography.

Be warned! This is a big site and you may have trouble connecting. You can get this directory at the following address:

> `http://info.cern.ch/`
> `hypertext/DataSources/WWW/`
> `Geographical.html`

Sun Microsystems's Web Site

Several other sites have proved useful to me. One of them is Sun Microsystems's Web site at the University of North Carolina—Chapel Hill. It connects to many government and political sources, both in the United States and in other countries. It is located at:

> `http://sunsite.unc.edu/`
> `unchome.html`

FedWorld Information Network

For U.S. Government Net resources, it is hard to beat the FedWorld Information Network. FedWorld is designed to be a one-stop source for links to government sites. You can reach it at:

`http://www.fedworld.gov`

Using WWW Search Pages To Find Other Sites

Besides accessing directories that give you pre-set sites of information, you can also perform keyword searches on the Internet. There are many of these search engines available on the Net.

Carnegie Mellon's Lycos

The most popular and well-known of these search engines is Carnegie

Mellon's Lycos catalog (see fig. 16.3). Currently, Lycos searches more than 1.75 million documents! To use Lycos, point your Web browser to `http://lycos.cs.cmu.edu/`.

World Wide Web Worm (WWWW)

If you would like to search both documents and URL locations, try the World Wide Web Worm (WWWW). The Worm builds an index and then lets you effectively conduct searches to find what you need. You can access WWWW at the following address:

`http://www.cs.colorado.edu/`
`mcbryan_merge/mcbryan/`
`WWWW.html`

Figure 16.3 `http://lycos.cs.cmu.edu/`
The Lycos catalog at Carnegie Mellon searches nearly two million documents for what you want.

WebCrawler

One search engine that I turn to frequently is the WebCrawler. This engine is really easy to use—just enter one or more keywords and click the Search button to get a list of sites with those keywords. The address for the WebCrawler Search Page is:

```
http://
webcrawler.cs.washington.edu/
WebCrawler/WebQuery.html
```

Each engine works differently, so the same query will give different results on each. If you don't find what you want on one, you can always try another.

The Centre Universitaire d'Informatique at the University of Geneva

There's also a directory of search engines to help you locate even more search engines. CUI (The Centre Universitaire d'Informatique at the University of Geneva) maintains one of the best "search for the searchers" sites. Its URL is:

```
http://cuiwww.unige.ch/
meta-index.html
```

Recommended Books on Using the Internet

This chapter has taken you on somewhat of a whirlwind tour of different resources you might use to get political information on the Internet. However, as is probably obvious, it would be impossible to cover everything you would need to know in one chapter.

Exactly how do you set bookmarks in Gopher? How do you control the way files are downloaded and uploaded when using FTP? What are all the shortcuts you can use to access newsgroups most effectively? These are all good questions. In fact, they all have good answers—but those answers can't all be found in one chapter.

If you find yourself wondering how to most effectively use all the resources mentioned in this chapter quickly and efficiently, you may want to check out some other Que titles that can help lead the way. Each one is designed to give you all the hints, shortcuts, and expert advice you'll need to be a true net surfer:

- Que's *Using the Internet* is a concise, user-friendly reference to the Internet. It includes a disk with Windows software for cruising the Internet.

- Que's *Special Edition Using the Internet*, Second Edition is using the Internet with guts! It includes more than 1,300 pages that tell you everything you need to know about the Internet. Also, it includes a CD with hundreds of megabytes of great software to help you.

- Que's *Special Edition Using the Internet with Your Mac* focuses on accessing the Internet through your Mac.

- Que's *Special Edition Using the World Wide Web* saves you time and effort by taking you step-by-step through how to get connected and how to discover the best online resources. It's the comprehensive guide to navigating the Web on the Internet.

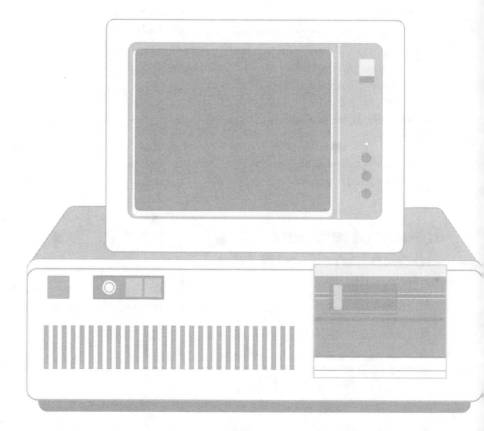

Chapter 17

Getting Going and Keeping Up on the Online Services

Here are quick tips for getting online and keeping up with the changing political scene.

In this chapter

- *How to subscribe to America Online, CompuServe, and Prodigy*
- *The costs of the three main commercial online services*
- *Internet access through commercial online services*

In other chapters

← *Specific political resources on each of the online services are covered in Part 1 through Part 4 of this book.*

The three top online services, America Online, CompuServe, and Prodigy, are all rich in resources for their subscribers. These resources include political documents, files, and forums. Although none of them has the range of resources that the Internet has, they are all more structured and easier to use than the Net. And because they all offer Internet access, one of them may be a good choice for you to participate in online politics.

This book explores some of the political resources on these services. In this chapter, you learn a little more about the services themselves, including how to get connected and what they charge. Beyond that, you will learn what tools they offer for keeping up with the changing political scene online. Finally, you'll learn about each service's Internet support, which allows you to use the political resources on the Net.

Politics on America Online

America Online (AOL) is the middle choice of the three online services when it comes to political information. It has more to offer than Prodigy, but somewhat less than CompuServe. One advantage of choosing AOL over the others is that it gathers its political resources together in one forum, making it easier to find things.

How to Subscribe, and What It Costs

You need the appropriate software to get online with America Online. You can find it at virtually any software store, or you can request a copy at 1-800-827-6364. Versions are available for DOS, Windows, and the Macintosh.

AOL has one pricing plan. A membership is $9.95 per month, and includes five free hours of connect time. Additional connect time is billed at $2.95 per hour. Member's Online Support is free of charge, but using the system to send a fax or printed mail, purchase things in the online store, or search the Mercury Center News database all incur additional charges.

Install the AOL software by following the instructions that came with it, and be sure to have your credit card handy. The software will get you set up and will automatically make you a subscriber to the system. From then on, when you log on to AOL, you'll see a screen similar to the one in figure 17.1.

America Online has sections dedicated to broad topics like Today's News, Computing, and Reference Desk. There's no option on the Main Menu devoted specifically to politics, but AOL does have such an area; it's called the Capital Connection.

Figure 17.1
AOL's opening screen covers broad topics.

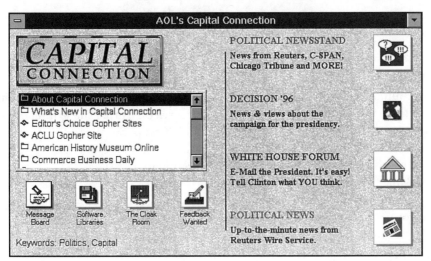

Figure 17.2 Keywords: Politics, Capital
AOL's Capital Connection is devoted specifically to politics.

Keeping Up with Politics on AOL

Capital Connection (Keywords: **Politics, Capital**) is where most political information resides on AOL. This forum is also the place to go for the latest news on politics and government. It has a variety of political information services and discussion areas. Forums cover topics such as the crisis in Haiti or the White House.

Another nice feature of AOL's Capital Connection is its integration with the Net. Many of the selections you can make in Capital Connection take you to a Gopher site, such as the ACLU Gopher Site option shown in figure 17.2.

Other resources in Capital Connection include 15 message boards, where members are invited to discuss everything from abortion to welfare. The Political Newsstand contains news stories from Reuters, C-SPAN, and other sources. The Political News section has up-to-the-minute news from Reuters.

The White House Forum contains press releases and other documents, as well as eight more message boards covering such issues as the State of the Union and policies. Decision '96 has the latest on the upcoming Presidential campaign.

As you can see, Capital Connection is the place to go when you want to keep up with politics on AOL. In particular, the What's New in Capital Connection directory lists recent additions.

Watch out for the This Week in Capital Connection directory in the About Capital Connection directory; all of the entries here were six months out of date when I last checked them.

Internet Access

Besides the Internet links in places like Capital Connection, AOL groups a number of Net tools in the Internet Connection (Keyword: **Internet**). AOL is the only one of the big three services that doesn't yet have a Web browser (AOL president Steve Case has made a preview version of Web browsers available for Windows users—a Mac version is soon to follow). However, it does provide a full range of other capabilities, as you can see in figure 17.3.

With the Mailing Lists and Newsgroups tools, you can take full advantage of the resources in the newsgroups and mailing lists sections throughout this book. The Gopher & WAIS Databases tool, combined with the FTP tool, give you access to all of the political Gopher and FTP sites described in the chapters. All of these tools work well; they're generally better than those on CompuServe and comparable to those on Prodigy.

Politics on CompuServe

CompuServe has the most comprehensive political coverage of the three major services. During the writing of this book, CompuServe usually had more material on whatever subject I was interested in.

How to Subscribe, and What It Costs

The CompuServe Information Manager (CIM) is an easy way to get connected to CompuServe. You can find it at virtually any software store, or you can request a copy at 1-800-848-8990. Versions are available for DOS, Windows, and the Macintosh.

CompuServe offers two pricing plans. The standard plan costs $9.95 per month, and provides unlimited access to over 100 basic services. This access is

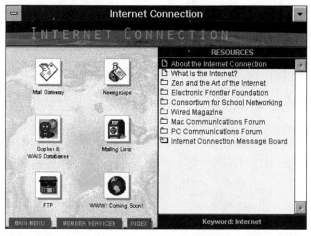

Figure 17.3 Keyword: `Internet`
AOL's Internet Connection provides several Net tools.

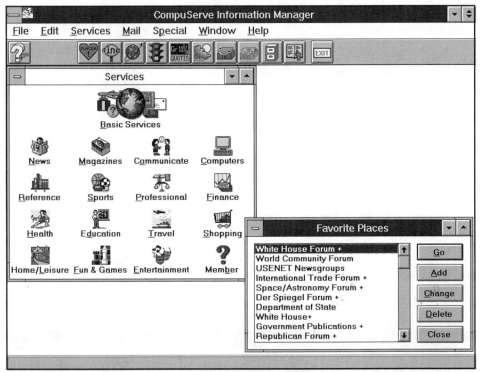

Figure 17.4

The opening screen of CompuServe Information Manager for Windows.

free of connect-time charges, meaning you could spend days connected to one of the basic services for your $9.95 fee. This plan includes free outgoing e-mail equivalent to around 90 three-page letters per month. CompuServe also offers an Alternative Pricing Plan. This plan has a $2.50 monthly fee, but charges connect-time fees for almost everything you do on the system. Depending on the speed of your modem, these fees run up to $22.80 per hour, making this alternative of little value to people interested in political information on CompuServe.

Unfortunately, the resources that have the political information in them are forums, which are considered to be

extended services. As such, they have an additional $4.80 per hour fee for their use. Expect to spend significantly more than $9.95 per month if you want to take advantage of the political materials on CompuServe.

To get started, follow the included directions on how to install and run the program. You'll then be asked if you want to join the service. Once you are a member, you'll see a screen similar to the one in figure 17.4 when you start WinCIM—the exact look is customizable.

CompuServe divides its content into a number of areas (such as News, Professional, Reference, and so on). There is no separate political section like on

AOL, but there's a lot of political material to be found.

Keeping Up with Politics on CompuServe

CompuServe doesn't have its political information all in one place like AOL. You have to find it. Fortunately, the Find tool—accessible from CIM's icon bar—does a good job of finding the information you request. This makes CompuServe a good choice if you know what political information you're looking for.

One place to look for political changes is the White House forum (see fig. 17.5). This forum is the place to discuss the Administration's plans for the country. Many events that aren't specifically related to the White House are mentioned in the messages that members post.

Another place to look for political changes is the What's New archive (Go: CIS:WNA-1). This is a searchable database that contains descriptions of new features and events on the system.

Internet Access

CompuServe recently unveiled its Web browser, which is a custom version of a commercial browser from Spry (see

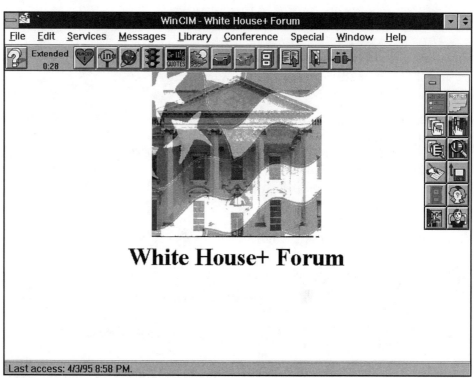

Figure 17.5 Go: CIS:WHITEHOUSE

CompuServe's White House forum is where the Administration's plans for the country are discussed.

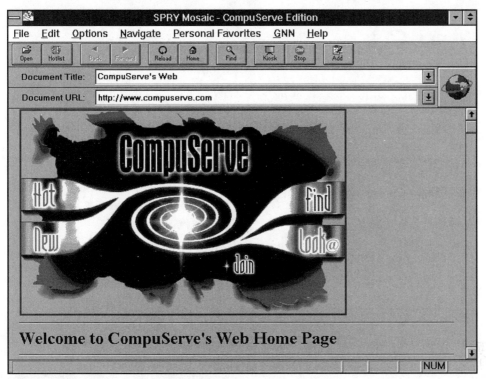

Figure 17.6 `http://www.compuserve.com`
CompuServe's Web browser, displaying CompuServe's home page on the Net.

fig. 17.6). The browser is cumbersome to use. You need to run a program called the CompuServe Internet Dialer, and then activate the Web browser after the dialer has made a connection. Use of the Internet, either through the Web browser or through CompuServe's other Net services, is billed at $2.50 per hour, after three free hours per month, for members who use the Standard Pricing Plan. For users who want more Net access, there is a new plan, called the Internet Club, that provides 20 free hours per month, with a fee of $1.95 per hour after that. This is available for an additional $15.00 fee per month.

Besides the new Web browser, CompuServe offers Telnet, FTP, and UseNet access to the Internet. You can reach these tools through the Internet Services area (`Go: CIS:INTERNET`).

Politics on Prodigy

Prodigy has the least political coverage of the major online services. It does, however, have a couple of places where you can get political information. Prodigy also provides a collection of Internet access tools, including a Web browser, that makes the Internet's political resources available to Prodigy subscribers.

How to Subscribe, and What It Costs

Like the software for AOL and CompuServe, the Prodigy software is widely available at software stores or by calling 1-800-776-3449. DOS, Windows, and Macintosh versions are available.

Prodigy offers a few different pricing plans. The monthly fee for the standard plan is $9.95, and includes 5 free hours. Additional hours are $2.95. Another option is the 30/30 Plan. This plan runs $29.95 per month, and includes 30 hours of access, with additional hours for $2.95.

Once you've installed the software and joined the service, you'll see a screen like the one shown in figure 17.7. The exact contents of the screen vary as different news, offers, and events are featured.

The different areas on Prodigy are selected using the buttons on the right side of the screen. The small amount of political information on the system is contained in the Reference area.

Keeping Up with Politics on Prodigy

Prodigy's political information is contained primarily in the White House Memo forum (Jump: **White House**). Like AOL's forum, the documents here come from the White House Office of

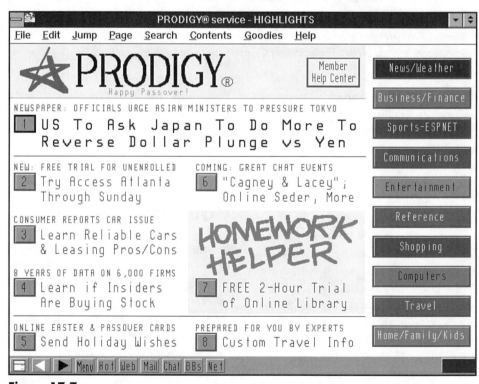

Figure 17.7
Prodigy's opening screen will vary to feature different news, offers, and events.

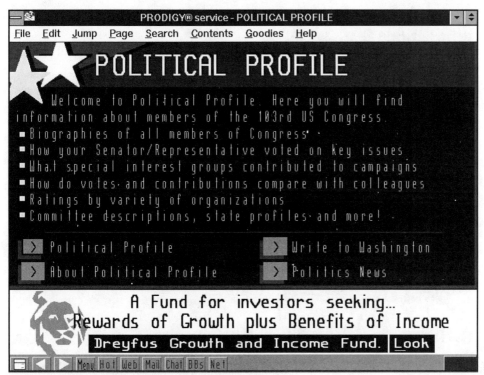

File   Edit   Jump   Page   Search   Contents   Goodies   Help

POLITICAL PROFILE

Welcome to Political Profile. Here you will find information about members of the 103rd US Congress.
- Biographies of all members of Congress·
- How your Senator/Representative voted on key issues
- What special interest groups contributed to campaigns
- How do votes·and contributions compare with colleagues
- Ratings by variety of organizations
- Committee descriptions, state profiles· and more!·

> Political Profile   > Write to Washington

> About Political Profile   > Politics News

A Fund for investors seeking...
Rewards of Growth plus Benefits of Income
Dreyfus Growth and Income Fund. | Look

Menu Hot Web Mail Chat BBs Net

Figure 17.8 Jump: POLITICAL PROFILE
Prodigy's Political Profile is easy to use.

Media Affairs. The documents are divided into six groups that you can browse through or search.

The other useful political resource on Prodigy is the Political Profile (see fig. 17.8). It contains information about all the members of Congress. Biographies, voting records, committee assignments, ratings by special-interest groups and more are all available here.

While the Political Profile is easy to use and contains a lot of useful material, there is one thing to watch out for—the information it returns may not be up to date. When I examined the information on Speaker Gingrich in April of 1995, some of his material did not reflect the election results from

November of 1994. Aside from that, the Political Profile section on Prodigy is the easiest and fastest way to get information about members of Congress.

Internet Access

Prodigy was the first of the online services to make a Web browser available. It's integrated into the system much better than CompuServe's browser; you activate it like any other Prodigy service, instead of running separate applications such as with CompuServe. Figure 17.9 shows Prodigy's Web browser displaying Prodigy's home page on the Web. Besides Web access, Prodigy offers UseNet newsgroups, FTP, Gopher, and e-mail.

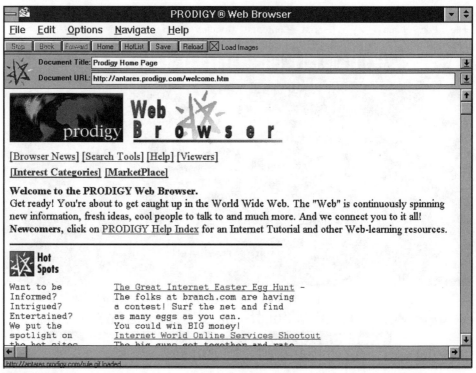

Figure 17.9 `http://antares.prodigy.com/welcome.htm`
Prodigy's Web browser, displaying Prodigy's home page on the Web.

INDEX

Supreme Court Decisions, 282-283, 290-291

Thomas Legislative Information Service, 278-279, 289

U.S. Budget Gopher, 290

United States Postal Service, 290

White House home page, 290

White House Publications Page, 276-277, 289

Arizona (az.politics UseNet newsgroup), 256, 271

Associated Press

Associated Press Wire search tool (The Activist's Oasis), 11

ClariNet e.News, 255

Association of Bay Area Governments home page, 272

atomic energy (International Atomic Energy Agency), 228

Australian Wildlife Protection Authority home page, 319-321, 325

az.politics UseNet newsgroup, 256, 271

B

Barloon, Bill, 302

Barlow, John Perry, 123-125, 131, 146

BBC home page, 229

BeastNet Archive FTP site, 141

Berkeley College Republican, 30-32, 39

Bilderbergers, 322

Bill of Rights

Bill of Rights home page, 159

Bill of Rights Journal Gopher, 158

Citizen's Guide to Individual Rights in America home page, 153, 158

Constitution of the United States (electronic versions) 152-153, 158

First Amendment issues

Amend1 free speech mailing list, 134-135, 155

American Communication Association Page, 135-137, 156

Church of Scientology, 137, 156

Vocal Point newsletter, 137

Fourth Amendment issues

alt.privacy, 135, 156

alt.privacy.clipper, 156

alt.security.pgp, 156

BlackNet, 142

clipper chip, 146, 158

Cryptography and PGP Page, 144-146, 157

Cryptography, PGP, and Privacy Page, 158

Electronic Frontier Foundation, 123-125, 131, 154-155

Privacy Rights Clearinghouse, 142-144, 157

Issues Forum (CompuServe), 155

Meanderings Newsletter home page, 159

Second Amendment issues

Citizens Committee for the Right to Keep and Bear Arms (CCRKBA), 138

Left Side of the Web, 157

Militia Watch on the Left Side of the Web, 140-141

misc.activism.militia, 134, 155

National Rifle Association (NRA), 138-140, 157

Patriot Archives Militia Directory, 141-142, 157

rec.guns, 156

Second Amendment Foundation (SAF), 138

Bill of Rights home page, 159

Bill of Rights Journal Gopher, 158

Bipartisan Commission on Entitlements and Tax Reform Web Page, 100, 164-165, 182

bit.listserv.govdoc-l UseNet newsgroup, 274

BlackNet, 142

Bob Reinhardt's RLC home page, 40

Bosnia

alt.current-events.bosnia, 296, 308

War in Bosnia—The Electronic Archives, 300-301, 309

Women for Women in Bosnia home page, 309

Boulder, CO

Boulder Community Network FreeNet, 262-263, 271-272

City of Boulder, CO home page, 261, 271

British Broadcasting Corporation home page, 229

Brittanica Online, 215, 228

Browne, Harry, 73, 75, 81

browsers (World Wide Web), 334

CompuServe browser, 350-351

NCSA Mosaic, 334

Netscape, 334

Prodigy browser, 353-354

URLs (Uniform Resource Locators), 334-335

Buchanan, Pat, 196

Mother Jones on Pat Buchanan home page, 204

Republican Primary page, 196

budget

1995 Federal Budget, 203

1996 Federal Budget, 191, 290

Bipartisan Commission on Entitlements and Tax Reform Web Page, 100, 164-165, 182

links (FreeNets), 272
LISTSERVs, 339
see also mailing lists
Lobbying/Advocacy Techniques,
14-15, 19
local governments
America on the Go bulletin
board (Prodigy), 269
Ann Arbor, Michigan
Gopher, 272
Boulder, CO
Boulder Community
Network, 262-263,
271-272
City of Boulder, CO
home page, 261, 271
California
Association of Bay Area
Governments, 272
California Counties and
Cities, 272
City Net home page,
265-266
current events
clari.local.headlines, 270
clari.news.usa.
gov.state+local,
254-255, 270
FreeNets
alt.online-service.
freenet, 256, 272
Cleveland FreeNet, 264
links, 272
NPTN (National Public
Telecomputing
Network), 264, 266,
271-272
New York City
(nyc.politics), 255-256,
270
Seattle (seattle.politics),
256
State and Local
Government Information
(U.S.) Gopher, 272
State and Local
Governments Page
(Library of Congress),
265, 272
Washington D.C.'s city
page, 271

LP (Libertarian Party) News,
64
LPUS mailing list, 79
Lycos, 342

M

magazines
Christian American, 91
Covert Action Quarterly,
207-208, 227
EXTRA! , 123
Forbes , 36
Mother Jones, 129, 196, 204
NATO Review , 219
Policy Review, 37
Wired , 131
see also zines
mailing lists, 8-10, 339
ACTIV-L LISTSERV, 10, 18
AIDS Patent, 182
Alternative Learning, 181
Amend1 free speech,
134-135, 155
Children's Rights, 227
A Conservative Mailing
List, 25, 39-40
Department of Health and
Human Services, 235, 250
e-mail clients
Eudora, 339
finding mailing lists, 340
Education Policy Analysis,
181
Education Reform
Newsletter, 181
FedTax-L, 188, 203
Judicial Affairs, 250
Libertarian
Announcements, 60-61
Libertarian mailing lists,
61, 79
LPUS mailing list, 79
moderators, 10
NATODATA, 227
Public Opinion on Foreign
Policy, 227
The Republican Liberty
Caucus Mailing List, 25,
39-40
SocNet, 84, 99

Sumeria Announcements,
324
Travel Advisories, 227
United We Stand America
mailing list, 101
Major Bureau of Labor
Statistics Programs, 189-190
Marcos, Subcomandante, *see*
Vincente, Rafael Guillen
Marrou, Andre, 72
Marxism, defined, 85
Massachusetts Institute
of Technology, *see* **MIT**
Meanderings Newsletter home
page, 159
media
FAIR: Fairness & Accuracy
in Reporting home page,
122-123, 130
"Media Tools and
Strategies," 17
Medicare, Retirement Living
forum (CompuServe), 179
messages, sending to White
House (alt.dear.whitehouse),
181
Mexico
Interview with
Subcomandante
Marcos, 309
Mexican Exiles for
Democracy, 304
NAFTA (North American
Free Trade Agreement),
216, 228-229
State Democratic Assembly
of the People of Chiapas,
304
YA BASTA!—The EZLN
Page, 303-304, 309
Michigan
Ann Arbor, Michigan
Gopher (government),
272
Michigan forum (America
Online), 268
military
clari.news.military, 226
Real Time Support for the
Warrior, 214-215, 228

INDEX

alt.rush-limbaugh, 39, 108, 128

alt.security.pgp, 156

alt.society.anarchy, 99

alt.society.civil-liberties, 79

alt.society.civil-liberty, 79

alt.society.conservatism, 25, 39-40

alt.society.generation-x, 99

alt.society.labor-unions, 187, 203

az.politics, 256, 271

bit.listserv.govdoc-l, 274

clari.loc.new-hampshire, 256, 271

clari.loc.new-hampshire.briefs, 271

clari.local.headlines, 270

clari.news.disaster, 226

clari.news.gov.state, 270

clari.news.labor.layoff, 203

clari.news.labor.strike, 203

clari.news.military, 226

clari.news.politics, 39

clari.news.terrorism, 296, 309

clari.news.top.world, 226

clari.news.usa.gov.financial, 187, 203

clari.news.usa.gov. foreign_policy, 206, 227

clari.news.usa.gov.misc, 162, 181

clari.news.usa.gov. personalities, 106-107, 127

clari.news.usa.gov. state+local, 254-255, 270

clari.news.usa.gov. white_house, 42-43, 55, 250

clari.news.usa.law.supreme, 250

clari.tw.health.aids, 182

clari.world.asia.japan, 324

clari.world.mideast.iraq, 309

comp.org.eff.talk, 18

courts.usa.federal.supreme, 235, 250, 275

dod.pb.nasa, 227

hierarchies, 337

misc.activism.militia, 134, 155

misc.activism.progressive, 18

misc.education, 181

misc.immigration.usa, 182

misc.taxes, 188, 203

moderators, 9, 10, 276

ne.politics, 55

newsreaders, 337
    finding UseNet
        addresses, 337-338
    Newswatcher, 337
    NewsXpress, 337
    Nuntius, 337
    WinVN, 337

nyc.politics, 255-256, 270

rec.guns, 156

seattle.politics, 256

soc.culture.burma, 308

soc.culture.native, 324

soc.culture.soviet, 324

talk.abortion, 135, 156

talk.environment, 99

talk.politics.libertarianism, 79

talk.politics.medicine, 182

talk.politics.misc, 55, 162-163, 181

Utah forum (America Online), 268

V

Vice President Al Gore's Town Meeting, 118, 129

Vice President Gore's biography home page, 129

Vice President Gore's home page, 129

Vincente, Rafael Guillen (*alias* Subcomandante Marcos), 309

Virginia forum (America Online), 267-268

Vocal Point newsletter, 137

Voice of America, 220-221, 229-230

voting issues
    Citizen's Guide to the
        National Voter
        Registration Act of 1993,
        92
    League of Women Voters
        of Iowa Home Page,
        92-93, 101
    Motor Voter Act, 92, 101

W

War in Bosnia—The Electronic Archives, 300-301, 309

Warren, Jim, 12-13, 157

Washington D.C.'s city page, 271

Weaver, J.B., 141

WebCrawler search engine, 343

welfare
    Catalog of Federal
        Domestic Assistance
        Gopher, 163-164, 182
    Department of Health and
        Human Services
        Abstracts Gopher, 167,
        182
        Mailing List, 235, 250
    Poverty and Welfare
        Gopher, 182
    Retirement Living forum
        (CompuServe), 179
    Special Report on Welfare
        Reform (America Online
        Capital Connection), 178

WELL (Whole Earth 'Lectronic Link), The, 15-16, 19, 131

What's Newt home page, 129

White House, 237
    alt.dear.whitehouse, 181
    clari.news.usa.gov.
        white_house, 42-43, 250
    FAQ on the White House,
        251
    Tours of the White House
        home page, 250
    White House document
        summaries home page, 56